Amazing Stories ~~of Man's~~ Beginnings

A fascinating spiritual and intellectual journey back through time and space. Beholding the glories of Ancient Kushite Civilizations Worldwide and the awesome wonder and wisdom of their creation stories.

Volume I

THIRD EDITION

Ishakamusa Barashango

AFRIKAN WORLD BOOKS

1356 W. NORTH AVE/POB 16447
BALTIMORE, MD 21217

TEL   410-383-2006   FAX   410-383-0511
WEB   www.afrikanworldbooks.com
EM   afrikanworldword@aol.com

•

April   2002

First Printing July 15, 1991

Cover: Elyn Powell

Dedication

To my good friend and brother, Mr. Robert Ellis. A human being in the truest sense of the word. With a soul as big as the universe. He is also one of the most optimistic persons on earth. A great humanitarian and an Afrikan who passionately loves his people with his whole mind, body and spirit.

Special Thanks

T o Brother William Barnes another Afrikan with the magnanimous spirit of our Positive Ancestors. Whose faith and patience was a key factor in helping to bring this project to fruition.

Publisher's Note

Afrikan Genesis: Amazing Stories of Man's Beginnings is Volume I of a four-volume series. In Volume II, *Afrikan Genesis: An Historical Reality*, we begin at 4.6 billion years ago, and take a spiritual fact finding journey through all the successive geological periods as we dock at each station along the way, we will carefully demonstrate their relevance to our people's historical reality.

Afrikan Genesis: An Historical Reality makes the scientific investigation of planet Earth's history and the evolution of man interesting and exciting to even the most casual reader.

Volume III, *Afrikan Genesis: A Narrative Commentary on the First Book of the Bible* is a verse by verse and story by story Afro-centric commentary on the Old Testament Book of Genesis which traces these scriptures back to the most ancient sacred writings of the *Book of the Coming Forth by Day and by Night* misnomered *The Egyptian Book of the Dead.*

Volume IV is entitled *Afrikan Genesis: Black Gods and Goddesses in the Land of Eden.* The basic objective of this work is to trace the gods and goddesses of worldwide mythologies, i.e., Kemetan, Greek, Roman, Scandinavian, etc., back to the original Afrikan kings and queens and heroes of whom they were symbols.

Dr. Ishakamusa Barashango
April 27, 1938 - January 14, 2004

TABLE OF CONTENTS

PREFACE

WHICH CAME FIRST?
THE CHICKEN OR THE EGG

This preface is intended as a rational approach to the age old evolutionist versus creationist debate. Although many may claim to, no one knows for certain the actual process which brought about the creation of the world and human beings. Was it the evolutionary course of "natural selection" or the hands of a Cosmic Deity or perhaps both? Maybe man will never know, but the contemplation of these concepts certainly do stimulate one's thought processes.

Which came first, the chicken or the egg, is an appropriate title for this preface because it recalls one of the main scientific symbols used in ancient cosmogonies (stories of creation) to pictographically describe the world's beginnings. At one time this seminal event was portrayed as being initiated by a huge cosmic egg from which this solar system was hatched. In another illustration planet Earth was an egg laid by the cosmic goose which is the basis for the Mother Goose story in today's fairy tales. In each instance these were mere mythological symbols applied by the ancients in their explanation of the origin of natural phenomena relative to this solar system and planet Earth.

The various creation stories invented by our ancient Afrikan ancestors indicate that they clearly understood the scientific principles represented by every mythological symbol. For every god and goddess was just another way of expressing some dimension of the Divine Intelligence in the universe as revealed in the laws of nature. Reflecting on this global cultural motif, paleoanthropologist Richard Leakey says "The full expression of story telling as a social cement comes, of course, with tribal myths, accounts of their people's creation. There is no human group on earth that cannot tell you how their ancestors came into being,..."* This we will be observing throughout this book as we take a fascinating spiritual and intellectual journey back through time and space visiting fabulous cities and magnificent civilizations all along the way.

People of the Lake by Richard Leakey and Roger Lewin, P. 177.

Again regarding the origin of planet Earth and its inhabitants, there are two main theories in existence which can expand into many other sub-theories. They are the Theory of Evolution and the Theory of Creationism. Both of them are theories. No matter how deeply one feels that he or she can substantiate either of them, they are still theories, and with a theory, putting it in plain language "it ain't necessarily so". It could be and it could not be. There seems to be enough evidence to support it, but there is no way we can actually prove it. When it becomes a natural law then it is science because the word science "to know" and only when you know for certain can you call it science. Even though the methodology employed is scientific in principle.

An hypothesis or theory is science in its stages of development, not exact. For the supposition is still being researched and investigated. Therefore, it cannot yet be absolutely proven.

In the first two volumes of the *Afrikan Genesis* series, we are presenting both the Theories of Creationism and Evolution to enhance our reader's knowledge and information, not to proselytize anyone to any particular way of thinking other than that of an Afrikan-centered worldview which encompasses an infinite spectrum of knowledge. It is also not our purpose to confuse our readers by presenting both sides of the story as regards the pros and cons of the Theories of Creationism and Evolution, but rather to provide them with samples of ideas in relationship to these theoretical arguments. The final conclusion, if any, is surely the perrogative of the reader. For we do fully trust our readers to do their own thinking and analysis which can be more accurate if one considers the many aspects of the subject in question.

Our major objective here is to demonstrate, whether you subscribe to either the Theory of Creationism or the Theory of Evolution or a combination of both—for each of them do contain elements of fact—their refutable reality is that according to both theories, humanity and its consequent civilizations began in Mother Alkebulan (Afrika). As a scientist it is my duty to unprejudiciously present both sides of the issue. This has been found the best way to arrive at any intelligent conclusions.

Again as a scientist, at the risk of being lampooned by both schools of thought, I must state the reality that the Theory of Evolution is based on hypothesis and the Theory of Creationism is based on a belief system. Both are supposition and guess work rather than incontestable proven facts. Furthermore, it would be quite arrogant to insist that there is only one way to answer the question of the world's origin. To think there is only one possibility as to how humans and the world were created is to be on a self-indulgent ego trip which places a prohibitive ceiling on mental growth. Each of the theories have plausible clues and probabilities, but neither of them can be considered absolute.

Perhaps at this juncture we may need to stop for a moment and define some of the terminologies we have been using;

1) Hypothesis — A Greek word meaning "to assume, to suppose, to lay a basis for",

2) Theory — from the Greek *theoria* - to see, to look at, to observe,

3) Science — from the Latin *scire* which means "to know".

Now let us view these definitions in relationship to the 5 basic stages of scientific investigation.

- Supposition — an assumption with less assurance than an hypothesis. Example, "Let us suppose that..." Best summed up in the word, maybe.

- Conjecture — a conclusion drawn from admittedly insufficient data. Example, "We surmise that..." Best summed up in the word, possibility.

- Hypothesis — a temporary explanation of an occurrence based on known data thus validating a basis for further research. Example, "It seems to be that..." Best summed up in the word, probable.

- Theory — an hypothesis so well substantuated as to be generally accepted. Example, "It appears to be..." Best summed up in the word, apparently (seemingly).

- Science — a body of actual facts systematically arranged and showing the operation of certain principles of natural law. Example, the law of gravity. Best summed up in the word(s), certainty (for certain).

Again we must remind ourselves that both the Theory of Creationism and the Theory of Evolution are ideas proposed by man to solve the mystery of his origin. Therefore, neither of the proponents of either school of thought can afford to be dogmatic. Thus it is expedient for arrogant exponents of either one or the other of the theories to get down off of their high horses of the egotistic desire to be totally right and admit that they do not really know and come together in a concerted effort to find—if it can be known by humans—the ultimate reality of the origin of things. For there are elements of truth in each of them. Another discussion of this topic from several different aspects will be presented in Volume Two of this series, *Afrikan Genesis: An Historical Reality* which is a study in Common Sense Geology and Grass Roots Anthropology. Until then let us conclude this preface by acknowledging the fact that it appears that Afrikans have always had a sense of being directly connected in a familial manner to a cosmic Intelligent Force in the universe generally expressed in terms of a Divine Creator though represented in myriad ways.

As the title of Volume One, *Afrikan Genesis: Amazing Stories of Man's Beginnings,* suggests, in this work we will be surveying some of the many different and exciting creation stories that were circulating in the ancient world and are still extant today. And though we may not solve the mystery of "which came first, the chicken or the egg", we will certainly have a good time trying.

INTRODUCTION
AIN'T NOTHING LIKE THE REAL THING BABY

The late song stylists Marvin Gaye and Tammi Terrell recorded a song-entitled *Ain't Nothing Like the Real Thing Baby*. These lyrics not only romantically expressed the feelings of the popular culture at the time but other aspects of the Black Experience as well, for Afrikan people were still struggling to gain some sense of reality in the midst of a filibustering white supremist controlled society. So it is even now especially in the study of world history which has been so grossly distorted by "the white man's declaration of black inferiority";[1] however, fortunately for us the subject of history which is a vital component of a people's self-concept has in recent years began to be put back in its proper perspective thanks to the heroic efforts of Afrikan-centered scholars. As this rediscovery process touches the lives of ever increasing numbers of our people it becomes clearly evident "there ain't nothing like the real thing".

One of the major psychological problems facing the race today is a distorted view of reality and if one's reality is distorted by his/her lack of understanding of the world and environment he/she lives in, it causes distorted experiences in his/her daily life, many times resulting in negative and self-destructive behavior often manifested in violence towards one's immediate family and community. Most behavioral patterns stem from self-concept and a very important element of self-concept is historical identity. If one seeks to historically identify with that which is other than the group which produced and nurtured them, then conflicting cross signals are set up in the psyche, often resulting in illogical reasoning and irrational behavior. If one out of ignorance endeavors to dismiss the importance of the race which gave him/her life in world history, then he/she would be in essence denouncing his/her own self-worth which can sometimes lead one to almost, without conscience, becoming an instrument of unseeming and violent acts perpetuated against his own kind.

The *Afrikan Genesis* series is an offering of rediscovery of our true historical reality and endeavors to aid our readers in answering such questions as; How did the universe, our solar system and the planet Earth come into being? Who were the first humans on planet Earth and how did they get here? These are just a few of the questions that human beings have asked and sought to answer

1

throughout the ages of man's existence and development. In all of humanity's quest for knowledge, these questions always seem to be somewhere at the top of the list.

In the past 400 years or so, many misleading ideas have been propagated about the world's beginnings and the establishment of its first civilizations. Yet recent rediscoveries and the careful examination of extant data reveals that contrary to what many of us have been erroneously taught, civilization did not begin in the so-called Middle East or on the Greek Isles but rather in the heart of Alkebulan (Afrika). For whatever the reason the forces of nature saw fit to create the Black Race first and to endow them with the wonderful gifts of the arts and sciences of civilization. Whether by the logical progression of natural selection or by the divine fiat of a supreme cosmic deity or by an harmonious synthesis of both evolution and creationism, one thing is for certain; in the beginning was the Black Race.

The intent of this series is not to contend, pro or con, the Theories of Evolution or Creationism, but rather to present both concepts for the reader's examination and to re-emphasize the undeniable fact that both theories testify to the preeminence of the Afrikan. Though the various scholarly viewpoints differ in approach and particulars, the underlying and connecting principle remain the same; Black People were here first. The Afrikan genesis of humanity is beyond any rational debate. Dr. John G. Jackson puts it even more succinctly. "The African genesis of the human race is now generally accepted in the realm of modern science as a fact beyond all dispute."[2] Therefore, "in the beginning was the Black man" is a reality that cannot be denied.

Through all the geological periods of planet Earth's development, Mother Alkebulan was being specially formed and extravagantly enriched with basic sources of material wealth ie, gold, diamonds, manganese, chrome, etc. because it was here and here alone that the first humans would evolve and create marvelous civilizations which became the matrix for all others. It was the Afrikans who first tamed the jungles and swamps teeming with venomous reptiles and lethal insects, who subduedthe deserts and established civilizations where once there was wilderness. This was not achieved any where else on Earth before it was accomplished in Alkebulan (Afrika). There is a wealth of information which traces the footsteps of these early inhabitants of the Earth from the most basic lifestyles of immediate survival to the evolution of great

2

kingdoms and magnificent civilizations which the original Black man and woman built and maintained all over the world. Dr. Chancellor Williams boldly affirms,

"The greatest of all issues is right here in the general agreement that at the very earliest period known to mankind an African civilization in the areas later called the Sudan and Egypt was fully developed with 'all the arts of civilized life already mature,' Its beginning being placed so far into the early history of the world that it is beyond the reach of man."[3]

The reason why this information is not common knowledge to the masses of Black People is because we are at war. The enemies of the world have been and still are concealing much of the rich priceless treasures of our true history in an effort to keep us in a perpetual state of mental, spiritual and economic enslavement. Dr. John Henrik Clarke reminds us,

"It is too often forgotten, when the Europeans emerged and began to extend themselves into the broader world of Africa and Asia during the Fifteen and Sixteenth Centuries, they went on to colonize most of mankind. Later, they would colonize world scholarship, mainly the writing of history. History was then written or rewritten to show or imply that Europeans were the only creators of what could be called a civilization. In order to accomplish this, the Europeans had to forget, or pretend to forget, all they previously knew about Africa."[4]

Dr. Maulana Karenga reenforces this reality.

"In fact, Europe declared that the more history you have, the more human you are and then set out to claim all relevant history and deny Blacks any...It is a fundamental fact that only humans have history and when Europe could claim without effective challenge during slavery and the colonization of African peoples and lands that Blacks had no history, they could and did also claim Blacks were not human. For to be denied historical achievement is to be placed outside of humanity, for only humans make history. The need, then, became one of rescuing and reconstructing Black history as a basis for and contribution to the rescue and reconstruction of Black humanity."[5]

To feed this ferocious dragon of white supremacy, the European world has motivated its captains of industry, moguls in the financial arena and the shakers and movers of other segments of their society to funnel many millions of dollars into those areas of

3

study and research which could be interpreted in such a way as to buttress their inflated self-concept, ie. archeology, anthropology, linguistics and other related fields. Because these disciplines give definition and cultural context to everything else in the world, European scholars set out to dominate these fields and recast their findings in the image of white supremacy. However, the historical reality of the Black Race's original place in the ancient world managed to survive through every effort to smother it in a verity of confusion. Among the ranks of Euro-centric thinkers,

> ''...the prevailing racist theories of history created a very real dilemma: How, in view of civilization's beginning in the Land of the Blacks, to explain their role in world history? Having successfully degraded the black race throughout the world and supported that degradation with their 'science' and religion, how now explain that this same black race was the first builders of the very civilization of which the Caucasian themselves are heirs?...''[6]

Most of white academia responded to this dilemma in the usual "stiff necked" irrational manner. They simply denied the compelling evidence of these ancient Afrikan High Culture civilizations by claiming them as their own. Therefore, as Dr. Carter G. Woodson so clearly points out in his book, *The Miseducation of the Negro*, the large majority of Afrikan people "educated" in the western world have only been taught about what other races—Europeans in particular—have done and that the only way we can ever be somebody is to imitate them instead of imitating ourselves, thus denying the reality of our own existence. Dr. Cheikh Anta Diop says,

> "This climate of alienation finally deeply affected the personality of the Negro, especially the educated Black who had had an opportunity to become conscious of world opinion about him and his people. It often happened that the Negro intellectual loses confidence in his own possibilities and in those of his race to such an extent that, despite the validity of the evidence presented...it will not be astonishing if some of us are still unable to believe that Blacks really played the earliest civilizing role in the world."[7]

When a people are robbed of the vital lifegiving knowledge of their own true history, they become lost and stray from the path of the high calling and holy purpose of their unique existence, for the spark that gives life meaning and purpose has been hidden from them. Consequently, the attitude of many of today's

4

unenlightened Black youth towards our history is "who cares about what happened back there in the past, all that is important is what's happening now." Surely only a people suffering from an acute "loss of memory" could produce children who would deny their own historical relevance. Dr. Asa G. Hilliard, III observes, "An individual that loses his or her memory is disabled. So it is with a people. African and African diasporan people have, in large measure, been deprived of the most important memories of history. Those who have enslaved and colonized Africans have understood fully the powerful role that history plays in the life of a people."[8]

As a result of being "robbed of a knowledge of self", all too many Black People are acting out of the context of their true natures. Some scramble their brains by incessantly listening to party music all day long and many of our youth often show outright disrespect to their elders or anyone else in the community without regard or consideration for the demoralizing effects of such actions. There is even in some Black communities an epidemic of child molestation. Now you know it is absolute insanity for individuals to traumatize future generations of their own people. Surely, it is not the true nature of the Afrikan soul. If anything, it is more indicative of European historical characteristics—mind you I am not stating this to be mean. In fact white scholars such as Will Durant and others write about it in their own works. See *Afrikan People and European Holidays: A Mental Genocide,* Book Two. Some Black school children have been led to believe that being studious is not "soulful". Some think of it as being "whitey's thing" and tend to intimidate or ostracize those students who are striving for excellence. It is not my objective hereto wring my hands and bemoan the negative aspects of the present state of the race, but rather to demonstrate some of the deleterious effects these negative thoughts and actions have on the race especially those of our people who have accepted what Rev. Jaramogi Agyeman refers to as "the white man's declaration of black inferiority"

Afrikan-centered educator, Abena Walker, admonishes that one of the ways that we can treat and remedy this pathology is to "...study our history and culture first then other peoples and cultures in relationship to who we are."[9] Dr. Yosef ben Jochannon offers a similar prognosis.

> "In order to make African Studies and Black Studies truly relevant, I am very strongly certain African and African-American (Caribbean peoples included) educators, historians, and other

5

writers dealing with the *BLACK EXPERIENCE*, must first attack and ferret-out the root-cause of the cancer of 'anti-Africanism' found in such abundance in the existing holdings and libraries, museums, and other literary depositories of the United States of America's private and public educational institutions.''[10]

Of course we are not suggesting that the study of our history is a cure-all for every ill, for we do understand that many of the problems which assault the psyche of the race are far more deep seated and complex than meet the eye, that the answers and solutions are by no means simple; nevertheless, a knowledge of our true history is an essential and logical place to start because truly a careful scientific investigation of the Afrikan in world history based on what Dr. Ivan Van Sertima calls "hard evidence" reveals there always has been and still is much more to us than the hand clapping, butt shaking, ball chasing, slap happy image the world generally holds of us.

The rediscovery of our glorious achievements in the past and present supply us with countless examples of Afrikan people's innate ability to be rational, practical, logical, deductive in our reasoning, analytical in our thought and provocative in our creations and yet still dance, sing, laugh and play in harmony with the rhythmic energy of timeless cosmic motion. The first mind to question life and find answers was the Afrikan mind. It was this mind which created and formed the sound mathematical basis for all tangible accomplishments. It was this soul born of the dark womb of the universe that obtained and maintained an everlasting connection with the umbilical cord of Divine intelligence. It was this chosen representative of the human species who continued age after age to generate and regenerate intuitive, clairvoyant, precognitive, psychokinetic, inspiration and spiritual oneness with the All and In All.

The Black Race must come to know and never forget that Mother Nature has blessed us with a generous supply of that special chemical ingredient which enabled Earthly humans to endure the scorching heat of the primordial Alkebulan plains and achieve in varying degrees the divine equilibrium of the harmonious development of mental, spiritual and physical being. This ''magic elixir'' which does not deteriorate with time is known as melanin. Melanin is the chemical which among others determines the intensity of skin pigmentation. The term ''melanin'' was associated with divinity in the ancient world. Renown historian Joel A. Rogers says,

6

"...the Black Aphrodite, later the Black Venus of the Romans and the Black Madonna of the Christians, was worshipped for her 'magical' powers in ancient Greece...This black goddess was also known an Melaina, 'The Black Lady',...Melanin, or the black pigment, in the human skin is derived from the name of this goddess (Greek: melos-anos, black)."[11] We will be dealing with this subject again in Volume Four of this series, *Afrikan Genesis: Black Gods and Goddesses in the Land of Eden*.

Dr. George G.M. James suggests that the study of the Afrikan in world history "is also going to mean a most important change in the mentality of the Black people: a change from an inferiority complex..."[12] In the mirror of history we behold a reflection of ourselves. A black Person's degree of consciousness as to his/her true history is directly related to his/her self-image. For the image a person/people hold of themselves is the regulator of all their thoughts and actions. Karenga analysizes this principle thusly,

> "...the enslavement and oppression of Africans was an appropriation of their labor and, thus, the effective interruption of their struggle to transform the world in their own image and interest. This appropriation and interruption led to historical amnesia i.e., loss of self consciousness based on historical practice and achievement. For we know ourselves by what we have done and do and when our labor is no longer ours and there are no records to reveal our true identity based on historical origin and practice as a people, how do we define and know ourselves? History, then, becomes the mirror through which we look to discover and know ourselves and our possibilities."[13]

Dr. Francis Cress Welsing says that "in most cases a person who thinks well of his/her self will not submit to or be satisfied with sub-standard behavior from his/herself or others towards him/her". Unless we as a people have a positive self image of who and what we are, no one else will. Those among us who do not possess this essential quality are like autumn leaves at the mercy of the winds, blown about by the public opinions and worldview of others which will have you going around doing any and everything, even that which breeds self-destruction. As it is exemplified on a collective level, so it is with the individual. One must acquire and maintain a positive self-image in order to do positive things and produce positive results. This state of mind is the determining factor as to how you will fare in any given situation no matter what the external circumstances. In short, before you can be good at anything, you must first have a good self concept. Speaking on how a lack of understanding of their true history tends to impair the self confidence of the leaders of many Afrikan nations today, John Henrik Clarke puts the question in his insightful booklet _Can African People Save Themselves?_ "Why do we import European and other foreigners to build roads, bridges, etc. when we have the technical skills to do it ourselves? Why are we purchasing shoes from Europe and other places when we have more than enough cows to make shoe leather right at home in Africa?"

Truly "the greatest of all treasures is the golden knowledge of self". A serious study of our true history is one of the master keys to unlocking that knowledge. Here are some additional reasons why Afrikan-centered scholars and behavioral scientists think that the study of history from an Afro-centric worldview is of such vital importance to the advancement of the race. Firstly, history helps us understand why the present world is the way it is. The lessons of history also provide us with clues as to how to change for the better those things which need changing. Without a clear grasp of world history and our rightful place in it, we will not know how to accurately interpret current events or adequately plan for our survival and victory over adverse circumstances presently or in the future. If one does not have a reasonable understanding of how things came to be, one will not be able to comprehend why circumstances and conditions are the way they are. Not knowing who you really are makes you ignorant of your place in the scheme of life and vulnerable to exploitation. Therefore, history can be a power tool in the hands of those of our people who sincerely desire to change things from what they are to what they should be. Dr. Imari A. Obadele makes this observation. "Humans are the only species capable of thinking in the past, present and future tense." As far as we know only non-human animals are confined to thinking and acting instinctively for the present or limited to preparing for the immediate future such as squirrels storing their nuts for the winter. Now if a person cannot get beyond that stage of existence, then one would have to question his/her respective order in the animal kingdom.

Secondly, to transcend the limitations of a purely biological existence, a person/people must have a sense of destiny. For this they must look to their history. Food, clothing, shelter and other biological needs should be balanced with the fulfillment of mental

8

and spiritual needs or as we have already discussed you will confine yourself to being just another animal. High ideals are one of the few factors that motivate humans to rise above basic biological desire and necessities. Without such ideals man is merely an evolving beast of the field, regardless as to how sophisticated he may appear to be. These high ideals are usually garnered from the great moments and cultural customs of a people's tradition and history. Therefore, we suggest that a sublime spiritual level of mental evolution can be achieved by many of our people, especially our youth, through the scientific investigation of Afrikan history particularly the ancient High Culture civilizations. Ancient history demonstrates with glowing examples the fact that through the ages Black People have been able to skillfully balance the intuitive and inspirational with deductive reasoning and experimentation. This balance gave our Afrikan ancestors a special characteristic edge in civilization building. I do truly believe that if we did it then, we can do it now; therefore, we must reach back deep into our cosmic souls and reconnect with our original divine nature.

Thirdly, there are many personal rewards to be gained from reflecting on Afrikan antiquity. Ours is a rich and vibrant history and if we embrace it and observe well its object lessons, it will open up new horizons. One passage of New Testament scripture states it this way, "...be not conformed to this world: but be ye transformed by the renewing of your mind,..."[14] For many of us a "renewing" of our weary and tired minds is a priceless reward unto itself. That stalwart Black Nationalist freedom fighter Malcolm X once declared, "Of all our studies, history is best qualified to reward all research." And so it is. For knowing our true history can provide you with a personal sense of our unique and special revelation to the world. It can motivate you to rediscover your innate ability to think in large dimensions

Finally, we should study our true history, if for no other reason then, as Manning Marible says, "We cannot wipe out the impact and effects of the past." Relative to our collective history, to attempt to do so would be spiritual and mental suicide. For a person/people without a memory (history) is in a pitiful and relatively helpless state as many of us were in the recent past until we began to come into what Messenger Muhammad coined as "a knowledge of self and kind". Therefore all praises are due to every teacher and scholar who has ever come into our midst while we were gripped in the

9

vise of white-supremacy and endeavored to bring us into the brilliant light of our true being. Of this sacred trust Drucilla Dunjee Houston wrote,

> "...from the oft repeated expression found by the author in research work, that 'what the ancients said about the Ethiopians [Afrikans] was fabulous.' Curiosity was aroused to go back over the story of the ancients to agree or draw new conclusions. The finds were so astonishing that the vow was made to spend upon this study many years if necessary. Like the 'Quest of the Holy Grail' the aim became sacred, for the trail led backward into the heart of all that the world holds most precious and to the primal roots from which all culture sprang."[15]

One of the main purposes for the writing of this series is to assist our readers in making the connection between those things one has seen and heard from the many streams of the everyday Black Experience and the documented evidence of the greatness of Afrikan People and their civilizations in world history. That is why we do our best to present factual data in juxtaposition to those elements most familiar to our readers.

It is in keeping with our commitment to the continuing policy of Fourth Dynasty Publishing Company to add something "new and unique" to the body of literature and informational materials known as the science of Afrikanology—that is the study of things Afrikan—and to participate in the great and exciting period of rediscovery being conducted by Afrikan-centered scholars in the present and to help translate this marvelous braintrust into the language and style of the "popular culture" that we do this. It is also our sincere hope that this knowledge may become the property of the masses and be regarded as a national and Pan Afrikan treasure beneficial to and enjoyed by all our people. We at Fourth Dynasty Publishing Company do truly believe that the potent knowledge of our glorious history should be collectively owned by our people and rewritten upon their hearts for unending generations to come. For it is written in one of the world's most ancient Afrikan history books "After those days, said the Lord, I will put my law in their inward parts, and write it in their hearts; and will be their God and they shall be my people."[16]

In keeping with this divine mandate, our daily prayer is that more and more Afrikan people from every walk of life, wherever we are in the world today will continue to organize and institute study groups and from these satellite bases establish research centers, community libraries, museums and even Afrikan-centered institutions of higher learning. Fortunately, you do not have to start out big to do this. All that is needed is a few sincere committed Brothers and Sisters who will lovingly join forces on a consistent basis, pool their resources, obtain a space, even if it is no more than a store front and build from there. You may be amazed at how far you can go with this once you set your mind to it. In fact there are already many such efforts in progress in many Afrikan communities. Most of them would be more than happy to network with you. Lord knows we certainly have an enlightened army of scholars and brain trusts to provide information and guidance for these endeavors.

Again I would remind you that Black People from all walks of life can participate in this process. What a glorious undertaking. What a marvelous vitality and positive stimulus this would/will bring to our community. For once the Black Race begins to obtain a sufficient and proficient "knowledge of self", it will be just a matter of time before many of us will be about the business of collectively transforming our communities and moving our race further along the high road of our rightful place in the sun. Helping to keep this idea alive and encouraging its fruition is the sacred goal and mission of Fourth Dynasty Publishing Company, as we strive to "attain victory in concert with other Afrikans of like mind and spirit".

CHAPTER ONE

JOURNEY TO THE ANCIENT AFRIKAN WISDOM OF ASTRO-MYTHOLOGICAL COSMOGONY

PRELUDE

Many of the ancients believed that the sun, the moon and the planets, with the stars beyond, moved around the Earth on great crystal spheres. The turning of these spheres was believed to produce beautiful, though inaudible celestial music. This music was called the "music of the spheres". Therefore it is only fitting that the title for this chapter came to me while I was listening to Pharaoh Sanders' version of Lonnie Liston Smith's spiritually transcendent composition *Astro Traveling*. While researching the subject, many ideas came to mind as to how to crystallize such an involved study into a concise heading that would be as clear as the streams that flowed through the old opulent Nubian valley known as the Table of the Sun. The beautiful strains of music helped the words to flow together. Thus the theme *Journey to the Ancient Afrikan Wisdom of Astromythological Cosmogony*.

Journey because we are spiritually going back in time as we seek to think as our ancestors thought when they were creating the timeless cycle of pictographic stories which they used to illustrate the principles of natural science. The original Afrikan scientists knew that knowledge was a basic source of power, that wisdom was the correct application of that knowledge and that knowledge can only be properly applied if there is understanding. And they used a variety of signs, symbols, myths and folkloric traditions to illustrate that reality. We do not here assume to exhaustively define the total meaning of ancient Kushite-Kemetan symbolism and sign language as we are certainly at a disadvantage being so far removed—tens of thousands of years removed—from the periods of their original conception. Our objective here is to explore and define this ancient sign language of astro-mythology making it intelligible to our present levels of relativity and understanding. We are certain that further light and clarification on these ancient sciences and their concomitant esoterical communications will be consistently forthcoming as more data is revealed through the collective efforts of committed Afrikanologists.

The study of ancient cosmogonies (creation stories) and cosmological (study of natural laws in the universe) myths is a complex and very involved pursuit. What is presented here is this author's Afro-centric views based upon the information presently available to me. In a study of this nature, it must always be kept in mind that the sign language of astro-mythology in the ancient cosmogonies was just another way of stating the scientific principles espoused by geologists, anthropologists and other branches of natural science in today's world. "Usually the most important myth in a culture, one that becomes the exemplary model for all other myths, is the cosmogonic myth. It relates how the entire world came into being."[17] This genre of myth generally involves a Divine Spirit which acts upon matter and produces water, earth, fire and air. This is the basic foundation of all creation stories which is what a cosmogonic myth is. The astro-mythological aspect is demonstrated by John G. Jackson, "In studying the mythology and religion of ancient Egypt [Kemet], it becomes apparent to any reader that he or she is contemplating a system of beliefs and rites based on the science of astronomy. The priest of ancient Egypt [Kemet] possessed a profound knowledge of astronomy, and this fact has been recognized by eminent modern scholars of the subject."[18] Understanding that all things in the cosmos whether earthly or heavenly was inter-related, the ancients believed there was usually an astronomic correlation or connection with human and terrestrial events. Thus the great body of astro-mythological creation stories that were so widely circulated in the ancient world.

THE PURPOSE AND FUNCTION OF CREATION STORIES

All peoples and great nations of antiquity endeavored to account for the origin of the world often using the same themes in a variety of cultural and historical applications and there are striking similarities in the pictures they drew. The constant reoccurrence of the symbology in vogue at the time testifies to the common matrix from which biblical and other creation myths were formed. And although the figures differ from myth to myth all the ancient stories intend simply to give a poetic accounting for cosmic origins.

Creation myths deal with the origin of the world and presuppose that in the beginning there was something uncreated and that

14

order was created out of chaos by a divine entity. The Kushite-Kemetan scientists of old perceived that everything in the ecological world had a mathematical balance and to them mathematics was not just happenstance. It suggested the existence of a preeminent intelligence—a Creative Force. This rationale on the part of the ancients is called "Theism" from the Greek _theos_ meaning "god" and implies that the world as we know it preceded from a divine being in the cosmos and that it was by the will of this Universal Intelligence that all things came to be.

How the ancients arrived at the conceptualization of the idea of a personal creator may be evident in the fact that as they observed how the invisible heat of the sun moves upon the elements of the soil and creates flowers, trees, food and other life giving substances and how the wind creates storms or pushes back the shadowy clouds in the sky to reveal the sunshine or that cosmic forces (natural law) reveals the well ordered structure of the universe and that even when you cannot see the sun on a cloudy day, you can still feel its heat and see the evidences of its creative power in the physical world, but probably the most profound sense of a Supreme Creative Force was in the power of parents to beget offspring.

The mystery of the fetus as it continued to grow in the darkness of the womb and develop through the successive stages of gestation then departing the portals of heaven and bursting forth into the light of this world appears to have, more than any other single factor, the deepest influence on the human psyche. Barbara Walker says,

> "Myths of creation generally present a symbolic view of birth. Conditions before creation suggest the uterine environment: darkness, liquid, stirring or churning movement, the 'eternal flux'...Often there is a suggestion of one entity inside another. 'When there was neither the creation, nor the sun, the moon, the planets, and the Earth, and then darkness was enveloped in Darkness'...Most creation myths speak of a splitting or an opening in the dark...The beginning of the existing world is signaled by the coming of light. Romans made the connection [which they borrowed from their Kemetan teachers] with birth quite clear: Juno Lucina was not only a creatress, but also the Mother who brought 'light' to the eyes to the newborn. The biblical God who said 'Let there be light' copied the word of the Goddess."

Many of the cosmogonic myths depicted the creation of the world as a dividing process. Darkness was divided from light and

15

dry land as a place for humans to breathe air was divided from the primal waters. Walker goes on to explain why the creation stories always spoke of light coming out of darkness.

"The prominence given everywhere to that moment of light suggest archetypal memories of the first impact of light on newborn eyes which have never seen light before. Like dreams of the individual unconscious, myths of the collective unconscious reveal hidden memories of the birth trauma. 'Locked up in the depths of our unconscious mind is the terrific impact of birth, the violent adventure that uprooted our pre-natal world.' It is also locked up in the symbolism of myths, projected on to the cosmic scale."[19]

MAKE IT BIGGER THAN LIFE AND THE PEOPLE WILL REMEMBER

There seems to be a basic human need for, even at times a demand for, the myths. Some psychologists think this need is as great in people today as ever it was in days gone by. "Indeed, most people will admit, if they are truthful, that they actually experience life on two levels—the scientific and the mythological...Myths provide a bridge between our outer 'realities' and the hope and fears of our dreams." As always seems to be the case, "...myths explain the phenomena of nature by drawing parallels between simple known things and those that are harder to grasp...Thus, out of common physical characteristics, symbolic equations are made, and one thing takes on the qualities of another."[20] Martin Bernal informs us that in the ancient world "...nearly all myths were based on one of two principles the miracle of sexual reproduction; and the intricate movements of the stars and other heavenly bodies. Although myth was couched in spectacular and fantastic terms,...it concealed an inner scientific truth which could be explained only in terms of science."[21] This astro-mythological method of recording and teaching scientific principles grew out of man's "...expression of his ultimate attitude to the universe, the summed-up meaning and proport of his whole consciousness of things."[22] Albert Churchward says that the myth "...as a mode of expression; and all its great primordial types are universal....There is a unity of origin for all mythology, as is demonstrated by a world-wide comparison of the great primary types."[23] And Bernal adds "...that all mythologies and religions can be traced back to one source, Egypt

16

[Kemet]."[24] The Kushite and Kemetan scientists used mythology as a method for teaching natural history. The myths were stories which helped to explain by means of something concrete and intelligible an abstract idea of such vague and difficult conceptions as creation, death and the place of humans in the universe. Their ultimate purpose was to explain why something exists or happens. This ancient form of myth-making was used as a process for relating the localized and temporal to the cosmic and eternal. The symbols of all the ancient mythologies have a scientific foundation and substance. The allegorical interpretations of myths and their symbology were an expression of the wisdom inherent in the High Culture Science of the ancient Kushites and Kemetans. In time mythological stories grew up about almost every object in nature. For example the rustling of the leaves was supposed to be the murmuring goddess who lived in the trees.

Having served as a vehicle for explaining the beginnings of the world and the universe and the creation of humans, the role of mythology in the human experience was continually expanded. Myths also began to account for how and why a people developed their own particular outlook and view of the world. Such questions as "How did they learn to make fire, fish, hunt, rear domestic animals, cultivate the earth, discover medicines, and, later, write?"[25] were often very esthetically and graphically answered through the facilitation of the myth as well. This in turn gave rise to the many stories which told of the universal Eden-like state of the planet Earth immediately after the dawn of its creation. "Plenty of food and water first made heaven palpable to primitive or archaic man on earth. Hence the primitive paradise was imaged as a field or garden of food. . . The tree of life was planted in the midst of the celestial oasis. . . A power of perennial renewal was perceived in nature, and this was manifested by successive births."[26]

One of the main ingredients of astro-mythology was the gods and goddesses who were viewed as presiding over the many aspects and manifestations of nature. Most of the names of the deities mentioned in ancient mythologies are based on an age old system of ancestor reverence. These symbols of cosmic phenomena were actual people who lived and functioned at a particular time and place in a nation's cultural history. Because they had manifested certain attributes and contributed so much to the collective well being of the community, their physical departure was so deeply felt at their passing that these exceptional men and women were

17

inducted into the god head. These gods and goddesses came to represent certain principles of astro and natural science. Churchward says "The gods of Egypt [Kemet], from the beginning, represented food and drink, not only as givers of sustenance—they were the sustenance in food and liquid. The Great Mother was the suckler, or wet-nurse. Hathor [Het Heru] offered food in the sycamore-fig, and Isis [Auset] in the persea-tree of life."[27] And the god Heru [Horus] was the light of day which helped to nourish the soil.

Just as there are many names and titles for Jesus and other Christian deities in many different languages and various forms of "revelation", so it was in ancient times when the Kushites and their Kemetan daughter traversed the globe spreading high culture. In each geographical location the principles of natural science took on the local coloring and language of the indigena. Each of these personified some principle of Mother Nature and Mother Sky.

"Ancient mythology, legend and parable, which even the later Nazarean [Jesus] did not hesitate to use, is a stupendous and glorious means of history recording...The characteristic trait of the myth is to convert reflection into history (a historical form). As in the epos, so in the myth, the historical element predominates. Facts (external events) often constitute the basis of the myth, and with these, religious ideas are interwoven... The idea that mythology is an allegorical interpretation of historical events or a natural phenomena to the masses, who are capable of grasping only a partial truth, was well established in Antiquity."[28]

There are 3 basic types of myth; the aesthetic myth which serves mainly as a source of entertainment and recreation. Stories of this type are usually very dramatic and/or tell of the amusing adventures of humans and animals. They play a very important part in the life of a people for they are more than just exciting or funny tales which help to make up the substance of happy gatherings. They always contain an object lesson designed to reinforce the value system of the community and enhance sociability.

Another class of story is the explanatory myth. These are generally taken more seriously and are usually regarded as sacred because they account for the origin of the world, the creation of humans and the reasons for sickness and death and oft times furnish revelations of a people's future existence on Earth as well as an individual's journey to the realm of the ancestors—the mystic

18

abode of life after death. It is from this type of myth that the various religious systems developed.

Then there is the heroic or historical myth which refers to important exploits of heroic deeds of past generations and are considered to be true. The sociological function of such stories is that they develop family pride, knit kinship bonds more firmly and serve to increase communal solidarity in the family, community, nation and race. In each of these classifications of myth can be found,

> "...the most profound truth and laws of God and Nature. Rightly understood, according to their real, esoteric, spiritual meaning, the myths, legends and parables bequeathed to us by ancient civilizations, are seen to combine rare beauty, grandeur and practicability of application."[29]

By all indications it appears that the major objective of the ancient myth makers was to help their students and others to remember and recall information through the system of psychopictographic imagery. Our primary focus in the succeeding chapters will be the explanatory or sacred myth as it relates to the creation of the world and humans—the cosmogonic myth. At this point in our study as we are preparing to analyze the Theory of Creationism as set forth in the various creation stories, it is appropriate to give some attention to the use and misuse of symbols as applied in ancient and modern mythology.

THERE SURE AIN'T NOTHING LIKE THE REAL THING

Throughout the ages there has been the problem of humans erroneously embracing the symbol as a substitute for reality. I suppose this is because the symbol of a person, place, thing or event is more obvious and often more tangible than the real thing which usually requires some degree of rational thought and analysis. It seems the average person would rather take the easy way out and focus on the symbol. That is why fantasy religions based solely on mythology bear such sway over the masses and help to keep the few in power over the many. So easily are people diverted from pursuing reality that power hungry individuals have been able to manipulate this human weakness to gain and maintain control over the gullible masses during many stages of human history. How did this happen? Why did it happen and why are

19

humans still slavishly wed to symbols today? Edgar J. Ridley in his article The Neurological Misadventure of Primordial Man in the autumn of 1982 edition of the periodical Black Male Female Relationships seeks to answer these questions. He says,

> "The axis on which world history turns is symbolism...It should be made clear here that a symbol is nothing but a representation of reality. In other words, a symbol is a substitute. A symbol, because it is a substitute, is a plastic entity. It is not real within itself, but a representation."[30]

The cosmogonies that we find in ancient Kemet, India and Babylonia and other stories of creation when they first began to be recited used the names of gods and goddesses as symbols of the myriad manifestations of the Creative Force. But as time went on the common man began to be separated from the higher knowledge and from his original keen awareness of his own spirituality. Then religion began to degenerate into forms and rituals which encouraged people to believe that these symbols were actually real. Now the scholars in Kemet, India, Babylonia and other centers of high culture civilization who were searching the skies with telescopes and analyzing the wonders of natural science knew better, but many of them let the average man believe this was true. So the common man was led into the trap of bowing down to images and statues and kissing venerated things and paying suppliant homage to one holy something or other.

As regrettable as this state of affairs was it is my duty as an honest Afrikan-centered scholar to bring out the bad as well as the good in our history and we cannot escape the fact that this was Black Folks doing it to Black Folks. Back then many power hungry individuals allowed the masses to literally worship them and to bow in reverence before statues which they knew had no life of their own for the priests and wise men were fully aware that if you created a thing how then could that thing be the Creator. How could it have power of its own generation. Granted there was knowledge among the Kemetan priests of the science of transferring energy from one object unto another, yet even with that the one who created the image and brought about the transference of energy to that thing could not rationally consider that thing to be greater than his or herself. So when we find some of our ancient kingdoms during certain periods of history at this stage we can readily see that this was not the best that we had originally produced from our high culture civilizations, but rather the lower elements of that culture. Reflecting on this Ridley strongly suggests that "...all religions, by virtue of their symbolic intent, would have to be re-evaluated for their distortion, due to the implicit and prevalent symbolic ingredient in all other world's religions."[31]

What has happened here in the instance of distorted symbology is that man no longer sees the symbol as a representation of something which in fact did or does exist, but he now views the symbol as being the thing itself. For example, a picture of you is a symbol of you, but the picture is not you. For your soul mate to embrace the picture and hug it and kiss it is a nice sentimental thing, but if they begin to do that quite often, you could safely say that person was having some neurological or psychological problems. And if your mate begins to prefer the picture to you, you would know beyond a shadow of a doubt that you were really in a "world of trouble" as far as the relationship was concerned. This is what man has done with mythology and religion. Those symbols which represented certain aspects and principles of the Creative Force in the universe, he no longer sees them as representing the principle or as something for him to focus on to bring the principle to mind. He now views the symbol as being real. So today many Black People will walk into a church with a picture of a blond-haired, blue-eyed white man and worship it as though it was the Almighty Creative Force itself. Ridley points to a remedy for this particular kind of mental illness. "Once Black People have the understanding of what a symbol really is there can be no confusion as to what is real and what is symbolic."[32]

In reference to the "confusion as to what is real and what is symbolic", I am reminded of an incident which took place in Houston, Texas. Two brethren of the cloth who had attended several of my my seminars there went back to their churches determined to set the historical and biblical record straight and they had two different experiences. One minister went back and read from the Bible where it says that Jesus had "hair like lamb's wool" and skin like "burnished bronze" and rightly interpreted this passage of scripture as describing the personage of a Black Man. Then he went on to quote historical documents which proved that Jesus was an Afrikan of the tribe of Judah, the darkest tribe in ancient Israel further building his case by presenting all the various evidences of historical reality we had studied in class. Then he boldly announced that they were going to remove all of the Euro-centric

21

images of Jesus from the church by the following Sunday and here is how the congregation responded. "We don't care what the Bible says. We don't care what history says and if you try to take those pictures and images down from the walls and from over the pulpit, the baptismal pool or from anywhere in this church, you had better find yourself another job some place else because you will no longer be pastoring here." The other preacher had a little more power in his church. He made a similar announcement and strongly stated in no uncertain terms that "By the next Sunday we will have disposed of all images of white deities because this is not the truth. They represent blatant lies and you have to stop having your children running in here looking up to a white man for the answer to their problems." And so during the following week it happened as he had said and at the removal of these images many of the people cried like babies as if "ole Massa was leaving the plantation, gone away never to come back again." Why was the emotional attachment to these white-supremist symbols of universal power so strongly demonstrated on each occasion? Why? Because the remnants of a slave mentality had many of the members of these congregations caught up in the symbol and one of the ways you can control the people is by taking them away from reality and keep them focused on the symbols.

Ridley reminds us that many of

> "...the rituals and superstitions of Afrikan people which emanated from the so-called spiritual experience became symbolic, lost all of its original qualitative power. Therefore, these rituals and superstitions lost all facsimile of being a liberating force for the growth, spirituality and power of all Afrikan people."[33]

Often people fight over the different symbols. Much blood has been foolishly shed through the annals of human history over them. And that is why I do not permit differences of religion to get in the way of my relationship to my beloved Black brothers and sisters. Neither will I allow a symbol to become a religion to me. On several occasions I have been vehemently denounced for this position. First I encountered a brother who was a born again Christian and he challenged me that if I did not accept his Jesus as my personal savior, I would be proscribed to eternal damnation. A few days later another brother who was a practitioner of a particular demonination of the religion of Islam consigned my soul to hell because I would not submit to his religious frame of reference. Then later on a Rastafarian told me I wasn't his brother because I didn't accept his way of life, nor did I understand Jah—the One Love as he did. This was amazing. I had three bloods in less than a week's time disown me as their brother and condemn me to oblivion simply because we do not share the same symbols. So you see, Brothers and Sisters, how devastating misplaced religious symbols can and have been. Therefore, my people for your own personal good in particular and the advance of the race in general, it is incumbent upon us to put the symbol in its proper perspective and deal with what it represents and not get lost in the symbol itself. It should be made very clear here that a symbol is nothing more or less than a representation. In other words a symbol is a substitute. Again Ridley says that many "Black People fail to realize that symbols and reality are indeed opposite. Black people fail to understand that 'symbols are essentially plastic'."[34]

In view of the present condition of many of our people throughout the world today who have been tossed and driven by every wind of doctrine like leaves at the mercy of a storm, I believe that we cannot over emphasize the fact that a symbol because it is a substitute is a plastic entity. It is not real within itself but a representation. Therefore, we reiterate, don't get caught up in the symbol. Get down to what the symbol represents and understand that symbols are only "mental representations of reality" not the reality itself. Otherwise the symbol is of no value to you whatsoever.

Ridley wisely advises,

"...we must realize that rituals, symbolism, superstition and tradition have not freed Afrikan people, and is not freeing Afrikan people in the diaspora. We wake up every morning as if it is the norm to be on the bottom the world over...and indeed, even though some of us wake up each morning like being on the bottom and servitude to white people is the norm, using symbols in place of ultimate reality, or spiritual impulses, produces a very, very frictional people who are continually in a state of conflict, jealousy and rivalry."

Commenting on many of those Black People who find it difficult to deal with reality, Ridley says,

"What I am stating here is that because Afrikan people around the world refuse, and continue to refuse, to act on, and understand, the difference between substance and symbols; because Afrikan people around the world choose to follow what is

23

symbolic and plastic, they continue and will continue, to be slaves to a white minority population...We have got to answer the question, if indeed we were so great, what happened? I say we were great. But any people who continually allow themselves to be led symbolically will disintegrate... Ultimate reality is simply what one experiences ultimately...It is beyond my comprehension why black people continue to opt for and be fooled by symbols."

And finally he says because of this misplaced neurotic attachment to symbols "most black scholars continue to function under the values and norms of white academia."[35]

Symbols have always been key to people in general and the Black Man in particular for well over 100,000 years. They probably started as ideograms and other pictographic messages which were necessary in the development and formulation of language before man acquired fluid writing skills for it seems that the cursive script was preceded by the picture symbols of Medu Netcher (hieroglyphics). So for all these years humans have been intimately relying on symbols, but now the symbols have man in a trap.

Instead of the average person using the symbols, the symbols are now being used by a handful to manipulate the masses. The people in power who are using the symbols know which buttons to push. They know just how to project them in the media and which words to use to get a particular emotional response. Normally they discourage an intelligent response because an intelligent response is an analytical response and once people become analytical they get to a point where they are no longer controlable, but if people blindly follow the symbols, the power brokers can press the right button and get a corresponding reaction or inaction. So my people we must get into the habit of emphasizing and re-emphasizing reality and not the symbol.

Brother Ridley suggests that we should dispose of all symbols. Yet after developing a habit for over 100,000 years, man is not likely to give up on his symbols. Therefore, those of us who have come to the light of understanding must now learn how to make plain what the symbol represents. The reality as opposed to focusing on the symbol. Many times in order to get a person back to reality you have to take them to the door of their symbol. But you must be careful to redefine and put that symbol in its proper perspective. This in and of itself is a powerful bit of knowledge to have and can be extremely useful to the average Black Person. Once he or she comes to fully understand this reality, he or she cannot be manipulated any longer. In fact one can in turn use certain symbolic words to press the emotional buttons of and to manipulate those who have been manipulating you. This question of separating the symbol from the reality and not being manipulated by the symbol is possibly one of the most important things that I will ever present to you, my people, throughout the course of my teaching and writing. Perhaps we can best overcome the pathological pitfalls of confusing symbols with reality by simply realizing that. . .

SYMBOLS WERE A MEANS OF COMMUNICATION IN THE ANCIENT WORLD

Though the symbol tells something about the phenomena, it is not the phenomena, i.e., stone images, religious symbols, etc.. The symbol is simply a key to unlocking the door behind which the true knowledge for solving the mysteries of life is rediscovered. For example, the profound and deep spiritual significance of water.

"Water had revealed the secret of creation in the life which came as food by water from the Mother-Earth in the unfathomable deep. The secret of water as a source of life was the primal mystery of the Egyptians [Kemetans]...Thus we have the Deep, the darkness of the face of the Deep [i.e. the Genesis story], the light breaking out of darkness, the waters and the life springing forth from the waters in the eatable plants."[36]

The first humans are symbolically portrayed as being molded out of the black clay of the womb of Mother Earth by a Divine Sculptor on the cosmic potter's wheel and we have already talked about the meaning of the symbology of the Universal Egg suspended in the primeval ocean as depicted in the creation myths.[37] Thus water as a symbol of these eternal principles was used in birth, rebirth and cleansing ceremonies, in fact, most all of the rituals and celebrations participated in by the ancients.

Frankfort says in *Ancient Egyptian Religion* that "...cosmic phenomena such as the course of the sun or moon, or the changeless rhythm of the seasons, reveal not only transcendent power but also order. In this lies their revelency to the affairs of man. They enable man to find, intuitively and imaginatively, answers to problems of his own existence: the problem of justice as the order of human society, the problem of survival after death

25

as the desired order of human life, or even the problem of meaning as related to the order of existence."[38] Higgins pinpointing one of the celestial aspects of mythological symbolism says "The sun himself, in his corporeal and visible form of a globe of fire,...was, for a long time, the sole trinity."[39] To the ancients the sun was a timely illustration of the age old concept of the Trinity. For example, the substance of the sun which cannot be seen or touched represented the hidden knowledge, strength and physical essence thereof, the powers of the masculine principle. The light and the rays which are beheld visually but cannot be touched with human hands or any instrument or vehicle of any kind represents offspring that is new life in the form of the child or children. The heat of the sun whose warm glow or elevated temperature can be experienced through physical sensation but cannot be seen with the naked eye represented the inspirational and motivational powers of the feminine principle. This all amounted to the Kushite-Kemetan concept of the Father, the Son and the Holy Ghost (Mother). The sun was not only emblematic but was also revered in all its aspects. In ancient times the golden orb was universally honored for its manifold blessings to our solar system in general and to the planet Earth and its inhabitants in particular. In those days great men and women who in their lives and work in the community had demonstrated certain of these lifegiving and sustaining attributes were symbolically deified. "Thus, there were sun gods representing the physical orb, the intellectual sun, the sun considered as the source of heat, and the source of light, the power of the sun, the sun in the firmament, and the sun in his resting place."[40]

This gave rise to the heroic myths as set forth in sacred texts and epic poems. These myths "...were the legendary history of kings and heroes, transformed into gods by the admiration of the nations."[41] As a matter of fact the word hero comes from Heru the Kemetan god of daylight—the second manifestation of the solar Trinity, one of the names of Horus.

> "The hero's deeds and inventions benefitted mankind both materially and spiritually... inventions of such extraordinary importance for survival were ascribed to cult heroes who had obviously been endowed with unusual talents...they served as models for people who had to live and struggle, suffer defeats, enjoy some triumphs, and die. Thus each epic forms a cycle analogous to the rise, zenith, and sinking of the sun each day."[42]

Of the magnificent architectural structures said to be built by many of the world's original heroes and heroines who were in actuality the kings and queens and master scientists of the ancient Kushite Empire during the Golden Age,[43] Cheikh Anta Diop says,

"These are found only in lands inhabited by Negroes or Negroids, or in places that they have frequented, the area that Speiser calls 'the great megolithic civilization', which extends from Afrika to India, Australia, South America, Spain, and Brittany."[44]

Most of these marvelous edifaces were dedicated to the ever prevading divine principles of procreation as was so clearly exemplified by the term Om inscribed on the inner walls of many of them.[45] Godfrey Higgins tells us that the letter O represents the 360 degree cycle of the cosmic scheme[46] which we will be discussing further on. The O in Om also symbolizes the womb of woman. And the letter M he says signified the numeral 40.[47] This we have found generally denotes the 40 week period of gestation during human pregnancy. It was one of the principle interpretations of the complex meaning of "Om" in ancient Kemet. Another indication of the sacred regard for procreation and motherhood as illustrated by the symbology of the Hapi (Nile) Valley high culture civilization.

Another distinguishing feature of the scientific symbology created by the original Black Race was the prolific use of animal images. As for example the serpent as initially employed in astromythology was a symbol of wisdom and immortality and at other times as a symbol of procreativity. Although regarded as an omen of death and evil by some cultures such as the Hebrews and the Babylonians, it was generally revered as an emblem of life as in the medical professions i.e. the entwined serpents of the caduceus which like the Rx insignia you see posted on drug stores and pharmaceuticals originated in ancient Kemet. According to Clymer the sign of the serpent was also used to illustrate the full spectrum of the 12 constellations. He says,

"In the most ancient maps, the zodiac was represented as a serpent banding the earth by holding its tail in its mouth. The band was sixteen degrees wide and, owing to the earth's movement around the sun, appeared partly above the equator for six months and below it for the other half of the year. The ancient Wise Men had basic scientific reasons for assigning the constellations and for drawing the figures around each."[48]

27

As to the profound meaning of animal images in the scientific records of high culture symbology Bernal says,

"...the zoolatry...of Egyptian [Kemetan] religion were merely an allegorical veneer for the masses: the priests, and/or those who had been initiated, knew that in reality the zoolatry and fantastic myths concealed deep abstractions and a profound understanding of the universe."[49]

In essence the symbolism of the ancient world as we examine it in retrospect provides us with some idea of

"How the primitive man observed the works and ways and on-goings of the intelligence thus manifested around him; how he copied where he could, and gradually found a line of his own in the scheme of development; how he honored these early teachers and instructors, and made their forms the pictures of the primal thoughts which they had evoked from his mind, is at length recorded in the system of hieroglyphic [Medu Netcher] symbols and mythology: and the illustrated proofs are extant to this day."[50]

As we draw to the close of this chapter, let us momentarily reflect on

THE ROLE OF WRITING IN ANCIENT SYMBOLOGY

In the older Kushite civilizations the knowledge of writing was universal throughout the populace,[51] but in the later Kemetan Empire, this basic literary function was assumed to be the perogative of the priests and aristocracy. Thus writing became a secretive art to the general masses. Eventually the written word was looked upon by them as being magical. At this time knowledge was largely conveyed to common man through the symbols demonstrated in elaborate rituals and richly imaginative legends and allegories. These manifestations deeply appealed to the spirit and emotions of the people. In this setting symbols increasingly grew in the nature of their significance and power. In essence they became bigger than life. Herein is how symbolism came to be a tool of manipulation of the few over the many.

Reflecting on this historically, we can readily see how misplaced symbolism was a major step in the wrong direction taken by the priestly repositories in the ancient High Culture System; for it helped to lay the basis for the future gullibility of the people. Because the knowledge of writing and other essential elements of civilization now became the exclusive property of the priests and hierarchy, it left the entire civilized infrastructure vulnerable. When powerful enemy forces invaded the land they had but to remove the head and the body was left weak and without direction. These various intermediate periods throughout the long history of the Kemetan Empire were plagued with great strife, decentralization and the destruction of vital information necessary to the well being of the people. Yusef ben Levi of the Kemetan Institute in Chicago, Illinois graphically describes one of these periods.

> "...a man goes out to plough with his shield, indeed, hearts are violent, pestilence is everywhere, blood is throughout the land, death is not lacking...Indeed, the land turns around like a potter's wheel; the robbers are possessors of riches and the rich man is become a plunderer... barbarians from abroad have come to Kemet...all is ruin."[52]

Here is a classic historic example of what extreme ends misplaced symbolic emphasis can lead to.

We have been discussing how symbols were created, why they were first used by Afrikan wise men and women of old and the manner in which they can be misunderstood. Now we will observe how they were originally applied to denote scientific principles and how we in our time can redirect them to that purpose.

CHAPTER TWO

THE KEMETAN COSMOGONICAL SPHERE IN
THE ANCIENT WORLD

PRELUDE

As we begin our studies of the many creation myths which describe in terms of each nation's and people's cultural experience their stories of the birth of the universe, we·will start with the first, ancient Kemet—the eldest daughter of the old Kushite World Empire—because the scientific principles illustrated in their astro-mythological symbolism —though varied in names and places according to geographical location—were universal. This we will clearly demonstrate as we move ahead in these studies. Dr. Cheikh Anta Diop informs us that the symbols of the gods and goddesses who played major and minor roles in the Kemetan cosmogony were conceived by the original Black Race. He says,

> "...authentic Egyptian [Kemetan] tradition, as old as recorded time and written into the *Texts of the Pyramids* and the *Book of the Dead*, teaches us in unequivocal terms that the Egyptian deities belonged to the Black race and were born in the south. Furthermore, the myth of Osiris [Ausuru] and Isis [Auset] points out a cultural trait characteristic of Black Africa: the cult of ancestors, the foundation of Negro religious life and of Egyptian [Kemetan] religion life...".[53]

The religious life of ancient Kemet was based on their world view as exemplified in the stories of creation and the origin of things. These ideas were essential to their daily life and was the impetus which helped to inspire their lofty achievements as witnessed in the tendency to build and do things on a grand scale i.e. the pyramids, the Ramesseum, Karnak, etc., and those gargantuan structures which their learned wise men raised all over the world at various periods of the Kemetan Nation's extreme longevity. To the Kemetan, like all Afrikans in their natural state, religion was as Dr. Chancellor Williams tells us "...something more than a subscribed-to system of beliefs, but a philosophy and actual way of living."[54]

This logical approach to religion was the cosmic glue which inextricably tied the Kemetan people to their Kushite roots for the word religion comes to us from the Latin *religio* meaning "to bind

31

or tie to". Unfortunately, in today's world having been taken out of its original Afrikan-centered cultural context and historical reality it often "binds" us to something to which we do not belong. But in the beginning this was not so, for to the Kemetans religion—before its later corruption by foreign invaders and unprincipled aristocratic clergy—was a force which stimulated the people to an elevated view of life and its experiences, and a highly spiritual awareness of unity with the total cosmos which was so dynamically demonstrated in their magnificent achievements. This eminent level of human attainment was motivated by a Kemetan religious philosophy of which Dr. Jackson reminds us, "the earliest religion of Egypt has been traced back to central Africa: the oldest structure [Kemet] of the people...was that which resembled the African in beliefs and practices."[55] Dr. Williams elucidates this still further.

"...African people are highly spiritual. A truly higher civilization can develop only from such a spiritual-moral foundation. Africans already possess the kind of spirit that should permeate their educational system, govern their economic activities, and guide their political actions. In practical every day living this would mean *actualizing* brotherhood and sisterhood through an each-for-all and all-for-each way of life, especially in economic activities...Now such a program would represent the triumph of the human spirit in deliberately placing human values above materialism...and develop a way of life expressly aimed at *actually* improving the conditions of existence for every human being."[56]

That is the way religion was practiced in the daily lifestyles of the populous of the original Kushite and Kemetan Empires and should be practiced by Afrikan People today.

Dr. Diop sums up why this understanding of the ancient Kushite-Kemetan world view is so important to us today. "A dynamic, modern contact with Egyptian [Kemetan] Antiquity would enable Blacks to discover increasingly each day the intimate relationship between all Blacks of the continent and the Mother Nile Valley."[57] The Hapi (Nile) Valley civilization was one of the pinnacles of human achievement. In fact, what our Afrikan ancestors accomplished during the classical development of the Kemetan Empire became a panacea for all succeeding civilizations and should serve as an inspiration to all Black People the world over. For in reality what the Kemetans did in their time is an innate and integral part of our natural African-centered being. Joel A. Rogers crystallizes this reality thusly,

32

"One's ancestry does not come out of the air. Though invisible it is as real as anything else on this planet. Every 'atom' of our ancestry could be accounted for. Many, many millions of individuals over vast centuries—individuals who lived and breathed even as ourselves—built it up as surely as the insects built up a coral reef. Had there been the tiniest break in our ancestral line we could not have been the individuals we now are. In fact, we might never have been born at all."[58]

THE PROFOUND MEANING OF KEMETAN ASTRO-MYTHOLOGICAL COSMOGONY

Kemetan mythology was inherited from the oldest in the world, the Kushite. The basic principles of Kemetan cosmogonies were primarily concerned with the manifold manifestations of nature: the sky, the earth, the wind, the sun, the moon, the stars, the Hapi River and the forces of reproduction. The origin and function of the various entities of the natural world were personified in the symbology of gods and goddesses. We will be examining some of these deified personalities up close in this chapter. As time progressed through the exceptionally long extent of the empire, creation legends continued to expand and became more and more complex as the levels of scientific knowledge were increasingly enhanced by the Kemetan's brain trust, ever renewing inquisitiveness and determination to solve the mysteries of the universe. Frankford says that the Kemetans combined "...a profound awareness of the complexity of the phenomenal world with that of a mystic bond uniting man and nature."[59]

Churchward tells us

"Egypt's [Kemet] knowledge of the beginnings was laboriously derived by the long, unceasing verification of scientific naturalists. Their astronomical knowledge did not find all from the Heavens ready made, nor was there any claim to a miraculous birth. It was gained by a long course of observation of all nature and nature's laws. Whatever they 'dug and worked for' was from reality —objectively—and everything they did was for a perpetual Symbol of the Truth."[60]

Kemetan scientists through their close observation of the heavens and the Earth

"...divided time, knew the true length of the year, and the precession of the equinoxes. By recording the rising and setting

33

of the stars, they understood the particular influences which proceed from the positions and conjunctions of all heavenly bodies, and therefore their priests, [could prophesy] as accurately as our modern astronomers... astral motion."[61]

Dr. John G. Jackson quoting from Albert Churchward's *Signs and Symbols of Primordial Man* says,

"What the knowledge of all this was old in Egypt [Kemet] before the Babylonians [usually credited with the invention of astronomy] even existed or knew anything about it. The Egyptians [Kemetans] had worked out all the architecture of the heavens and their priests had carried the same with them to all parts of the world—not only the Northern heavens but the Southern, as well. Probably they worked out the South before the North, and the Druids and the Mayas and the Incas knew it all from the priests of Egypt [Kemet],..."[62]

Then Jackson puts this in even clearer perspective by stating,

"In studying the mythology and religion of ancient Egypt, it becomes apparent to any reader that he or she is contemplating a system of beliefs and rites based on the science of astronomy. The priests of ancient Egypt possessed a profound knowledge of astronomy, and this fact has been recognized by eminent modern students of the subject."[63]

The Kemetans even expressed the science of astromythology in musical compositions which they called "the music of the spheres". It is said that their orchestral scores were superior to later ones which evolved in the ancient world. They were among the first to invent musical instruments such as harps which were elaborately constructed and artistically formed from the finest woods and other costly materials. They also created a multiplicity of wind and percussion instruments. They were considered in antiquity to be the best music teachers in the world. Students from India, Arabia, and Greece as well as all the other surrounding nations came to be taught at the feet of Kemetan maestros. Blavatsky says,

"They understood thoroughly well how to extract harmonious sounds out of an instrument by adding stings to it, as well as the multiplication of notes by shortening the strings upon its neck; which knowledge shows a great progress in the musical art. Speaking of harps, in a tomb at Thebes [Wo'se] Bruce remarks that, 'they overturned all the accounts hitherto given of the earlier state of music and musical instruments in the East,

34

and are all together, in their form, ornaments and compass, an incontestable proof, *stronger than a thousand Greek quotations*, that geometry, drawing, mechanics, and music were at the greatest perfection when these instruments were made; and that the period from which we date the invention of these arts was only the *beginning of the era of their restoration*'."[64]

It is also reported that Kemetan medical doctors used music as an aid in physical and spiritual healing. The music they created was so in tune with the cosmos that it became a standard ingredient in the cure for illnesses.[65]

Wow! Those were some "bad brothers and sisters" back in those times. I must need stop here because there is so much more that I could say about this music it would take up the rest of this book and many more, but suffice it to say no doubt John Coltrane, Mary Lou Williams, Theolonius Monk, Charlie "Yardbird" Parker, Charles Mingus, Pharaoh Sanders and a host of other highly spiritual musicians have tapped into sundry dimensions of this ancient Afrikan "music of the spheres".

THE UNITY OF THE ONE IN KEMETAN SYMBOLOGY

The sum total of Kemetan astro-mythology was expressed in myriad symbolic representations indicative of their intimate relationship with the laws of nature. These Afrikans viewed all things in the world as emanating from a cosmic unity-the unity of The One. "The Egyptians [Kemetans] lived in very close contact with nature and found (as we have seen) in the recurring events of the farmer's year experiences pregnant with meaning...". Therefore we must ever bear in mind as we contemplate Kemetan symbolism that they had a "...deep emotional involvement in such natural phenomena as the sun's course or the rise and fall of the Nile [Hapi]."[66]

The Afrikan's "deep emotional involvement" with nature formed the basis for the creation stories recited in the body of oral and literary education material known as Kemetan cosmogony. The Kemetan affinity with nature was also dynamically expressed in the symbolism of zootypes. Churchward says,

"The living Ideographs or Zootypes were primary, and can be traced to their original habitat or home, Africa, and to nowhere else upon the surface of the earth...the Zootype

35

became and was the image of the superhuman power; for example, the Mother-Earth as a giver of water was imaged as a Water-Cow...Female Hippopotamus... Seb, the Father of Food, was imaged by the Goose that laid the eggs."[67]

Churchward goes on to dispel the fallacy of the allegations that the Kemetans literally worshipped animals by clarifying the reasons as to why animals that possessed certain distinct attributes were identified with the superhuman powers of nature.

"The Animals and Birds, etc., were ever superhuman, therefore were adopted as Zoo types and as primary representations of the superhuman Powers of the Elements. They were adopted as primitive Ideographs, and they were adapted for use and consciously stamped for their representative value, not ignorantly worshipped."[68]

Many of these animals such as the elephant, the lion and the bull were adopted as totemic symbols because of their enormous physical strength which far exceeded that of humans. As to the typification of the bull which was personified in Ausuru (Osiris) as a token of the fecundating powers of the Hapi River inundations, Drucilla Houston says, "No intelligent Egyptian worshipped the bull. It was only the symbol that represented Osiris [Ausuru]."[69] Churchward adds, "The root of these things lies far beyond the Anthropomorphic representation...".[70]

The creatures of the animal kingdom became emblematic of the diverse manifestations of natural phenomena in Afrikan literature and were applied as figures for instruction in their colleges and universities. In the elaborate Kemetan temple edifices, classroom and courtyard sessions were facilitated by master teachers who instructively stimulated the imagination of their students through the animation of zootypical symbology. Even in today's Euro-centric dominated society zoolatry continued to exist as a means of getting attention and focusing it for instruction or subliminal affirmation, i.e., the eagle insignia of the USA, the lion of Britain, the bear of Russia, etc, all zootypes. Children are admonished about forest fires by Smokey the Bear and the birth of a child is said to be a visit from the stork. Now there are thousands of examples of this kind of idiographic emphasis in the present world, but no one is accused of actually worshipping these symbols. Resting on the foregoing historical documentation and present data, I submit that the Kemetans were not likely to be inclined towards worshipping animals as deities but rather they had a deep abiding reverence for their attributes which manifested certain aspects of the cosmic creative powers present in all living things. The powers of nature which emanate from the unity of the "One" as symbolized in Zootypes were further perceived in their infinite dimensions through the process of personification. Thus the intricate pantheon of Kushite and Kemetan gods and goddesses. Strange as it may seem to today's way of thinking these deities were characteristic of an all pervading monotheism that was central to Afrikan thought.

Blavatsky says,

> "Despite their apparent Polytheism, the ancients —those of the educated class at all levels—were entirely monotheistical; this, and too, ages upon ages before the days of Moses... *Eminate men were called gods by the ancients*. The deification of mortal men... is no more a proof against their monotheism than the monument-building of modern Christians, who erect statues to their heroes..."[71]

The various names of the gods and goddesses that come down to us from ancient Kemet is indicative of the different schools of thought set forth by the instructors in the High Culture universities over a period of some 18,000 years. The respective deities were "all-comprehensive" and thoroughly harmonized in ancient Afrikan monotheism which clearly demonstrates "...the tolerant wisdom with which they had done justice to the many-sidedness of reality."[72] The Kemetans perceived of the "unity of The One" the "one power" from which they received "a multiplicity of answers" to life's mysteries.

According to Dr. Charles Finch originally the pivotal axis of the philosophy of Kemetan cosmogony was the idea that "the universe was created in an equilibrium and it is the subtle and complex interplay between the light and dark that gives our universe its form and its reality. In the Deified Man the paragon of Egyptian soul science, the opposites are united and transcended."[73] Dr. George GM James adds that the further purpose of the Kemetan high culture learning system was "...the deification of man, and taught that the soul of man if liberated from its bodily fetters, could enable him to become godlike and see the Gods in this life and attain the beatific vision and hold communion with the Immortals." This self realization experience was a manifestation of "...the liberation of the mind from its finite consciousness, when it becomes

37

one and is identified with the Infinite."[74] Barbara Walker, in the book *The Women's Encyclopedia of Myths and Secrets*, gives us a clue as to how these originally lofty ideals and precepts were later degenerated into superstitious idolotry wherein the common man was bound in spiritual servitude to the handiwork of the ecclesiastical aristocracy. "After the 20th Dynasty the early religion of Egypt [Kemet] was fragmented and lost in confusion under the rule of new patriarchal gods...Buge says, 'knowledge of the early dynastic religion of Egypt possessed by the priests in general after, let us say 1200 B.C., was expremely vague and uncertain. The result of this was to create in their religion a confusion which is practically unbounded'."[75] Classical Kemetan religion once described the world as "an optimistic vision of an ordered cosmos" and Drucilla Houston informs us, "The priests cast of Egypt [Kemet] had been Ethiopian [Kushite] and the first rulers priest-kings. As they were overthrown the priesthood was not able so perfectly to dominate the thought of the empire. When the priests of Amen, the Ethiopian priesthood immigrated to Napata it is clear why Egypt lost the inner meaning of the religious cults."[76]

For a summary analysis of the astro-mythological symbolism of Kemetan cosmogonies, we turn to a quote from the textbook *Man's Religions*.

> "Of all these apparently contradictory descriptions and metaphors it has been very sensibly said: 'As no symbol can encompass the whole essence of what it stands for, an increase in the number of symbols might well have appeared enlightening rather than confusing,' because 'a multitude of mythological concepts may exist for any single entity'...all are an evidence of the existence of the many-faceted cosmic order...Its awesome actuality is represented by _Maat_, a term which as concept means world order and as goddess stands for the truth, reality, and justice prevailing behind the changing scenes of life, now and hereafter."[77]

THE PERSONIFICATION OF PRIMAL FORCES AND CREATIVE ENERGIES IN KEMETAN COSMOGONY

"...The primeval scenery of the Nile [Hapi] Valley which was independent of the labor of man and which played a predominant part in the religious imagination of the Egyptians [Kemetan]"[78] stimulated them to be among the first thinkers to propose a theory concerning the origins of living things and the variations that arise in them. Actually the Kushites or perhaps their predecessors, the Nubian-Grimaldi, were the first to initially conceptualize these contemplations which in fact gives them the honor of being the authors of the science of natural history.

The ancient Kemetans, inspired by the annual overflowing of the Hapi, its role in the germination of seed planted in the rich alluvial deposits which produced an ultra abundance of life giving food and the swarms of marine life which soon sprang forth in the pools of water left behind after the inundation subsided, imagined that in the beginning the universe was filled with a primordial ocean called Nun or Nuni. They envisioned Nun as being a boundless spherical body of water in the shape of a cosmic egg which completely filled the universe. According to this theorem water was the underlying principle of all things. Everything in existence on Earth had arisen from the fathomless deep. The land upon which this planet's inhabitants lived and walked was initially a condensation of the primeval waters of Nuni and was first composed of the primordial mud out of which life was generated in the biological world. This applies to chemicals, plants, animals, and humans as well as our entire solar system. Diop tells us that in Kemetan cosmogony Nun represented "primitive nothingness" in the form of "uncreated matter" and "this primitive matter contained, in the form of principals, all possible beings." And he says that this eminent primal force

"...also contained the god of potential development, Khepru (Ptah). As soon as the primitive nothingness created...the demiurge, its role ended. Henceforth the thread would be unbroken until the advent of Osiris, Isis, and Horus [Ausaru, Auset and Heru], ancestors of the Egyptians. The primitive Trinity then moved from the scale of the universe to that of man..."[79]

A concept which later European Christians reduced to the limit of their scientific understanding after they had barely forced the closing of the Afrikan mystery schools around 1600 years ago. As recently as 1954 Dr. George GM James was still reminding us that these ideas originally created by the superior intelligence of our Afrikan ancestors "have never been clearly understood by Europeans."[80] We will be discussing the subject of the primeval waters

and its attendant scienfitic deity symbols in Chapters 9, 10, and 11.
To the Kemetans

"...the story of the creation held the clue to the understanding to the present and it was for this reason that accounts of
the creation were commented upon and elaborated with
unvarying interest. They did not merely satisfy intellectual
curiosity; they did not merely answer the theoretical question
how things came into being;... In Egypt [Kemet] the creation
stories displayed, with a clarity...the articulation of the existing order and the interelation and significance of its component parts.
The social order was part of the cosmic order. All
theological schools agreed that...[it] had been introduced at
the time of creation."[81]

John G. Jackson says,

"Ancient Egyptians contended that it was in their country, the
oldest in the world, that the gods fashioned the first of all
human beings out of a handful of mud moistened by the
lifegiving water of the 'Blessed Nile'. Likewise, Creation stories
have come from many other parts of Africa (Ethiopia, Tanzania,
Zimbabwe, Congo, Ghana, Nigeria, etc.)."[82]

Remember these "gods" were personifications of primal forces
and creative energies. Here is a role call of some of the cosmic
characters who stared in the Kemetan creation drama which was
copied and recopied in so many varying interpretations that it eventually influenced the entire world.

NETER-NU—"THE ONE", the first cause, the Divine Intelligence, the sum total of everything, the limitless boundless inex-
haustible source of life, the all and in all, the first and the last points
of everything past present and future equivalent of today's concept of the one invisible God represented by the 360 degree symbol
with a dot in its center.

NUN or NUNI—The Primeval Waters which contained the
germ of all matter. A colossal ocean of billowing fathomless depth
churning with the energy of Neter-Nu. Symbolically represented
by the cosmic egg and the Zootype of a maternal serpent wrapped
around the egg and sometimes as a frog. Originally personified
as a woman giving birth, later as a man standing waist high in water
with both arms uplifted supporting the ship of the sun.

PTAH or PTAH-TATEN—The Primeval Hill rising from the
cosmic ocean of Nuni. The formative matter of which the Earth

40

is made. Represented by a scarab beetle pushing the ball of the sun before it. Personified as a man shaping the cosmic egg on a potter's wheel. At certain periods of the Empire, Ptah was depicted as a mummy with the staff of the 7 levels of paradise and holding the ankh of eternal life in each hand.

ATUM—The atom which permeates and exists in all matter. Described as creative vibration, divine utterance, the moving power of the spoken word which called all things into being. Represented by the golden orb of the sun and a male lion with ruffled mane. Personified as a man surrounded by the sun disc and sitting in a boat.

SHU—First of the 8 gods (forces) of nature created by Atum/Atom. Shu was the air and its chemical components; hydrogen, oxygen, nitrogen and carbon. The space between earth and sky, the wind, the breath of life, the essence of atmospheric spirit that must be inhaled by all living things on Earth. Represented by a feather and the Zootype of a roaring or panting lion. Personified as a man with upraised arms bearing the sceptre of power in one hand and the 4 pillars of heaven (the cardinal points of the constellations) in the other with a crown of twin feathers on his head.

TEFNUT—Second of the 8 gods (forces) of nature created by Atum/Atom. Sister and wife of Shu. She was moisture, the dew, humidity, rain and anything liquid or wet. Represented by a cup of water with the Zootype of a Uraeus (Kemetan cobra) symbolic of the power over life and death and personified as a woman with the head of a lioness crowned with the solar disc.

GEB or SEB—Third of the 8 gods (forces) of nature created by Atum/Atom. Geb was the earth which sprouted forth vegetation. The brother and consort of Nut, the Sky Goddess. He was the local mountains and valleys of the Earth's surface. Originally represented as Mother Goose who laid the golden egg of the sun and in the later patriarchal eras after foreign domination in Kemet as a gander. Personified as a man laying on his back with vegetation growing from his body and an erect penis pointed upward towards the Sky Goddess Nut.

NUT or NUIT—The Fourth of the 8 gods (forces) of nature created by Atum/Atom. She was the waters of the atmospheric heaven. The bejeweled sky who gave birth to Ra (the sun) every morning, supreme symbol of femininity. Represented in Zootype

41

as the celestial cow and sometimes as a cat with the headdress of a Uraeus and a sun disc. Depicted as "a woman arched over the earth touching the ends of the Earth with her toes and fingertips",[83] her body elaborately adorned with the stars of heaven. On occasion Nut was personified as a woman bearing a water pot on her head, the Kemetan hieroglyph for mother's womb.[84]

AUSARU (Gk. Osiris)—Number five of the eight gods (forces) of nature created by Atum/Atqm. Most revered of the Kemetan deity symbols. He was the masculine principle of Hapi (the Nile River) which annually overflowed to germinate the rich soil of the surrounding area, the father of agriculture and of wine making and beer brewing in Kemet. This historical personage who once lived and breathed among men and reigned over early Kemet as its first king eventually became the personification of the moon which gives light to the night sky. And the most honored symbol of death, burial and resurrection.

Throughout all the dynasties of ancient Kemet Ausaru was paid homage as the savior of the world. He was also typified as the supreme ruler of the dead. All departed souls had to stand before Ausaru (Osiris) on the day of judgement. In Volume Four of this series, we will be discussing in detail how and why this Afrikan attained such an exceptional degree of exalted respect in the hearts and minds of the ancient Kemetans.

Ausar was represented as a green mummy wielding the ankh of eternal life and the sceptre of imperial power as he presided on the throne of judgement in the court of man's last Rite of Passage. He was depicted in Zootype as an ever potent regenerating bull. His chief emblem was the all-seeing eye.

AUSET (Gk. Isis)—Perhaps even more venerated than Ausaru (Osiris) was Auset (Isis), the sixth member of the eight gods (forces) of nature created by Atum/Atom. She was the black soil of the Hapi Valley, the mother principle typified by many phases of nature, the feminine aspect of the moon. She is said to have resurrected Ausaru and restored him to life. Of all these things she was the absolute personification.

Wife and sister of Ausaru, first Queen of Kemet, the actual inaugurator of agriculture in that nation. Auset and her son Heru were worshipped all over the world. She was the original prototype of the Madonna and Child from which all the others were copied.

Often portrayed as the body of a woman with the head of a cow wearing a headdress of the sun disc flanked by large curvaceous animal horns. Then again as a woman with protruding breasts extended to nurture the world holding a sceptre intertwined with lotus blossoms in one hand and the ankh of eternal life in the other wearing a crown in the shape of a throne. Hers was the divine lap upon which all the pharaohs sat. Volumes have been and still can be written about this Afrikan woman who was regarded as the ultimate female and made such a profound impression on the world that people have been exulting her attributes throughout the ages.

SUT or SET—Seventh member of the Ennead—the eight gods (forces) of nature created by Atum/Atom. Originally he represented persistence in the face of nature's sometimes austere aspects, i.e. the intense heat of summer, the harsh dryness of the desert, sand storms, typhoons, drought and the dark of night which covers the Earth after sunset. "In the early dynasties he was a beneficent god, and one whose favor was sought after by the living and by the dead, and so late as the IX Dynasty kings delighted to call themselves 'beloved of Set'."[85]

After the XXII Dynasty the Asian invaders' fear of and uncertainty about the darkness of night caused them to view day and night as being in opposition because they did not possess the knowledge nor understanding of the Kemetan astronomical science which enabled these Afrikans to behold the glory and wonder of the night sky in the stellar heaven. Therefore, the Asian and Eurasian interlopers perceived of this daily dance of the sun on its axis as an eternal battle between Sut (the night) and Heru (the day) so Sut eventually became Set the nemesis of Ausaru (Osiris) and his son Heru.

Set is said to have lured Ausaru into a banquet hall; chopped him in 14 pieces and scattered them to the 4 winds. This explains, according to the widely circulated anthropomorphic tale, why the light of the moon in its 28 day cycle is engaged in a constant death and renewal struggle, 14 days of which darkness reigns supreme at night. Then for 14 days the silver orb gradually resurrects into the brightness of a full moon. The priests of the Hapi Valley also identified Sut with the eclipse and the waning of the moon.

Set was represented zootypically as a zebra and at times as a man with the head of a strange looking animal with long floppy ears resembling a donkey. There is much explaining to do as to how Set who was initially revered as Sut the tranquil peace and

43

restfullness of nighttime came to be shrouded with ominous characteristics. This of course we will set about doing in *Afrikan Genesis,* Volume Four. However, just here we will say generally Afrikans did not perceive of the forces of nature in terms of good or evil. They believed whatever the manifestation of the cosmic forces "if there was a will, there was a way" to deal with it. Usually they sought to ascertain a way as to how they might harmonize with the force being expressed rather than perceiving themselves as being in opposition to it, for to the Afrikan all things came from the Boundless Womb of the Cosmos.

NEBT-HET or NEPHTHYS—Last member of the eight gods (forces) of nature created by Atum/Atom. She was the dark part of the dawn in the shadowy cloak of twilight; the tender side of the night; the tranquil ethers which make darkness peaceful and serene; she typifies spiritual understanding; a sign that all adversity, uncertainty and enigmas can be turned to your advantage, all stumbling stones can be repositioned and stacked as stepping stones which can take you to the heavens of personal attainment. Kemetans called her Lady of the House, she was the friend of the deceased in the judgement hall of Ausaru, the sister of Ausaru and Auset and sister and wife of Sut (Set), pictured with beautiful multicolored wings, one pointed down and crossed over her sister Auset's in front of Ausaru's throne and the other in like fashion pointed upward over his head from behind the throne.

Nabthet is a constant companion of her twin sister Auset who was one with her in mourning and in the search for the 14 pieces of Ausaru and stood with her as a guardian angel at the right side of (Auset on the left) or behind his throne. The deeper significance of Nebt-Het and Auset's function in this capacity is discussed in *Afrikan Woman: The Original Guardian Angel* by this author.

Represented in Zootype as a vulture symbolizing her ability to make the best of a bad situation, that is to say to create something of value from that which has been cast aside. Personified as a woman with breasts that had no nipples wearing a crown in the shape of an incense burner on her head signifying she exclusively functioned in the etheral and spiritual realm.

Additional meanings of the names of these gods and goddesses and the definitive roles they play in Kemetan cosmogony will be discussed at length in Chapters Ten and Eleven in which we will be discussing some of the details of the Memphite Drama, the original creation story.

CHAPTER THREE

THE GLOBAL INFLUENCE OF ANCIENT AFRIKAN COSMOGONICAL SCIENCE IN SUMER AND ARABIA

PRELUDE

The creation stories of Kush and Kemet were told and retold many times in many ways and in many places. Let us now visit some of these exotic countries and distant lands of the past who first received their art, learning and science from Alkebulan. Our first stop on the journey is ancient Sumer.

One of the first areas to be colonized by the Kemetans was Sumer in the Land Between the Two Rivers (the Tigris and Euphrates) which the indigena called Chaldea and the Greeks referred to as Mesopotamia presently known as the southern portion of Iraq. Somewhere between 10,000 and 5,000 BCE[86] a contingent of Kushite-Kemetans led an expedition there and established a colony which eventually blossomed into the Sumerian Empire with its capitol at Ur.[87] According to recent archaeological rediscoveries, Kemetan agricultural sciences transplanted crop growing and harvesting techniques along with animal husbandry to that location ca. 10,000 BCE.[88]

Renown Afrikanologist Dr. John G. Jackson quoting Dr. H.R. Hall of the Department of Egyptian and Assyrian Antiquities of the British Museum reports,

> "The Sumerian culture springs into our view ready made...we have no knowledge of the time when the Sumerians were savages; when we first meet with them, in the Fourth Millenium B.C., they are already a civilized metal using people, living in great and populous cities, possessing a complicated system of writing and living under the government of firmly established civil and religious dynasties and hierachies...".[89]

Drucilla Houston asked the question "What was the original race of these Sumerians?"[90] W.E.B. Dubois answers.

> "Before the year four thousand B.C. there is evidence that Negroid Dravidians and Mongoloid Sumerians ruled in southern Asia, in Asia Minor. And in the valley of the

45

Tigris-Euphrates. Negroids followed them under Sargon, and Sargon boasted that 'he commanded the black heads and ruled them.' "[91]

Runoko Rashidi adds,

"The Sumerians did after all, call themselves the black-headed people, and their most powerful and pious people, such as Gudea of Lagash, consistently chose very dark, and preferably black stone for their statuary representations. There is also no doubt that the oldest and most exalted Sumerian deity was Anu, a name that loudly recalls the thriving and widely-spread black civilizers found at history's dawn in Africa, Asia and even Europe."[92]

Houston says "...overlapping of the genealogy of antiquity... serves to unite the Chaldeans with the Old Race of the upper Nile, as does their building the temple of Anu another name of the original Cushite family."[93] Diop corroborates, "...the first Mesopotamian civilizations were black. Elam and Susa, it must not be forgotten...were black cities. But the movement was out of Egypt, the Egyptian influence spread through all of western Asia."[94]

Jackson assures us that

"The Sumerian's stories of their origins definitely points to Egypt and Ethiopia as their original homeland...the myths, legends, and traditions of the Sumerians definitely point to Africa as the original home of the Sumerians...Sir Henry Rawlinson called these people Kushite."[95]

And Chancellor Williams relates an old Sumerian legend, "What became of the Black People of Sumer? The traveler asked the old man 'for ancient records show that the people of Sumer were Black. What happened to them?' 'Ah,' the old man sighed. 'They lost their history, so they died..."[96]

THE HIGH CULTURE CIVILIZATION OF THE SUMERIAN BLACK HEADS

Dr. Walther Hinz tells us in his obviously patriarchal view that the people of this region had "...an uncommon reverence and a respect for eternal womanhood..."[97] The land abounded in oracular shrines attended by Afrikoid women who gave vital advice on "political, governmental and military matters". They also served as repositories for historical records. These priestesses were a sort of prototype of the west Alkebulan griots who could recall generations of history going back hundreds or even thousands of years. The Black Sumerians believed that they were not totally bound by predestined fate. They perceived of themselves as having the innate ability to alter circumstances and conditions not only in the present but to a large degree in the future as well. So they often sought the advice of their "oracular priestesses" as to "the most advantageous action to take".[98]

It had long been a custom of their pharaonic predecessors to marry high priestesses from Nubia. The Kemetan ruler viewed this act as a sure means to securing the throne for these women were said to possess clairvoyant powers which would insure the continuity of the king's reign. That is why in turn female prophetesses played such a dominant role in Sumerian political affairs. Originally this idea was symbolically represented by huge twin statues of bare breasted women with the body of a winged lion which guarded the gates of Sumerian and other Chaldean cities. Entering the city through the "winged gates" was symbolic of "rebirth" thus passing through the city gates was symbolic of passing the sacred lips of the vagina to partake of the joys of heaven.[99]

Concerning ancient Sumer's particular type of cuneiform writing, Merlin Stone says,

"Texts revealed that it was the Goddess Nidaba in Sumer who was paid honor as the one who initially invented clay tablets and the art of writing. She appeared in that position earlier than any of the male deities who later replaced her. . . earliest examples of written language [cuneiform] so far discovered. . .were. . .located in Sumer, at the temple of the Queen of Heaven. . .a most convincing argument that it may have actually been woman who pressed those first meaningful marks into wet clay."[100]

The Sumerian goddess Nidaba was a type of Auset (Isis) who was formerly credited with the invention of cursive writing in Kush and Medu Netcher hieroglyphic in Kemet and the paper (papyrus) upon which it was written at least 10,000 years earlier than cuneiform in Chaldea. Jackson informs us, "Around 4000 B.C., the Sumerians had attained a high level of civilization in the plains of Shinar. They tilled the soil, practiced irrigation, erected cities, reared cattle, and invented the system of cuneiform writing which they bequeathed to their Semitic successors."[101]

It is also reported that the Sumerians masterfully sailed the Persian Gulf about this time in the tradition of their Kushite-Kemetan ancestors who were regularly making 400 mile voyages to Byblos in Lebanon to sell paper (papyrus rolls) and trade in other commodities. As a matter of fact, James Bailey "...was particularly impressed by a great body of evidence linking the Sumerians with Brazil and Mexico as early as 2370 BC."[102] This should not be surprising as it is quite well known among historians that the Kushites and the Kemetans were ardent sailors of the high seas dating incredibly far back in antiquity. Evidence of this is seen in their architectural marvels which exist on every continent.

"The Sumerians achieved such excellence in the various arts and sciences that none of the future cultures of Mesopotamia ever rose to their level. 'Babylonian science,' as Dr. Briffault pointed out, 'was exactly as far advanced in the nebulous dawn of Sumerian culture as it was nearly 4,000 years later when the Greeks came to gather up its crumbs. Not a single aspect or feature of the Babylonian civilization shows in the course of the thousands of years of its supremacy the slightest indication of advance or development'."[103]

THE SUMERIAN STORY OF CREATION

"One Sumerian prayer goes as follows: 'Here oh ye regions the praise of Queen Nana, Magnify the Creatress, exalt the dignified, Exalt the glorious One, draw nigh upon the Mighty Lady'."[104] Sumerian theologians perceived of humans as having been created from clay by the Great Mother Creatress whom they called Mama Aruru and represented with the ideogram for the boundless sea. (cp. Kemetan Nuni) From her primordial ocean emerged Anu, the sky-god, the "pristine king and ruler" of the gods (forces) and his consort the goddess Ki, mother-earth, often symbolically depicted as being venerably draped in the floral garments of her exalted station.

"...united as though they were a large mountain in the midst of the sea. An [Anu] and Ki produced within or between them Enlil, air, and as the air began to stir in the darkness within the mountain, it separated sky and earth. Then to see better, Enlil begot the moon-god Nanna, who in turn begot the sun-god Utu, presumably to make the light brighter. By this time the world had come into being, for the sky [An/Anu] by expansion of the air below (Enlil) had reached a great height, and the earth (Ki) had made a solid floor below, with

48

sun and moon to bring light. When air moved across earth (or when Enlil united with his mother Ki) and received the aid of water (Enki), plants and animals came into being."[105]

Finally man was created by the divine unction of Mama Aruru who moved upon Ki the Mother Earth and Enki the water god to erotically spawn the clay (mud) from which she fashioned humans. According to Sumerian Astro-Mythological scientists, all of these phases of creation were accomplished through the power of divine utterance (cp. Kemetan Atum who spoke all things into being). This creation story as recorded in the book *Man's Religions* sheds some light on the Sumerians profound knowledge of natural science which they had received from the Kushite-Kemetans.

Following are some descriptions of the deity symbols portrayed in the Sumerian Creation Drama;

MAMA ARURU or NAMMU: Represents the seminal life-giving fluid inherent in all living things and the fact that life on Earth began in the sea.

ANU or AN: Is the volt of heaven which revealed the celestial entities at night and the clouds which contained the seminal rains by day. (cp. Kemetan Nut) The Sumerian Creation story reversed the personified roled of the sky and the earth. In the Memphite Drama of Kemet, the sku, Nuit, is a feminine principle and the earth, Geb, is masculine. This is a prime example of how different geographical locations brought local color to basic Kemetan Cosmogony. In Sumer, Anu was called the father of the Gods in honor of the Anu people from Kemet who founded its civilization.

KI or NINMAH: The womb of Mother Earth which receives seed and bears fruit, the bountiful nurturing bosom that feeds every living creature, the primary source of all products and wealth. (cp. Kemetan Geb)

ENLIL: The space between sky and earth; the air we breathe; the chemical compounds of the wind, hydrogen, oxygen, nitrogen and carbon which enables Earth to be a habitable place. (cp. Shu, the god/force of air in Kemetan cosmogony)

INANNA: Nanna the moon god as set forth in the above quotation is a misconception because the Sumerians viewed Inanna the goddess of love wrapped in the silvery negligee of moonlight as the queen of the night sky. Like Auset the Kemetan goddess of love, comfort and inspiration she was most venerated through the land.

49

UTU: The sun god is also taken out of context in the above document for it is not the moon which gives light to the sun but rather the silver orb gets its glowing illumination from the supreme body in our solar system—the sun. Historical evidence attests to the fact that the Sumerians were well aware of this scientific reality. Indeed the Kushites and Kemetans who first taught them were in possession of this knowledge as demonstrated in the symbolic representations of Atum or Amen-Ra the sun god, father of Ausaru and Auset who typified the male and female aspects of the moon.

ENKI: The water god originally portrayed in Kemetan cosmogony as Tefnut the goddess of moisture and liquid, the continuity of the primeval ocean as experienced in all complex living organisms. According to the above rendition of the story "plants and animals came into being" through the interrelationship of Enlil (air) the initial preparatory force for life on the planet and Ki (earth) which produced vegetation and other sustained elements vital to the support of life on Earth and Enki (water) which comprises 70 percent of the human anatomy and a great portion of other living things.

The creation of man as expressed in the symbology of Mama Aruru, Ki and Enki indicates the spermatozoa (seminal fluid) of Enki impregnating the earthen body of Ki and being formed in the embryo of the womb while suspended in the life sustaining crucible of maternal fluid which has the same chemical composition as sea water. The ancient Sumerians, like most other Afrikans in their right mind, placed great emphasis on the natural phenomena of sexual union as the primary source of joy and regeneration on a spiritual as well as a physical plane. Every year at the autumnal equinox —Dumuzi—representing all animal and plant life—returned to the warm embrace of Inanna in her aspect as earth, the passionate consort. According to Sumerian natural scientist, this sacred union revitalized and made fertile all plant life every spring. Consequently each new year the Sumerians celebrated the Akitu festival which culminated in the ritual re-enactment of the king in the role of Dumuzi united with the high priestess in the role of Inanna. These holy nuptials took place in a golden bed amidst hanging gardens atop the seventh level of a Ziggarut tower. In the Sumerian belief system, this annual sacred sexual union endowed the king with the inspiration of new life, renewed energy and divine strength to rule the nation.[106]

All in all the symbology of Sumerian cosmogony expressed their conceptualization of creation and its ever evolving continuity.

50

"Heaven, earth, air and water were regarded as the four major components of the universe. The act of creation was accomplished through utterance of the divine word. The creating deity had merely to lay his [or her] plans and pronounce the name of the thing which was to be created. To keep the cosmos in continuous and harmonious operation and to avoid confusion and conflict, the gods devised the *me*, a set of universal and unchangeable rules and laws which all animate and inanimate beings were obliged to obey."[107]

Around 2,000 BCE semi-barbarous Asians (so-called Semitics) invaded the land between the two rivers and after gradually co-opting Sumerian culture they proceeded to pervert many of its original lofty concepts and superimposed male deities over female deities. Having no real understanding of what they were stealing during their occupation of Sumer, the patriarchal Semitics enforced the transition from Mother-Goddess veneration to the worship of a masculine god as supreme subsequently demurring the exalted status of black Sumerian women.[108]

One of the black rulers who valiantly resisted this incursion was Gudea, prince of Lagash, who preserved Kushite-Sumerian culture and learning almost single-handedly. A stone figure of him sculptured from black stone is inscribed with cuneiform symbols praising his deeds and wishing him long life.[109]

We will now geographically backtrack a little and head our scholarly caravan toward Arabia.

ARABIA: LAND OF FLYING CARPETS, GENIES AND FABLED ENCHANTMENTS

The stories of Arabian Nights with its flying carpets and giant genies have inspired children and adults alike of many lands with awe and delight. Drucilla Dunjee Houston informs us, "They were a collection of tales from the widespread colonies of the Cushite race. The richest of the tales came from India, the cradle of story and fable. Many came from Baghdad the royal city of the eastern caliphs."[110] Famed for its golden domed palaces and wondrous delights she adds that the Arabian Nights were pictographic recollections "...from a higher and more perfect civilization" originally penned in "Himyaritic writing, which is a form of the primitive African language and has no relation to the Semitic tongues."[111] The most fanciful of these tales were "... Arabian

51

legends, springing from the same sources as those of the Egyptian manuscripts. Lenormant says, 'We may perceive in all this the remembrance of a powerful empire founded by Cushites in very early ages.' "[112] This particular tribe of Kushites was known as Adites and "...were depicted as men of gigantic stature."[113] Reflection on their lives and deeds inspired the imagination of ancient writers with the model for the wise genies who possessed magical powers so often encountered in the Arabian Nights stories.

The flying carpets and other mythological vehicles of flight may also have been a recollection of ancient Kushite aeronautics. Again Houston says,

> "...The wonderful Ethiopians who produced fadeless colors that have held their hues for thousands of years who drilled through solid rock and were masters of many other lost arts, and who many scientists believe must have understood electricity, who made metal figures that could move and speak and may have invented flying machines, for the 'flying horse Pegasus' and the 'ram of the golden fleece' may not have been mere fairy tales."[114]

The Arabian peninsula is approximately 50 percent desert, the whole country being 1,100,000 square miles with 500,000 square miles of arid regions abounding in sand dunes. These regions are called Arabia Deserta. Here temperatures in the summer months can be as high as 130 degrees Fahrenheit. The northwest sector was referred to in ancient times as Arabia Petrea, that is stony Arabia, because of its abundance of granite and Nubian sandstone which Kemetan architects and stone masons somehow managed to transport in 150 ton chunks over a distance of some 600 miles to the Hapi Valley where they used it in the building of the pyramids and other huge structures.

Then there was Arabia Felix, happy Arabia. This rainbathed area of southern Arabia was named so because

> "here existed to almost our times the late flowers of a rich primeval civilization, which did not spring from the Semitic race, which is in possession of Arabia today...this country abounded in riches and especially in spices and is now called Hedjaz. It is much celebrated because the cities of Mecca and Medina are situated in it."[115]

This area was once ruled by Kushite queens as the eastern province of the kingdom of Sheba (Seba). Houston states in regards to the whole of the peninsula, "In general features, Arabia

52

resembles the African Sahara of which it is but a continuation. Its general characteristics are African."[116] She further informs us "Arabia was originally settled by two distinct races, an earlier Cushite Ethiopian race and a later Semitic Arabian. The Cushites were the original Arabians..."[117]

ARCHITECTURAL GIANTS OF THE "OLD RACE"

Around 17,000 years ago the ancient black Adite giants and the Anu of the "Old Race" journeyed from Kemet and "crossed over the Red Sea to establish settlements along the coastal plain" and shortly thereafter built Kushite civilizations in stony Arabia and Arabia Felix.[118] Albert Churchward corroborates Drucilla Houston, Cheikh Anta Diop and Sterling Means by informing us that

"Commentators of the Koran repeat the ancient traditions concerning the Adite ancestors of the Arab race, proving that originally they were... giants of prodigious size and stature,...of the past generations who left Egypt...".[119]

Clearing up some of the incorrect notions in relation to early Arabian chronology, Houston writes, "Modern history speaks of the Semitic conquest of Babylon as early as 4500 B.C. which is erroneous unless they explain that these Arabians were Cushite Arabian, another division of the race of the black Sumerians. The line of Sargon 3800 B.C. was of the same race. Each one of these early Arabian conquests was of African Arabs."[120] She further and unequivocally establishes the historical reality that

"To the Cushite race belonged the oldest and purest Arabian blood. They were the original Arabians and the creators of the ancient civilization, evidences of which may be seen in the stupendous ruins to be found in every part of the country."[121]

Houston also tells us that the "Himyaritic Arabians" were still referring to themselves as Ethiopians in "diplomatic and elevated circles" in 1926 when her treatise *The Wonderful Ethiopians of the Ancient Cushite Empire* was first published.[122]

Even when its ancient glory was beginning to wane in the days of Alexander of Macedon [misnomered the Great-ca. 332 B.C.E.] they were still considered by the Greeks to be the "richest nation of the world"[123] and today throughout the old territory of Arabia Felix now called Yemen

> "...are to be found gigantic ruins which bewilder the beholder, who cannot understand how they were raised by human hands. They were built by the same race that reared the columns at Belbec and Karnak. These original Arabians were spoken of by later Arabs as Adites, men of Ad, giants of old...these Cushite Arabians were a fine race of remarkable stature and dark complexion"[124]

who constructed a civilization which in many ways equaled that of its Kemetan motherland and flourished side by side with the Kushite Eden-like empires of Sumer, Persia, India and later Babylon.

THE VIOLENT DELUGE OF THE "FLOOD OF AREM"

The High Culture Civilization of Kushite-Arabia like many another ancient black civilization in that region of the world was eventually violently disrupted by a wave of Semitic speaking Eurasian invaders to whom the ancient records refer to as the "flood of Arem". They entered Arabia from the north around 1800 B.C.E. and through the horrid tactics of their "merciless tortures" and cruel methods of conquest they drove many of the indigenous descendants of Kushite royal families to Yemen and other areas to the south. That is why even unto this day, the greatest concentration of the jet-black descendants of old Kushite Arabia is still in the southern portion of the Arabian peninsula.[125] The original Kushite Arabians had always been "...given to a settled life and not to the wandering habits of the Semitic Arabians. They were fond of village life, society, the dance, and music."[126] According to Houston the so-called Semitic Arabians "...had entered Arabia after the extended empire of the Cushite Arabians had declined and disunited. The Semitic Arabian lived a rude nomadic life in obscurity until 700 A.D., (CE)."[127]

She also informs us that this semi-barbarous branch of Afro-Asian and Caucasoid admixture of Semitic peoples were "...quite unlike in nature to the Cushite and Hebrew stock, which in early ages must have been deeply permeated with Ethiopian blood.[128] Recently this author read an article in *The Washington Post* reporting that a certain Arab nation was currently driving Blacks from all walks of life out of the land, even so far as to be escorting them to the borders; entire communities have vanished.[129]

In reference to the wandering descendants of the "flood of Arem" who later inhabited portions of northern Arabia, Douglass Fox in an introduction to some of the studies of German cultural anthropologist Professor Leo Frobenius published between 1921-1924 and in the year 1931 described the Semitic Arab as

> "...a nomad," who "pendulates to and fro, carrying merchandise or driving his flocks of sheep, goats, or camels. It is a matter of indifference to him whether he sleeps in the oasis or the town. The shepherd moves from one grazing area to another. The merchant travels between his establishments in two or more widely separated towns. These are equipped with wives and other household goods, but are not, psychologically, homes."[130]

This brings to mind the fact that planet Earth has never really "psychologically" been a home to the wandering Caucasoid cousins of the Semitic Arabs who, since they have come into world power, have increased the pace of living to the death defying speed of the jet and atomic age moving frenziedly from one world crisis to another always teetering on the brink of total human annihilation and planetary destruction.[131]

Oh, how the truly human soul longs for the peace and tranquil longevity of the ancient Kushite and other Afrikan civilizations which generally flourished in cosmic harmony before the restless descendants of the Cro-magnon stormed upon the world scene with the twin pathologies of the "Chronos" (time) and suicidal syndromes.[132] That is why it is so important for we who are the "stunned survivors of the Afrikan holocaust"[133] to be reawakened to the "knowledge of self" through the resurrection and redemption of our true history, culture and Afrikan genius so that we may mentally, physically and spiritually get back in step with the cosmic rhythm of Divine eternalness. Though presently for reasons of economic survival many Afrikan people globally are forced to reckon with white-supremist Euro-centric time frames, we must at one and the same time always maintain within our Afrikan souls an harmonic balance with the divine universal laws of the cosmic scheme as we struggle to change things from what they are to what they ought to be. The signs of the times indicate that that day is surely close at hand. So above all things we must always stay in tune with "the One"—the boundless height and depth of our own Afrikan souls.

THE CENTRAL THEME OF
ORIGINAL KUSHITE ARABIAN COSMOGONY

Long before the coming of the violent "flood of Arem" the ancient deities of the Arabian cosmogony like other Kushite civilizations were of maternal descent. [134] The supreme symbol in the land was a huge black stone, probably a meteorite for Dr. Yusef ben Jochannon informs us that "a black stone's remains from a meteorite. . .was imported into Arabia by the Africans of Ethiopia (Abyssinians) when they ruled Arabia and Persia, and all the way into India-to the Ganges." [135]

Later Islamic Àrabs called this venerated object the Kaaba. In Kushite Arabian cosmogonical science, this black stone represented the navel of the universe which fell to Earth from the belly of the cosmic Mother-Creatress[136] known to them as Umm Attar[137] and at other times as Allat. Again Dr. ben Jochannon instructs us that

"...the worship of El Ka'aba, whom the people of Arabia worshipped along with the Goddess Al'lat... was extremely important, since Mohamet's family worshipped both El'Kaba and Al'lat...Note that the name 'AL'LAT' was the origin of the later word 'AL'LAH,' or 'SUPREME GOD.'" [138]

And Barbara Walker relates,

"Before Islam arrived in the 7th Century A.D., Arabia was matriarchal for over a thousand years of recorded history. The Annals of Ashurbanipal said Arabia was governed by queens for as long as anyone could remember. The land's original ALLAH was Al-Lat,...at Mecca the Goddess was Shaybah or Sheba, the Old Woman, worshipped as a black aniconic stone...the same Black Stone now enshrined in the KAABA at Mecca was her feminine symbol, marked by the sign of the Yoni and covered like the ancient Mother by a veil." [139]

While we are on this subject, I would like to say to my Muslim brothers and sisters that in presenting these facts it is not my intention to offend anyone's religious sensibilities. Yet I might add, neither can I allow myself to be restricted by any particular doctrine or religious philosophy. I would also remind you that even

56

though this author holds a degree in Christian theology, I am not bound by that either. Our approach here is strictly scientific. We are presenting historical information that is verifiable through scholarly documentation for Dr. Yusef ben Jochannon informs us

"all religions originated in Africa...however, it must be made very clear that the Africans, those who are very much cognizant of their historical heritage, do not hold Christianity, Judaism or Islam in any higher esteem than they hold their own religions which have not been corrupted by slavery, colonialism or cultural genocide."[140]

Having said that with a undying love for all Black People and "malice towards none", we resume our initial trend of thought.

Once again we call upon Drucilla Dunjee Houston.

"Let us examine the passage of the Semitic Arabians across Africa. Was his influence for the making of civilization? They burned the priceless collection of books that made up the Alexandrian library, in which were locked up the secrets of the lost arts and the knowledge of the origin of civilization. So great was the number of books that 6 months was needed for the consumption of this precious fuel...[Consequently] the Semitic Arabian race has not been noted for any creative or constructive qualities and until united in conquest with the more ancient Cushite race was wholly destructive."[141]

Touching on the antiquity of Kushite Arabian literary arts she writes,

"Gibbon speaks of the times of ignorance that preceded Mohammed. This is true if we speak of Semitic Arabia, but later research has revealed a different source for the literature of the land. Britannica says of Arabia (Vol. 2, p. 230), 'Arabia if poor in monuments is superabundantly rich in manuscripts. There are verses inscribed to the kings and heroes of Yemen dated a thousand years or more before the Christian era. We find undeniable specimens of at least two full centuries before Mohammed,...this was the Arabian heritage of splendor from the magnificence of Cushite Arabian days which the prodigality of the later caliphs sought to imitate."[142]

ARABIAN COSMOGONY AFTER THE COMING OF ISLAM

The Prophet Mohammed was from the Koreysh Tribe which claimed descent from Ismael through Haggar the Kemetan.[143]

Renown historian Joel A. Rogers reports that the Prophet Mohammed ibn Abdullah was a "bluish-colored" Black Man with "frizzly" hair and Afrikoid features and that his mother as well as his grandfather Abd el Mottalib were Afrikans.[144] And though

> "Mohammed furnished the executive ability and generalship for the new faith...Bilal provided much of the inspiration...After listening to him, the soldiers of Mohammed whipped to frenzy, were ready to hurl themselves against any foe."[145]

Dr. Ben adds,

> "Bilal, the former Afrikan slave was responsible for the creation of much of what Moslems past and present believe about paradise (heaven); also many of their first original prayers and doctrines... Bilal, the Black Abyssinian,...established the fundamentals of Islam."[146]

The basic tenets of the Arabian creation story since the inception of Islam are essentially the same as the Judeo-Christian. For a general overview of Mohammedian Cosmogony, as quoted in *The Muslim Dictionary*, let us draw upon some quotes from the Qur'an.

Surah L.38—"We created the heavens and the earth and all that is between them in six days, nor did any sense of weariness touch Us."

Surah XLI.9-12—"Do you indeed disbelieve in Him who in two days created the Earth? Do you assign Him equals? The Lord of the Worlds is He...He applied Himself to the heaven, which was but smoke: and to it and to the Earth He said, 'Some ye, in obedience or against your will?' and they both said 'we come obedient' and He completed them as seven heavens in two days, and in each heaven made known its office; and We furnished the lower heavens with lights and guardian angels. This is the disposition of the Almighty, the all-knowing one."

Surah XVI.3—"...Man hath He created out of a moist germ; yet lo! man is an open caviller. And the cattle! for you hath He created them,...".

Surah XXXV.12—"God created you of dust-then of the germs of life-then made you two sexes." According to the Muslim tradition "God created the Earth on Saturday, the hills on Sunday, the trees on Monday, all unpleasant things on Tuesday, the light on Wednesday, the beasts on Thursday, and Adam, who was the last of creation, was created after the time of afternoon prayers on Friday."[147]

Encyclopedia Britannica provides us with this brief summation of some of the compenents of Islamic Cosmogonical thought.

> "God created the world in six days, and set Adam in the garden of paradise, but, tempted by Satan, Adam fell, intermediate between men and angels are the Jinn, male and female, created from fire; some are believers, others are infidels. The devil is sometimes described as one of the angels, sometimes as one of the jinn; he was expelled from heaven because he refused to prostrate himself before Adam at his Lord's command."[148]

The intricacies of Hebrew, Christian and Islamic creation stories and how they were transplanted from Kushite-Kemetan Astro-Mythological Cosmogony will be thoroughly explored in Volume Three of this series, *Afrikan Genesis: A Narrative Commentary of the First Book of the Bible*. In Volume Four of this series, *Afrikan Genesis: Black Gods and Goddesses in the Land of Eden*, we will be touching of the unique version on Islamic Cosmogony as developed by the Messenger Elijah Muhammad in the Nation of Islam theology.

Now let us travel back to more ancient times as we prepare to visit the exotic land of Kushite-Persia.

CHAPTER FOUR

THE GLOBAL INFLUENCE OF AFRIKAN COSMOGONICAL SCIENCE IN PERSIA

GLORIES OF THE ANCIENT KUSHITE-PERSIAN EMPIRE

Now on our journey we arrive in old Persia with its bustling marketplaces trading in all sorts of merchandise. Incense from the kingdom of Sheba perfumes the air. Beautiful strains from a Kemetan orchestra float upon the ethers as lovely voluptuous sable dancers from India with delicate little bells dangling from their wrists and ankles ignite the senses. Tumbling acrobats from China vie with an exhibition of Mongolian wrestlers for the attention of the strolling crowds. Elegant ostrich feathers from Nubia wave gracefully in the breeze as the aroma of delectable dishes from every land tempts the palates of all within their range. An occasional bejewelled elephant transporting some official dignitary lumbers through the street as many in the crowd admiringly step aside to give them plenty of room. In the distance a caravan of long necked dromedary camels pass by the east gate.

It seems as though merchants everywhere are calling attention to their internationally renown Persian carpets spread out in an array of intoxicating colors and patterns which dazzle all potential customers who see them. Among the many Persian treasures is a:

"...great carpet of white brocade 450 feet long and 90 feet broad with a border worked in precious stones to represent a garden of flowers, the leaves formed of emeralds, the blossoms of rubies, sapphires and pearls."[149]

The design of this magnificent piece serves as a matrix for the timeless beauty of many another Persian carpet tapestry and shawl which make up some of the ever enduring products that come down to us from the old Kushite race. Just now a contingent of mahogany colored Persian soldiers in route to relieve the sentinels from atop the walls and at the gates of the city proudly stride past sparkling fountains gracefully gushing forth miniature geysers with tiny droplets that rise, spin, descend and splash like aquatic ballerinas upon a stage of shimmering sunshine then collectively rise again sending forth ripples of prismatic spray.

61

In the midst of all this emerges a very tall, white bearded, navy blue-black man clad in a a bright red hooded robe trimmed in gold and silver brocade holding a multi-colored egg in one hand, he points to it and speaks in a full resonant voice with the authority and power of one who really knows as he beckons "gather around my friends and let me tell you the story of how all things began". We draw nigh listening to him very carefully and suddenly like the rest of the congregation we find ourselves completely enthralled as he eloquently recites the Persian version of the Kushite-Kemetan cosmogony.

THE ORIGINAL PERSIAN STORY OF CREATION

This most learned and eloquent sage continues, "Long ago and far away", he begins, "when there was no space or time Mother Anihita[150] filled the universe and in the midst of her cosmic womb suspended in the essence of life was the divine egg. At Anihita's utterance the sacred egg was ablaze with ultra-brilliant flames. There was an awesome rumble of thunder when she clapped her hands and a billion arrows of lightening filled the darkness with light. The light she called Mithras and darkness she called Mithra. Darkness and light sang and danced together for a time to the music of the spheres. Fire and water kissed each other in passionate embrace. From their divine electrifying copulation planet Earth and all the orbital spheres were born. The holy placenta thereof became matter, the tangible essence of all things. Then Anihita commanded darkness to rule the night and light to rule the day. Each night when the golden orb reposes in the western sky the two cosmic lovers are reunited and every morning at twilight you can see them tenderly embracing when Mithra presents her lover with a bouquet of violet and rosy clouds at dawn as they depart with the blush of a good-bye kiss.

With a sigh the great Anihita sent forth the four winds to cover the whole Earth to separate the celestial waters from the terrestrial mud and with an aria of everlasting love the Cosmic Mother sang and the waters gathered together to form the Seven Seas and their myriad children and grandchildren. The dry land burst forth with verdant foliage fresh with her manifold divine fragrances. With one hand Anihita held her flaming cosmic egg and with the other she reached in and drew forth cosmic dust splattering the night sky with the twelve constellations and its deep purple tapestry with a thousand twinkling eye. Then gently crushing the cosmic egg between her heavenly thighs, she sent forth new life, male and female created she them. There with infinite affection she bathed them in the mother of all rivers baptizing them with the perpetual power of love that they might multiply and fill the Earth. When the Great Mother had made an end of all these wondrous things, she sang a joyous song and in one brief moment she became that song causing herself to permeate all living things. Thus Mama Anihita is still with us to this day for her divine intelligence is present in each and everyone of you under the sound of my voice."

As we stood entranced in thought contemplating the wonder of all that he had said, suddenly he was no more. And the place where once this giant of a man had stood was now an empty space. Yet we could all feel the warm glow of his presence. Who was this man? Is this the one called Zoroaster, the Prophet? For surely we have heard many rumors of those who said they have seen him and always they speak reverently of his deep dark color as black as the midnight sky and his ardent visage shining like a cluster of many stars.[151] Some say he is a mystic from the hills of Kilimanjaro where he is nurtured by seven daughters of the moon and that he has travelled to many lands and places and seen many things. Others say he is a wise man of untold centuries who was once a prince in one of the old Kushite kingdoms of long, long ago. One day they said he forsook palace live, donned simple clothes and left the capitol city of his homeland to travel the world in search of answers to questions of the mysteries of life and death. They say he comes with the morning breeze at the first breath of spring and departs with the sigh of eventide at the early signs of autumn. We will probably never know for sure who this venerable Black Man was or is but this we do know, we will never forget him.

THE FABULOUS CITY OF SUSA AT THE CROSSROADS OF THE WORLD

As we continue to meander awestruck through this city of enchantment, we inquire of a passerby with a most benevolent continence wearing golden sandals and draped in a resplendent Kente cloth sarong "Peace be unto you, my Sister. Would you please tell us what place this is?" She charmingly returns the greeting, "Peace be unto you, my beloved people." And informs us that we are standing at the cross road of the world in the fabulous city of Susa. "Legend has it", she relates in a euphonious manner, "that Amenhotep III, Pharaoh of Kemet built this metropolis about 500 years ago[152] however," she continued, "we do know for certain that this city was erected by Kushites from the Mother Continent and that it served as a royal residence for Amenhotep whom the Greeks called Memmon whenever he visited the eastern extremity of his vast empire."[153] When she had made an end of saying these things with the words of peace she graciously took her leave of us. There was a pleasant murmur in our hearts, especially the brothers, as we watched her shapely form slowly fade away in the distance.

Amidst all the city's activities, there is still an aura of calm in the air coupled with a kind of gladness to be alive here in this wonderful place. The evening shadows fall as we continue to behold the tranquility and inner peace reflected upon the countless faces who pass before us going happily about their sundry tasks. The majority of them are of the old Kushite racial stock who came to this region from Alkebulan a very long time ago and remnants of their marvelous civilizations and culture are still extant for all to enjoy. Ah, it is so good to be an Afrikan, to be of a people hailed and respected the world over.

A VISIT TO THE NATIONAL ARCHIVES OF THE "OLD RACE"

Before taking our leave of this land, let us visit the National Archives and review some of ancient Persia's history before it was stolen from them.[154] Our investigation reveals that from earliest times the Persians were called Elamites. The Elamites were Black men with short wooly hair who lived in the highlands of southern Mesopotamia. They like the inhabitants of India and other surrounding areas were a strain of the old Kushite race.[155] These Elamites in concert with expeditions of High Culture Scientists from Kush and Kemet laid the foundations of and established what was to become the Persian Empire.

One of the last of the kings of the "Old Race" who tried to reunite the many nations and kingdoms of this ancient Kushite Empire after it had been violently disrupted by several Eurasian invasions was Cyrus the Great who reigned between 550-529

BCE.[156] We are informed that his true name was Kurush a variant of Kush. The engravings of his image on his tomb is that of a Kushite.[157]

One of Cyrus' many valiant efforts in stemming the tide of the plague of the barbarous Scythian hordes and their encroaching threat to civilization[158] is described thusly, "There the beseeching cries of their women and the challenge to their valor and patriotism caused Persia to turn with ferocity and thrust back the foe. Astyages fell back to the vicinity of the Persian capitol and there in the watches of the night Cyrus surprised them. The victory was on the side of the Persians. Astyages was overtaken and captured. The Medes welcomed Cyrus as a deliverer from the rising domination from incoming usurping Turanian Scyths."[159] As a result of this victory, the Scythian's encroaching threat to civilization was checked in that region and throughout the Fertile Crescent for some two centuries.

Even the Hebrew prophets had foretold and hailed the arrival of Cyrus the Great in Palestine. Prior to Cyrus' liberating campaigns in Persia and neighboring nations it is reported that in 640 BCE, Susa the capitol city of Kushite-Persia was immensely ravaged. Professor Runoko Rashidi reports:

"When after many years of hard and intense fighting the Assyrians finally took Susa, they savaged it with a ferocity rarely equaled in human history. Ashrubanipal's own text recalled in horribly triumphant detail the looting and razing of temples, the destruction of sacred groves, the desecration of royal tombs, the seizure of Elamite gods, the removal of royal memorials, 'the sowing of ruined ground with salt, and the deportation of people, livestock, and even rubble from the devastated city. The style of the reports suggests that the destruction of Susa was a sweepingly calculated effort designed to shock the entire world and proclaim Susa's total earthly eradication."[160]

Yet in spite of this particular event of Eurasian wanton desolation, Cyrus and his descendants managed to salvage and largely restore the beautiful metropolis of Susa. And this eastern jewel of revitalized Kushite and Kemetan engineering and architectural genius would continue to flourish until it was sacked around 321 BCE by the Greeks under Alexander who plundered and destroyed its center of high culture. This is why "later Persians were utterly ignorant of the history of their country before Alexander."[161]

SAGA OF AN INDOMITABLE KING IN
"THE LAND OF THE BOW"

Now let us return for a moment to the vantage point of the 20th Century and reflect on the later years of Persia's history. Drucilla Houston tells us "the native Persians of today are sadly degenerated from constant mixture with foreign races."[162]

Some scholars believe the destruction of Persia and its capitol may have been a manifestation of the immutable Law of Karma, that is to say "the chickens coming home to roost". For Cyrus' successor, Cambyses, descecrated the holy land of Kemet and put Pharaoh Amasis II to death in 525 BCE. This pharaoh was the very one who had relaxed the laws of his ancestors and opened the door for Persian scholars of Eurasian extraction and Greeks to study in the Mystery System High Culture institutions in Kemet.[163] Diop says that from then on Kemet was continually dominated by foreigners.[164]

Cambyses also had designs on doing the same thing further south in Ethiopia (Kush) in the Land of the Bow. In preparation for his planned invasion of Kush (Ethiopia), Cambyses employed members from a neighboring tribe of Nilotic nomads who were themselves Kushites. They had lived along the Red Sea coast and could fluently speak the language of the greater Kushite kingdoms in the region. These mercenary spies masquerading as emissaries met with a most formidable ruler of the united Kushite kingdoms in the Nubian district, King Nastesen,[165] who responded to their ambassadorial pretenses conversely. "The king of Persia has not sent you with these presents because he puts a high value upon being my friend. You have come to get information about my kingdom; therefore, you are liars, and that king is a bad man. Had he any respect for what is right, he would not have coveted any other kingdom than his own, nor made slaves of a people who have done him no wrong. So take him this bow, and tell him that the king of Ethiopia has some advice to give him: when the Persians can draw a bow of this size thus easily, then let him raise an army of superior strength and invade the country of the long-lived Ethiopians. Till then, let him thank the gods for not turning the thoughts of the children of Ethiopia to foreign conquest. He then unstrung the bow, put it into the hands of the Ichthyophagi, [fish eating ambassadors].[166]

Upon receiving this message, Cambyses was so angered

"...he at once began his march against Ethiopia, without any orders for the provision of supplies, and without for a moment considering the fact that he was to take his men to the ends of the Earth. He lost his wits completely and, like the mad man he was, the moment he heard what the Ichthyophagi had to say, off he went with his whole force of infantry, leaving behind the Greeks who were serving under him...Then with his remaining forces he continued his march towards Ethiopia. They had not, however, covered a fifth of the distance, when everything in the nature of provisions gave out, and the men were forced to eat the pack-animals until they, too were all gone...Once they had reached the desert some of them were reduced to the dreadful expedient of cannibalism. One man in 10 was chosen by lot to be the victim. This was too much even for Cambyses; when it was reported to him, he abandoned the expedition, marched back, and arrived at Thebes with greatly reduced numbers. From Thebes he went down to Memphis and allowed the Greeks to sail home. So ended the expedition against Ethiopia."[167]

We are told that Cambyses, spurred by greed by the reports of the enormous wealth (especially gold) and power of the Kushites of Nubia, attempted a second expedition against them. The results of which were recorded in an inscription in the holy city of Napata wherein the great king Nastesen who came from the tribe of the Macrobian giants descended from the "Old Race describes "...How he had beaten the troops of 'Kembasuden (Cambyses)' and taken all their ships..." and how "Cambyses retreated from his encounters with the wise and pugnacious Macrobians, insulted, shaken and humiliated."[168]

THE WHITE SUPREMIST CORRUPTION OF PERSIAN COSMOGONY

In later years when Persia was completely overrun by Greeks and other Indo-European races the original Persian version of Kushite-Kemetan cosmogonical science was co-opted and recast in the image of the white supremist patriarchal system. The cosmic egg was portrayed as being viciously cracked by Ahriman formerly a benevolent serpent symbol of the creator of the material world who represented, in the symbology of the high science of Persian cosmogony, the primary stages of vegetation and other life forms

67

in the dark womb of the Earth. The Persians, who had like other nations in Mesopotamia, received their science and culture from the Kushite-Kemetans and believed the earth had hatched from a "giant cosmic egg" which was their way of explaining the 360 degree circular principle in the universe. This knowledge was based on the ancient High Culture astronomers' observation of celestial eliptical orbits which the also identified with the diptical (oval) shape of the female vagina and ovaries (eggs), and the cycle of the seasons. It was upon this correlation and analysis that the foundation of agricultural science and all the other disciplines which strang from it was constructed and developed throughout the ages of early civilizations.

Because most of the Eurasians and Indo-Europeans came from the harsh environment of the Caucasian steeps as opposed to the general abundance of the lands inhabited by Kushite peoples, and due to the utter lack of respect for the science of agriculture and their ignorance of astronomy by the Scythian descendents of the Indo-Europeans,[169] they turned the Ahriman symbol into Angra Mainyu an evil spirit who mixed good with evil in the universe by releasing twenty-four demons into the world when he severed the cosmic egg. The sexually maladjusted Indo-Europeans also transformed Ahuru a feminine aspect of sunlight into a male deity Ahura-Mazda[170] who was said to defeat the darkness of Ahriman every morning and will at the end of the world violently destroy the night for all eternity. Then completely ignoring the original Kushite symbology of King Mithras, who after his death came to represent "the luminous sky in general",[171] and the fact that he was initially depicted as a Black Man,[172] the later Iranian (white) Persians transmuted Mithra—originally the feminine aspect of the Mithras/Mithra union of light and darkness[173]—into first an androgynous then finally a caucasianized patriarchal god of rain and the sun who all by himself created life from the blood of a bull. The symbol in this instance instead of being used to illustrate potent copulation and fecundation with the "Cow of Heaven", as demonstrated in Kemetan astro-mythological cosmogony, was applied as a device to entirely eliminate the feminine principle altogether.

Barbara Walker explains this manifestation of "ambiguous sexual dimorphism" in the following manner:

> "To eliminate the female principle from their creation myth,
> Mithraists [caucasianized Persians] replaced the Mother of All

68

Living in the primal garden of paradise (Pairidaeza) with the bull named Sole-Created. Instead of Eve, this bull was the partner of the first man. All creatures were born from the bull's blood. Yet the bull's birth-giving was oddly female-imitative. The animal was castrated and sacrificed, and its blood was delivered to the moon for magical fructification, the moon being the source of woman's magic...".[174]

The old Kushite Persians called the moon Metra or Matra which to them meant "mother whose love penetrates everywhere". The Iranian Mithra is generally portrayed in their caves and temples as a white male astride a bull holding him by the horns and stabbing him to death. Jackson tells us that "the horned bull was symbolic of the horned [crescent] moon".[175]

In essence, this violent imagery designated the supposed triumph of paternal Mithrasism over the maternal religion of Ausar (Osiris) and Auset (Isis) so widely revered throughout the world, especially in the days of the Roman Empire during the early years of Europeanized white supremist patriarchal Christianity which, in its turn, gradually replaced white supremist Mithrasism in Europe during the 3rd Century. The Indo-European usage of the term "Mithras" meant "cow-murderer" and is known to us today through the Germanic word _mord_, in English "murderer".[176]

> "Like early Christianity, Mithrasism was an ascetic anti-female religion. Its priesthood consisted of celibate men only. Women were forbidden to enter Mithrasic temples...Some resemblances between Christianity and Mithrasism were so close that even St. Augustine [one of the indigenous Afrikan early church fathers] declared the priests of Mithras worshipped the same deity as he did."[177]

In fact, the parallels between the stories of the life, death and resurrection of Jesus ben Joseph (Christ) and Mithras so closely resemble each other it is often difficult to distinguish one from the other. Dr. John G. Jackson, in his book _Man, God and Civilization_ on page 132-133, provides us with a very good comparative parallel of the lives of these two savior gods. The cult of the Caucasianized savior god Mithras was for a long time a thorn in the side of early European Christianity for it

> "...was the leading rival of Christianity in Rome, and more successful than Christianity for the first four centuries of the 'Christian' Era. In 307 A.D. the Emperor officially designated Mithras "Protector of the Empire."[178]

From the foregoing documentation we can clearly ascertain how the religion of white supremist Mithrasism, which arose ca. 300 BCE when black Mithras was identified with Helios, the Greek version of Ra, the Kemetan god of the sun and later introduced into Rome about 68 BCE long after the domination of Indo-European Iranians in old Persia, eventually usurped the scientific principles of Afro-centric Mithrasism as related to us by our mystic friend when we visited the ancient city of Susa.

With this understanding we must keep in mind that many different accounts of the original Kushite creation story were told again and again throughout the ancient world. In fact some of the unique particulars of the Persian version are very similar to the creation stories of India. Therefore, it is fitting that we should now turn our attention to that ancient land of mystery renown for its mystic traditions of yoga and transcendental meditation. Once known as Kindu-Kush, this country produced music and paid homage to the serpentine fires of the Kundalini as represented by the living cobra in the same tradition as their Kemetan brothers in the Motherland showed reverence for the fiery sting and medicinal powers of the Kemetan cobra's (asp's) venom as depicted by the symbol of the Ureas worn upon the face of the double crown of the pharaohs.

CHAPTER FIVE

MYSTIC INDIA LAND OF THE BLACK BUDDHAS
TRAVELING SAFELY ACROSS A
RIVER OF CROCODILES

We for a time now resume our spiritual and intellectual journeys to ancient lands as we cross the Indus River and travel through the Indus Valley to old Hindu Kush.[179] As we are ferried across the Indus we see long snouted, armor backed crocodiles slithering in a scampering manner from the banks of the shore as they splash down into the murky waters opening their huge mouths with ominous hissing while displaying to us their awesomely sharp spiked teeth. This river, like the Hapi (Nile) in Kemet abound in these descendents of Mesozoic Mosasaurs (large sea lizards who lived c. 70 million years ago. Fortunately for us the aquatic vehicle in which we are traveling is very well constructed and superbly piloted by strong and agile ferrymen.

According to historian W.B. Chandler "As the Nile was to Egypt, and the Tigris and Euphrates was to Sumer, so the Indus River was to the Harappan Civilization. It is appropriate that India's name derives from the river which nourished her earliest peoples. (Interestingly enough, early Indians knew this river as the Sindhu, and the region around it as the Sind. Persians, who had difficulty pronouncing the letter S called it Hindu. From Persia to Greece the word spread and in time the land became known as Hindustan and its inhabitants Hindustanis or Hindus.)"[180] Houston tells us that all Hindus before Alexander of Macedon (ca. 331 BCE) were black.[181] In fact, the name India means black.[182]

A VISIT TO THE PERFUMED GARDENS
OF "ANCESTORS HILL"

It is a matter of historical record that the whole culture of this sub-continent is but a continuation of Kush and Kemet for we are told that from Kush "...he (Osiris) passed through Arabia, bordering upon the Red Sea as far as to India...he built many cities in India, one of which he called Nysa, willing to have remembrance of that (Nysa) in Egypt where he was brought up."[183] And that the Hindu Kushites in turn became "...colonialists sent from India, who follow their forefathers in matters of wisdom."[184] The dark-skinned, broad-nosed people[185] we encounter as we sojourn in India reflect the Afrikoid features of the old Kushite race who were pre-eminent and predominant here from earliest times.[186] In the 20th Century they would come to be known as Dravidians.[187] The gods and goddesses of these people which represented to them the per-sonifications of the forces of nature were cast in their own beautiful black image.

We now enter the great city of Mohenjho Daro (Mound of the Ancestors) with its massive temples and elaborate pagodas sur-rounded by lush perfumed gardens, sparkling fountains and cascading waters that shimmer in the brilliant noon day sun as they gently flow into tranquil reflection pools graced by colorful lily pods. As we stroll through its broad well-paved tree-lined streets, for a brief moment we think we see our mystic friend again standing by a kinky haired shrine of a halo-headed Buddha with a multitude of people gathered about him as they listen in delightful ecstasy at his strange enchanting words. This time he spoke the names of Maya, Kali-Ma, Indra, Vishnu, Brahma, Shiva, Krishna, and Buddha. Suddenly our attention is breathtakingly redirected as we look about us and behold the many fabulously engraved shrines and temples decorated with stone portraits of many of the Afrikoid deities of the Indian pantheon which span centuries of Kushite-Hindu history. We first glimpse a voluptuous sculpture of Maya draped in rainbow colored cloth. In ancient India's version of the Kushite-Kemetan Astro-Mythological Cosmogony, she represents the cosmic womb—conception and the unending continued pro-creation of life forms in the material world.

MAMA MAIA: THE CELESTIAL MIRROR OF CREATION

Maia or Maya as she is most widely known is the Indian rendi-tion of the Kemetan deity Auset. In ancient Hindu-Kushite cosmogony noted for its adoration of mother goddess symbolism and religious philosophies with attributes so firmly based in fam-ily and ancestral tradition, Maya is indicative of the Mother Creatress of "all things made of matter and perceptible to the senses", the reality of "existence in the material cosmos". Dark mother-womb which spans the chasm between the creation of each new world. "Bridging the periods of watery chaos between them

72

by preserving the seeds of future life."[188] In this aspect, Maya resembles the Kemetan Nuni as the primal abyss containing the male and the female generative powers. Often symbolized by the shape of an upright pole (male linga) fixed in the female yoni in the shape of a boat floating in the shimmering sky of the watery firmament which she moves to the divine act of procreation by the inspiration of their infinite passion and love.[189]

Mama Maya is also associated with the rainbow. "The rainbow's seven colors represented the seven celestial spheres and the rainbow-hues veils of Maya, the Goddess working behind the veil to manifest the material world in its many-colored complexities.[190] All her priestesses here in India wear the sacred multi-colored veils as do the daughters of Auset who dance the dance of the seven stoles in the Kemetan holy rites. Many centuries later, this same time honored tradition would come to be known as the Dance of the Seven Veils which according to the Christian mythology of the New Testament would be danced by Salome to entertain King Herod, a practice, the meaning of which would come to be greatly misunderstood and shrouded in obscurity by women hating European Christian interpreters of Hebrew biblical mythology.

The month of May derived from her name is also sacred to Maya. The moon is referred to as her celestial mirror and according to the dusky inhabitants of this land, from time immemorial a great festival is celebrated annually in India on the day of the full moon in the month of May and the Hindu-Kushites said this practice gave impetus to May Day celebrations around the world. All of which include the ritual of dancing around the May pole decorated with multi-colored ribbons that fan out from the pole's center and is held in the hands of each of the participants who dance in a circular fashion. Universally the May pole symbolizes the Lingham (male phallus) blissfully inserted in the Yoni (female vagina) of Mother-Earth as does the huge stone Stele of Kemet represents the holy union of Ausaru and Auset.

In the original Kushite-Kemetan Astro-Mythological Cosmogony and even unto the 20th Century of the Common Era, in many parts of India, especially those still inhabited by the Dravidian (Harappan) descendents of the "Old Race", agricultural work is still determined by the phases of the moon.[191] The most favored color of the rainbow to Maya—who is oft times depicted as a stunningly black and beautiful multi-breasted nurturer to the

73

world—is blue. We are also informed by Hindu-Kushite scholars that in the distant land of the Mayan people who dwell across the Ethiopian (Atlantic) Ocean on the other side of the world, their lovely sable skinned women wear blue colored jewels in their left nostrils as a sign of their devotion to Maya and her manifold blessings to these children of the sun whose civilization many scholars believe is respectfully named after her.[192]

To the later Greeks she will come to be known as the great goddess of the May time festival whom they called Maia. The Indus Valley natural scientists also refer to her as the Maia-Kali "who made the universe by her magic powers"[193] and through the timeless ages in southern India she would still be revered and known to them as Amma "the ancient of days" even after centuries of cruel disruptive Aryan (Indo-European) domination.[194]

KALI-MA: THE REVELATION OF LIFE'S UNENDING CYCLE

The next sacred icon we encounter is an awesome portrayal of Kali-Ma carved from jet black onyx stone and delicately trimmed in bright red. We are informed by HinduKushite scholars that these colors are favored by Kali-Ma because all the colors of nature's spectrum disappear into the dark of night to be born again at dawn. So too do "all things enter Kali-Ma to be reincarnated and come forth from The Beautiful One" to the newness of life, and just as the red hot magma of the Pre-Cambrian Era at the embryonic stages of the world's creation spewed forth like an ocean of blood at the moment of birth, so also does the scientific symbol of Kali-Ma, represented by the color red, signify the natural forces which produce earthquakes, erupting volcanos and catastrophic floods. For she is emblematic of nature in all its aspects including the cycle of life and death.[195]

At times Kali-Ma was depicted through grotesque imagery to illustrate India's Kushite master scientist's understanding of the reality that though Mother Nature may sometimes be made manifest in very harsh ways such as earthquakes, erupting volcanos, violent storms, floods, plagues and draught, death as well as life has a necessary role to play in the animal kingdom in order to maintain a natural ecological balance. This realization synchronized with the general belief that reincarnation occurred in ever

74

renewing cycles is taught in their mystic institutions of higher learning as a kind of esoteric theory of evolution. To the Indus Valley High Culture Civilizations, Kali-Ma was an archetypal image of Mother-Earth in her dual aspect as womb and tomb.[196] Eternal in the cycle of life, she represents birth and death.

Kali-Ma is also a spiritual symbol of the world's fertilizing waters. Through life's cycles she is always an integral part of cosmic energy in Tantric prayers. It is said of her:

"she feeds him as a mother feeds her child, and he becomes immortal: 'Deathless are those who have fed at the breast of the Mother of the Universe'... Contrary to the west's ideas of her as a purely destructive Goddess, she was the fount of every kind of love which flowed into the world...through her agents on earth, women."[197]

At the time of death one is said to be touched by the peaceful kiss of Kali-Ma while being received into the blissful arms of the Shakti and returned physically and spiritually to the womb of the cosmos and reunited with Maya's "Oceanic Being". The symbol of her Kundalini spiral is found engraved on Nubian-Grimaldi tombs dating back over 40,000 years ago. Walker informs us:

"As Kundalini the Female Serpent she resembled the archaic Egyptian serpent-mother said to have created the world. It was said of Kundalini that at the beginning of the universe, she starts to uncoil in a 'spiral line movement which is the movement of creation'. This spiral line was vitally important in late Paleolithic [Old Stone Age] and Neolithic [New Stone Age] religious symbolism, representing death and rebirth as movement into the disappearing-point of formlessness, and out of it again, to a new world of form. Spirals therefore appeared on tombs, as one of the world's first mystical symbols."[198]

Some Hindu-Kushite Mythologists teach that it was through Kali's creative utterance OM that all things came into being. An idea which would many centuries later be assumed by the Christians and called the Logos—the word of God.[199] She is also credited in the original Afrikan-Hindu mythos with the invention of language and early writing in India which she derived from "primordial creative energy expressed in sound."[200] She is fervently praised by her devotees especially the males for blessing humanity with maithuna, a transcendental method of sexual intercourse performed as one of the five sacred gifts of Kali-Ma. The others being woman, food, wine, and the high content of nourishing brain 'ood and other stimulating properties in fish.[201]

In man's earthly life "women represented her spirit in m rtal flesh. 'The Divine Mother first appears in and as Her worshippers earthly mother, then as his wife; thirdly as Kalika, She reveals Herself in old age, disease and death.'" She is "...the formless condition she assumed between creation, when all the elements were dissolved in her primordial substance."[202] In a sacred prose poem, the god Vishnu hails her as the

> "Material cause of all change, manifestation and destruction...the whole Universe rest upon Her, rises out of Her and melts away into Her. From Her are crystallized the original elements and qualities which construct the apparent worlds. She is both mother and grave..."[203]

Other enthusiasts pray to her chanting "O Mother! Cause and Mother of the World! Thou art the One Primodial Being, Mother of innumerable creatures, Creatrix of the very gods."[204]

The destroyer aspect of Mother Nature as symbolized in the Kali-Ma principle of Hindu natural science would come to be greatly over exaggerate by later semi-barbaric Aryan invaders whose lack of understanding of the god-force and its multiple expressions in India's High Culture Science would cause them to dub her the "goddess of Disease" and to project this original dual faceted Kushite deity into the Indo-European version of Brahminism as a singularly grotesque malcontent. Still in many other areas of the world she will continue to be venerated. Globally she is also known by the title of "Cunti" or "Kunda", a term originally applied with great respect which since European world domination has come to be used in a derogatory manner in reference to the female of the species.

The Phoenicians while circumnavigating the world as they followed the old Kushite sea routes[205] dubbed the straits of Gibraltar "Calpe" another form of the name Kali. "Because it was consider the passage to the western paradise" of the Great Mother where the Bronzed-skinned Maya and Inca people dwelled.[206] In Saxon Europe where remnants of the Black Celtic culture survived,[207] Kali-Ma would come to be called Kale or Cale from which comes the English word calendar. In ancient Kymry (Kemetan) Ireland[208] her priestesses were called Kelles hence in modern English the name Kelley.[209]

In the Hindu-Kushite cosmogony, Kali-Ma is the symbol of the never ending cycle of life, the continuity of birth and death in the universal creative process. Life ever renewed from the womb to the tomb.

SISTER GANGA: THE SANCTIFIED DAUGHTER OF THE HIMALAYAN MOUNTAINS

As we continue to sojourn here in the Indus Valley, we overhear exciting tidbits of vital historical information from devotees preparing to make the annual pilgrimage to the Ganges River in the northeastern region of this sub-continent. The indigenous ebony inhabitants of the land tell us that this great body of flowing waters is called Mother Ganga, the Holiest of All Rivers. It is also called Sarasvati, the "Flowing One" whose sacred waters are essential to the anointing, purification and baptism of kings.[210]

The river Ganges is also referred to as the daughter of Nanda Devi one of the Himilaya Mountains formed during the early periods in Earth's geological development. Her lifegiving waters cascade down the steeps of the Nandi Devi bestowing many rich blessings on the land below. Barbara Walker says that, "Ganges waters represented baptism and redemption." and "heaps of sin accumulated by a sinner during millions of births are destroyed by the mere contact of a wind charged with her vapor...As fire consumes fuel, so this stream consume the sins of the wicked."[211]

The name of the mountain source of the Ganges River, Nanda Devi, means "Blessed Goddess". The term "devi" is variously translated "Holy Goddess" and "Divine Yoni".[212] In the 20th Century, it is used to denote a female opera singer called a diva. Because in ancient times one nations' deities (gods and goddesses) would many times be thought of as his enemy's devil later patriarchal and misogynistic Indo-European Aryans translated the sacred title "diva" and "devi" to the word devil. The appellation devil, from the Greek *diabolos*, means "one who spawns and stirs up evil disruption and destruction".[213]

Historian Joel A. Rogers informs us that originally the Ganges River was called Chiliaros then renamed in honor of a Kushite king Ganges who helped to maintain a great black civilization in the surrounding lands on the bank of its waters many centuries before the arrival of the Aryans and Mongols.[214]

The Ganges River is also associated with the goddess Sarasvati whom the inhabitants of this region say invented the alphabet and music. Savasvati is also known as Savitri "a name of the Hindu Goddess as mother of civilization, she who brought forth music and literature, rhythm, time, measurements, day and night, memory, conquest, victory, yoga, and religion, as well as many spirits of civilized arts;..."[215] Sarasvati is also sometimes known as Sara "the Daughter of the Sun" and "the wife of Brahma, though the creative Goddess preceded Brahma, and became his consort only after the [Indo-European Aryan] Brahman cult claimed her as a source of his power."[216]

In the Hindu-Kushite cosmogony, Ganga-Sarasvati is a scientific symbol of the fructifying and purifying river of life that flows from the Eternal Stream which was their way of demonstrating the prominent role of great rivers, in this case the Ganges, in the establishment and maintenance of Hindu-Kushite civilization in the Ganges Valley of India.

UNION WITH THE SHAKTI:
A SURE PATH TO ABSOLUTE REALITY

Our thoughts return now to the Indus Valley where in the midst of all the wonderful and instructive iconography we notice many representations of the Lingham and the Yoni a clear graphic indication of the holy and sacred regard the Hindu-Kushites have for the Divine blessing of human sexuality. The supreme symbol in India's Astro-Mythological Cosmogony is the Shri-Yantra a double triangle intertwined. According to the euradite Hindu-Kushite gurus focusing on this design while in transcendental meditation will assist the devotee in achieving total unity with "The One".[217] This sacred sign would many centuries later be misinterpreted by European Jews as the Magen David, the Star of David or Solomon's Seal. Barbara Walker says the age old Shri-Yantra of Hindu-Kush:

"had nothing to do with either David or Solomon it was not mentioned in Jewish literature until the 12th Century A.D. and was not adopted as a Jewish emblem until the 17th Century. The real history of the hexagram began with Tantric Hinduism [initially a branch of Afrikan High Culture Science] where it represented union of the sexes."[218]

The Shri-Yantra is also typified by such symbols as the Maypole which represented the generating power of the Lingham firmly implanted in the Yonic circle surrounded by verdant grass and beautiful flowers. This circle, a sign of Mother Earth's womb is called the Holy of Holies".[219]

Arrangements of this type can be found in the center of all of India's temples. Many times it is represented by a huge marble pillar that connects the floor of the temple with a domed ceiling decorated with similartudes of the gods and goddesses amid stellar configurations denoting the Divine Union of "Heaven and Earth" signifying that through intimate and reverent contact with Mother-Earth especially in the person of the Black Woman, man enters through the gateway of the vulva major into paradise, the "Holy of Holies" which puts him in direct communication with the Divine Universal Intelligence.

To the original Hindu-Kushite theologians of India, the intimate relationship of man and woman was the most direct way to God, the best and highest form of prayer. In stark contrast to the absolute sacredness of this philosophic principle of natural science was the later Aryan corruption and total debasement of human sexuality. Their descendants eventually reversed the meaning of this holy act and taught that meditation and absentia of female contact, that is celibacy, was the panacea for spiritual attunement. Many, many centuries later the Roman Catholic priesthood would adopt this practice of taking a vow of celibacy. They are said to be married to Christ, a male deity. This demonstrates once again that unfortunately somehow throughout history since the emergence of and our contact with Cro-Magnon and his Caucasian posterity what had been from time immemorial sacred to the Black Man and Woman—the original humans on this planet—was co-opted by the white man and inverted to mean something evil. For more information along these lines, read *Afrikan People and European Holidays: A Mental Genocide*, Book II, pages 20-23 by this author.

The exalted concept of the Lingham and the Yoni represented to the original Black Race of India the vital principle of male and female genitalia in holy union. To them it was the most profound manifestation of Cosmic Oneness. Lingham and Yoni is also known as Yab-Yum and Om-Um. In China it is called the Ying and Yang. Around the globe it is known as the "Jewel in the Lotus"[220] Even in 20th Century terms male testicles would come to be referred to as "the family jewels".

The Indus Valley inhabitants emphasis on the unity of the male and female principle as a means of insuring the creation of new

79

of new generations provided them with much inspiration and impetus to create their High Culture Civilization. The doctrine of the efficacy of sexual joy and procreation illustrated in India's manifold art forms are an integral part of the philosophy and science of "Absolute Reality" through union with one's Shakti. The designation Shakti means "Cosmic energy". The Shakti epitomizes the energizing emanating souls of humans and deities alike. She is a vehicle for stirring up the active energies of gods and men, the heat and passion of life.

> "She implies 'power, ability, capacity, faculty, strength, prowess; regal power; the power of composition, poetic power, genius; the power or signification of a word or term; the power inherent in cause to produce its necessary effect..."[221]

All the male deities of India are said to have a Shakti without which they are powerless to act. Hers is the force which makes a hero fearless in the face of danger and death. The Hindu-Kushites, as many other Afrikan peoples around the world, believe that without his "Lady Love", his Shakti, neither Earthly man nor cosmic god can realize his greatest potential.[222] The Shakti is often referred to as man's guardian angel in the "spirit world" who makes herself incarnate in his Earthly feminine mate or mates. Just as Auset and Nebthet are called the wives and guardian angels of Ausaru in some Kemetan texts, the brilliant wise men of India teach that woman is "life itself" and the proper mental, spiritual and sexual union with her is the gateway to mental expansion and total enlightenment. A Hindu-Kushite "synonym for 'woman' was Shaktiman, 'Mind of Shakti' or 'Possessor of Shakti'."[223] The figure of the Shakti represents one of the maternal aspects of the Divine Intelligence "and as such stands for the spontaneous loving and joyful acceptance of life's tangible realities".[224]

Hindu-Kushite pundits teach that at the moment of death, a man's spiritual Shakti which is a reflection of his Earthly soul mate/mates pierces the darkness with her lovely form and continence and receives him into her divine bosom to partake of eternal bliss. In the case of a man with many wives, his spiritual Shakti is manifested as a composite of the best of their collective attributes. This concept of the Shakti's embrace at death dates all the way back to Nubian-Grimaldi times when the deceased was interred with voluptuous Afrikoid female figurines.

In Hindu-Kushite cosmogony, the Shakti represents the union of male and female forces in absolute harmony, sexual joy and procreation in cosmic balance. The everlasting posterity of all created beings.

THE COSMIC DANCE OF INDRA IN THE MIDST OF MAYA-KALI

The next manifestation of cosmic god forces of nature that quickens our attention is an elegantly embossed relief of Indra who represents the Archeozoic Age in the geological time frame (c. 4.6-2.5 Billion B.P.) which experienced many heated electrical storms of enormous degrees in the planet's atmosphere accompanied by constantly reoccuring red hot magma from earthquakes and rumbling volcanos. This vibrant activity helped to mold and shape the planet Earth and as it gradually cooled off the perpetual motion prepared the globe as a fit habitation for myriad organic forms some of which eventually evolved into the human species. So says the brilliant men and women of high intellect in the Indus Valley.

Indra is an old Kushite storm deity[225] who is depicted in Hindu-Kushite Astro-Mythological Cosmogony erotically dancing with his Shakti to the cosmic rhythms and music of the spheres as they stir up heat and energy in the midst of Mama Maya's dark and watery womb thereby acting as a divine catalyst for the everlasting stimulation of the Lingham and Yoni in all Earthly creatures.[226]

In Hindu-Kushite cosmogony Indra in union with his Shakti is scientifically symbolized as an activator for terrestrial posterity. The heat which stimulates life ever increasing through perpetual motion.

VISHNU AND THE TEN AVATARS OF EVOLUTION

Being surrounded by the Indian Ocean, the third largest ocean in the world on three sides, India's scientists are ever sensitive to the essential role in water and aquatic creatures in the evolution and maintenance of life on Earth. So it is only natural that they should give considerable attention to this idea in their symbology. The concept of the universal permeation of sea water and its animate residents is stunningly exemplified in a bronze effigy of Manu (equivalent of the Hebrew Adam) emerging from the mouth of Vishnu in the form of a fish. This majestic figure luminously projects its message to us through the reflection of the noon day sun.

The heat is intense. Yet somehow we cannot manage to disengage ourselves from observing all the wondrous similatudes around us and the profound lessons of natural science they project. Before entering into the cool relief of the sanctuary of the temple shrine, we will endure the heat for yet a little while longer as we contemplate the meaning of this beautiful work of art. The name of the fish symbol, our guide tells us, is Vishnu which means "one who embraces and expands". Vishnu is also known as "the penetrator".[227] His chief sign is the Lingham-Yoni in the form of a circle with a cross in its center. Vishnu is most often portrayed with his Shakti, Lakshmi, the goddess of material wealth who wears "the many colored veils of Maya".[228]

The other character depicted in this iconography is Manu, the first ancestor of man according to Hindu-Kushite cosmogony. He is said to have survived a great flood with the assistance of the great sea serpent Vasuki (one of the manifestations of Vishnu) who safely guided his ark through the turbulent waters.[229] Hindu-Kushite scholars tell us the archaic form of Manu is synonymous with the Kemetan feminine designation Ma Nu and was at the time of the foundation of Indus Valley civilization identified with Nu or Nuni and represented by a huge fish.[230] They also inform us that the masculine aspect of Manu was initially associated with Menes seemingly relative to Aha Menes who united upper and lower Kemet (Egypt) ca. 5500 BCE. They affirm that this is another indication of the Kushite-Kemetan origin of Indus Valley High Culture Civilization.[231]

Houston tells us that the laws for governance in old Kushite India was called the Code of Manu. This code has regulated the moral and social life in India from the most ancient times. Central to its precepts—as in many other Black lands—was maternal authority as the foundation of all civil law.[232]

In time the original Kushite code, the Law of Manu, would come to be co-opted and corrupted by Indo-Europeans into a cruel instrument of oppression and repression against the indigenous Black populations of India—the Aryan—Brahmin Caste System.[233] This venomous system would be interjected into the Manu Code ca. 100 CE.[234]

82

As we now enter into the exhilarating atmosphere of a temple-university classroom overlooking the cool refreshing waters of a murmuring brook, our learned mentors begin to instruct us on the symbology of the ten mythological Avatars of evolution as illustrated in the incarnations of Vishnu;

1) Matsya-Vishnu, the great fish representing the dominance of sea creatures during the Paleozoic Era (c. 600-225 Million B.P.)

2) Kurm-Vishnu, the giant tortoise representing the preeminence of the reptile during the Mesozoic Era (c. 225-70 Million B.P.)

3) Varaha-Vishnu, the mammoth boar representing the early profusion of mammals in the Cenozoic Era (c. 70-1 Million B.P.)

4) Nara-sing-Vishnu, a robust man-lion resembling *Kenyapithecus (Ramapithecus)* who emerged in equatorial Alkebulan (c. 14 Million B.P.) and symbolizing the exceptional physical strength of the Earth's early manlike creatures. Nara-sing-Vishnu represents the last animal stage before the evolution of the hominid line of apemen and humans.

5) Vamuna-Vishnu, a dwarf resembling the *Anzaniapithecus* stage of human development between 4-2 million years ago representing one of the early stages in the development of the human species.

6) Parasu-rama-Vishnu, a human form not yet perfected resembling the *Homo erectus* and archaic *Homo sapiens* between 1 1/2 million to 300,000 years ago. Parasu-rama-Vishnu represents an advanced stage of hominid (the family of apemen and humans) development.

7) Rama-Chandra, the hero of the epic poem Ramayana, a physically perfect man, a *Homo sapien sapien*, who, among his closest friends, was a verbally articulate monkey and the army of apes who helped him defeat his adversaries.

8) Is Christna, an advanced *Homo sapien sapien* (modern human), a being with high technological skills denoting the last 20,000 years of the Holocene Period.

9) Buddha who signifies spiritually enlightened humanity and a general ever reoccurring resurrection to the eternal principles of the Black Man's original High Culture Science. This especially applies to 20th Century born-again Afrikans renewed in consciousness, wisdom and understanding.

10) Kalki-avatarum, humanity in complete harmony with the cosmos after the last great world catastrophe. This manifestation of Vishnu represents the state of a new world "the garden replanted" the supreme aim and objective of evolution.*

In summary the wise sages tell us that in the HinduKushite cosmogony, Vishnu and his ten manifestations are symbolic of the preeminence of the sea and the many evolutionary stages of creation and finally the ultimate salvation of the total harmony of mind, body and spirit. As we listen to this astonishing information being shared with us, we are completely enthralled in its wondrous depth and amazed at the wisdom of our Hindu-Kushite instructors who seem to possess a knowledge that stretches ad infinitum from the remotest past and on into the future.

Though what they have just taught us is a system of scientific symbols meant to be understood allegorically, this very old concept from the remotest of times as it was being reiterated through the mythos of Vishnu's incarnations is to us as we sit fixed in our seats in the temple classrooms with its pleasant smelling sandalwood and cedar furniture, many scented lighted candles and fragrant incense a vehicle for transcendental astro-traveling. Wow! What a journey.

THE PASSION DANCE OF SHIVA IN THE HEART OF THE UNIVERSE

The evening shadows begin to fall. My, how time has passed while we were being instructed in the temple. As we step through the golden doors of this elaborate edifice and descend the inlaid jeweled steps to the pavement of one of Mohenjo-Daro's broad avenues, we behold a morphologic silver cast of the multi-limbed Shiva passionately embracing his consort Parvati and displaying a luminous ruby in the center of this forehead to symbolize spiritual and intellectual attainment through union with the Shakti. Shiva also bears upon his head an emblem of the crescent moon, the sign of Maya denoting his attunement and direct contact with this Maternal Creative Force.[235]

---

* The various geological stages of planet Earth's development and the evolutionary growth of the human species will be discussed in detail in Volume Two of this series.

The god Shiva is also known as Sthanu meaning "pillar" or "pole" which signifies the male phallus in Hindu-Kushite natural scientific cosmogonical symbology.[236] This deity is often referred to as Mahakala "The Great Black One" and is seldom depicted alone. "...for his power depended on his union with Kali, his feminine energy, without whom he could not act."[237]

The name of his consort Parvati means "Mother-Earth" and is one of the many appellations of Kali-Ma. "As Kali's consort, Shiva bore the title of "Lord of Yoga"...yoga meant to link, join, or unite, like the English derivative 'yoke'. It was the term for sexual union between the Tantric sadhu and his yogini, or Shakti, in imitation of the union between Kali and Shiva."[238]

Sometimes Shiva is called "Lord of the Dance" when in estactic embrace of his Shakti as they dance the "Dance of Life,...directing and controlling by its rhythm the constant movement in time and space of all material things." The esoteric teachings of the Hindu-Kushite sages tell us that this dance is performed in the "Center of the Universe" which is located within the human heart. They impress upon us "...that (1) the heartbeat is the basic rhythm to which all human music is related, because it is heard even by the unborn infant in the paradise-state of intrauterine life, and it is never forgotten; and (2) each human being secretly regards his own heart as the center of the universe indeed, therefore the god is located within the core of man's own self."[239]

Shiva attains "universal energy" through union with his divine Shakti. To optimize this energy he applies the system of maithuna, the method of controlling his own orgasmic pleasure while insuring that of his partner. In this manner, he is able to fully partake of her lifegiving and enlightening sexual energy.[240] This method of Spiritual Illumination and power has been practiced by the priests of Kemet every since the foundation of their High Culture Civilization in the Hapi (Nile) Valley. In our day song stylist Aretha Franklin defines this divine union as "getting in the spirit in the dark" and Marvin Gaye refers to it as "sexual healing".

The cosmological sciences of ancient India teach that it is through yoga (linking) with the Goddess that Shiva became "Bindu" the spark of creation[241] and so it is also on the Earthly plain with the Black Man and Woman become one in erotic love. Each time they do this in the context of being properly balanced mentally and spiritually, this sacred act is supposed to take them further into the heights and depths of Cosmic Revelation and inspire them to accomplish great deeds in their lives. In our day, that mu:. have been what Jackie Wilson meant when he sang "your love keeps lifting me higher and higher". Hindu-Kushite men and women of letters teach that "coitus is a repetition of the creation of the world, the religious moment in which the self obtains the beatitude."[242] This particular aspect of ancient Afrikan High Culture Science was first taught in India by priest-scholars from the Hapi Valley many many years ago.

Hindu-Kushite master thinkers affirm the fact that early India's adoration of the Shiva force as it is manifested in natural phenomena was pure and its sexual rites were highly spiritual, but later Aryan-Brahmins, being morally debased, would pervert the worship of Shiva even unto the practice of human sacrifice and the burning of a man's widow on the funeral pyre. Sycthic twisted degenerated rites so transformed Shiva veneration from its original form and practice that 20th Century Afrikan historian, Drucilla Houston in 1926 would deny that ancient Kushites had anything to do with Shiva whatsoever.[243] However, further research by other 20th Century Afrikanologists have proven Kushite disassociation from the ancient Hindu high culture symbol of the Shiva principle to be untenable.[244] One of the foremost scholars of Asian Antiquities, Runoko Rashidi, says that Shiva was originally an Afrikan deity.[245]

So to put this discussion in the light of historical reality, we must recall and clearly understand that the original meaning of the scientific symbol of Shiva in HinduKushite cosmogony before the invasion of India by Eurasian foreigners from the north denoted cosmic intellect, the motivating power of the Supreme Being and divine healing through sexual harmony with the Shakti and the sexual union as an act to help perpetuate the ever renewing cycles of creation in the world.

BRAHMA: THE MISPLACED SON OF MAMA MAYA

Just ahead of us on a reverently chiseled collage of the gods and goddesses resplendently displayed over the doorway of a shrine to Lord Krishna, we see a small four-faced figure of Brahma. "Rising from the center of this relief in a lotus-blossom throne over Krsna's [Krishna's] extended right arm..."[246] At first a rather insignificant deity in the Hindu-Kushite pantheon, Brahman's archaic

86

name is Rudra Mokshakala "Liberated Black Rudra",[247] god of the woodlands and wild animals. He is often associated with Ogun, the Orisha of iron and war of the Yoruba people who migrated from the Hapi Valley to west Alkebulan and would be later identified with the Greco-Roman god of war, Mars.[248]

Originally Brahma was just one of the sons of Maya. His eventual exalted position in the Hindu cosmogony was never fully accepted by the indigenous Black populations of India. Barbara Walker says "Brahma...worship never struck vital roots in the popular folk soil. He was used mainly to support the caste system. Today Brahma is so relatively unimportant that only one or two temples in all India are reserved for his exclusive worship."[249] Later patriarchal Indo-Aryan Brahmins would seek to totally eliminate the feminine aspect of creation by referring to Brahma as "the Birthless One" is spite of the fact that the older Kushite scriptures referred to him as a child of Mother Maya.[250] Barbara Walker tells us:

"The older dharma (holy law) said the worst of crimes was killing a woman of female child, because it meant killing unborn generations. However, like most patriarchal systems, Brahminism lifted the taboo on male aggression against females, and claimed that it was better to kill women that to insult Brahmins: 'to revile and calumniate a worshipper of the Supreme Brahman is a sin ten million times worst than that of killing a woman.' Like the medieval Christian Church, Brahman priests made rules for rigid control of wives, and... reversed the old system of matrilineal inheritance, insisting that property must pass from father to son."[251]

One of the examples of an habitual Indo-European trait is clearly indicated in the fact that "...wherever [Aryan] Brahmins found a god whom it was politic to reverence they made him one of their own."[252] The Indo-European Aryans were also wont to impose their perverted concept of Brahminism upon the indigena through the means of cruel and horrific tortures. Thus we behold in this again the historical reality that generally what was good and sacred to the Afrikan became perverted and the original high ideals were distained by the many Eurasian and Indo-European invasions of our lands. These violent and vile interlopers were never able to fully comprehend the real meaning of the scientific symbols used in our most ancient High Culture Systems. So they would co-opt and misinterpret them in their desperate attempts to redefine all things in the image of white-supremacy. Here is a classic case of

87

this type of zenophobia (fear of other peoples and cultures) in the Aryans blatant distortions of the original functions of the Hindu-Kushite deity Brahma.

According to ancient Hindu-Kushite scriptures, the scientific symbol of Brahma represents no real significant contribution to the creation of the world. Rudra Makshakala Brahma as was said was basically a deity of the woodlands and wild animals who during times of escalated national defense would be accorded special attention as he was also the Hindu god of war at which time he would be given the exalted and honored title of Black Liberator. But in that the way of the Hindu-Kushite of India as it is with most Afrikan people was not to be preoccupied with constant war and conquest, the Brahman symbol was assigned to a minor function during the long peaceful period that was the preferred state of the highly civilized Hindu-Kushites who originally occupied the Indus and Ganges Valleys.

LORD KRISHNA:
THE BLACK MESSIAH OF INDIA

Now as we turn our attention again to the collage of the gods and godesses over the doorway of the temple shrine, we notice that at the center of and the most dominant figure in this relief is ''...the form of Krsna [Krishna], the supreme warrior, asleep on the coils of the giant multi-headed serpent, Ananta.''[253] Krishna, a prophet who lived and manifested incredible deeds in India around 1200 BCE, is regarded as the 8th evolutionary incarnation of Vishnu[254] and would come to be the most celebrated deity of the Hindu-Kushite pantheon. Krishna, the Black Messiah of India, is an aboriginal deity of the original Black inhabitants of the Indus Valley.

He is often regarded as a reincarnation of Ausaru of Kemet and precedes by many centuries the Aryan exaltation of the lesser god, Brahma, whom they recast in the image of white-supremacy. Houston says, ''Krishna which means black was taken out of the old cult and incorporated in Brahminism, anything to insure the strengthening of the claim of the [Aryan] Brahmin to the priesthood.''[255] Jackson corroborates this by informing us that in most Indian art ''Krisha is depicted as a man of black complexion, and the name Krisha literally means the black.''[256] Rogers adds another dimension to this historical reality by informing us that,

88

"the earliest gods and messiahs on all the continents were black. Research has yielded an impressive amount of material on the subject. It will be seen, too, that the messiahs, some of whom lived many centuries before Christ, had lives which so closely paralleled that of Christ that it seems most likely that the story of the latter was adapted from them. Moreover, the word, Christ, comes from the Indian, Krishna or Chrishna, which means 'The Black One.' "[257] And Walker says, "Unlike the western Christos, however, Krishna was an erotic god...His favorite mistress was the insatiable Radha,...".[258]

The correlation between Krishna and the later Christian Christ will be further discussed in a forthcoming work by this author entitled *Black Historical Facts on the Life of Jesus*. Krishna in his turn had many incarnations. Rama, the hero of the epic poem Ramayana, is reputed to be one of them.[259] Rama Krishna is vividly described in this ancient Hindu-Kushite epic poem as a mighty warrior flying through the air in fire spitting rocket ships while defending his homeland against the encroaching Aryan armies.[260] Led by the valiant Rama Krishna, the normally peaceful Kushites of the Indus Valley were for a time victorious over the ultra-violent Indo-European invaders from the north.

In the Hindu-Kushite cosmogony Krishna represents the eighth evolutionary incarnation of Vishnu, the last 20,000 years of *Homo sapien sapien's*(modern man's) growth and advancement.

THE PROCESSION OF THE BUDDHAS

We pass by, once again, a statue of the Buddha where we momentarily saw our mystic friend whom we first encountered in Persia. The place is a graciously appointed courtyard with lily pod garnished reflection pools, hanging gardens, an infinite variety of shrubs and trees and an array of beautiful flowers of every type and color. In the midst of this serene environment is an immense stone effigy of a broad-nosed, thick-lipped, kinky-haired Afrikan reposed with legs crossed and palms upturned in the meditative position of the Lotus. The inscription at the base of the statue reads "The Buddha" which is a title of great honor and respect meaning "The Enlightened One".

Buddha, the ninth avatar of Vishnu, represents a general resurrection to the Eternal Principles of the Black Man's original High Culture Science. One of the many names of the Buddhas who

89

appeared through many successive incarnations on Earth was Siddhartha meaning "Rich in Yogic Power". The most famous of the Buddhas, Gatuma, appeared around the 5th or 6th Centuries BCE was born of the very beautiful blue-black Maia, a high priestess and Earthly incarnation of Mama Maya.[261] It is said that this particular Buddha attained enlightenment while poised in the lotus position under the Bo tree which is sacred to the Great Cosmic Mother Maya.

Drucilla Houston tells us that Hindu-Kushite Buddhists have the highest respect and tender regard for their women. For instance, in Buddhist literature "the poems describe their character and relations with women as pure and noble...They are full of tenderness and female charm, like the mass element of India that was once Buddhist." Other poetic utterances of ancient India "reveals the high moral status of the female sex. A deep feeling of tenderness and regard for women is invariably represented."[262]

All the original Buddhas prior to Eurasian and Aryan occupation and influence had "A well-known aphorism...'Buddhahood [enlightenment] resides in the vulva (yoni)'." Even in spite of "...the constant tension between ascetic and sensual elements." of Buddhism, the sacred relationship of the feminine principle was consistently reasserted and generally superseded celibate Buddhism.[263]

The sacred symbols of the Buddhas are the same as those of Heru (Horus) of Kemet. Touching on the three dimensions of Buddha, Rogers says "the personifications of the Buddha of India are three; the past, the present, and the future; they are generally represented half-naked with wooly heads in a sitting posture." The English scholar Godfrey Higgins declares:

> "that the Buddhist were Negroes [Blacks] the icons of their God clearly prove...this...[and] prejudice wears away when I go to the precursors of the Brahmins, the Buddhist, and when I reflect upon the skill of the Fine Arts which they must have possessed when they executed the most beautiful and the most ancient sculptures in the museum of the India House and the knowledge of astronomy shown in their cycles of stone."[264]

Affirming that the Afrikaness of the Buddhas is plainly evidenced by irrefutable data, Higgins goes on to state that,

> "the religion of Buddha of India is well known to have been very ancient. In the most ancient temples scattered throughout Asia, where his worship is yet continued, he is found Black

as jet, with the flat face, thick lips and curly hair of the Negro...the religion of the Negro god is found in the ruins of his temples and other circumstances to have been spread over an immense extent of country. Even to the remotest part of Britain; and to have been professed by devotees inconceivably numerous."[265]

Another 19th Century English scholar of this genre wrote:

"it is certain that the Black Buddha of India was imaged in the Negroid type. In the black Negro god, whether called Buddha or Sut-Nahsi, we have a datum...The people who first fashioned and worshipped the divine image in the Negroid mold of humanity must, according to all knowledge of human nature, have been Negroes themselves. For blackness is not merely mystical, the features and hair of Buddha belong to the black race and Nashi is the Negro name."[266]

According to Houston:

"The older temples of India are to Buddha. His worship was anterior to that or Brahma...Buddhism was older than Buddha-Gautema, who was only one of the incarnations of the old faith...the dates of the incarnations of Buddha ranged from 2450 B.C. to 453 B.C.. Buddhism was the evolution of many centuries. It sprang from some earlier form of Cushite faith. Buddhist when they pray call upon 'Ad'. The early Cushites were [known as] Adites."[267]

Some of the major dates of the incarnations of Buddha are:

- India, 1366 BCE, the first Buddha born of a Black Woman named Maia and depicted with a brilliant halo around his black woolly head. His symbols are the cross and the tetragramadon (swastika). of Twa origin.

- Japan, 1000 BCE-where he is also represented with Afrikoid features and kinky hair.

- India, 721 BCE-where he is delivered by his mother Maya (Maia) to the accompaniment of flowers, music and perfumed air. "His woolly head was rayed; his complexion jet black and his hair.[268]

This last reference is probably to Buddha Gautema who is said to have forbidden the worship of himself and graven images and requested of his disciples that they not deify or build any temples to him after his death or found a new religion in his name. A request that would be totally ignored by succeeding generations of

91

Buddhists for "the religion of Buddha of India...is found in the ruins of his temples and other circumstances to have been spread over an immense extent of country,..." and it is geographically diffused all over the globe.

In Hindu-Kushite cosmogony, Buddha, as was said, represents a general resurrection of the eternal principles of the Black Race's original High Culture Science. The final preparation before the last stage of human evolution; total harmony with the cosmos a time when as Hindu-Kushite sages believe when all evil, sickness and physical death will be eradicated from planet Earth and a new creation will begin.

While taking this intellectual and spiritual journey to ancient Kushite India, we have in consciousness been modulating chronologically between the old Indus Valley civilizations, the later Aryan Indo-European period of domination and the 20th Century. We will now, though somewhat reluctantly, return wholly to our present time frame as we continue our investigation into the original high culture civilization of the Hindu-Kushites.

SUMMATION OF THE GODS AND GODDESSES OF BLACK INDIA

Again we remind our readers that what we have been discussing here in this chapter is another dimension of one of the many versions of the original Kushite-Kemetan Astro-Mythological Cosmogony. The same basic creation story was told repeatedly in many different ways throughout the ancient world. In Indus Valley High Culture Cosmogonic Science as in all other Kushite civilizations around the globe, the status of maternal deities was preeminent and supreme because of the ancient Kushite's esteemed reverence for the feminine principle. At one time there were many more goddesses than gods in India. Houston reminds us that "the spirit of the Cushite was to honor and exalt women, therefore lineage was there traced."[269] "In later periods of Indian history, as in many other areas where the worship of the male deity was superimposed upon the female religion, many people, perhaps those who remained in more insulated areas, still retained the worship of the Goddess."[270] Somewhere between 561 and 600 BCE, the teachings of the great sage, Buddha Gautema, helped to restore mother reverence in India after one of the many Aryan invasions.

92

All the above god and goddess symbols played a role in Hindu-Kushite cosmogony and like its predecessor, Kemet, India had many creation stories during its long antiquity as a nation. Instead of telling the various stories, which space in this particular work would not permit, we have given the scientific meaning of their deity symbols, so whenever our readers should encounter some form(s) of Indian Cosmogony, they will have the key to interpreting the principles conveyed therein.

CHAPTER SIX

EPIC POEMS OF COSMIC HEROES THE SACRED SCRIPTURES OF COSMIC ADVENTURERS

The original Vedas and other sacred writings of ancient India are the books which tell the stories of the god and goddess forces of nature personified in Hindu-Kushite rulers and sages. On our spiritual visit to ancient Mohenjo-daro, we were edified and illuminated by studying the iconography of these age old heroes and heroines whose legendary lives caused them to be identified with the powers of nature and elevated to the level of a godhead.

The original Vedas appear in 5 collections comprising more than 100 books. Rig-veda pictures a strong people singing with joy at the world's beginning. Yajur-veda contains prayers and litanies of Hindu-Kushite worship services. Sama-veda is a book of hymns sang in adoration of the scientific symbols of the gods and goddesses. The Sutras encompasses the laws, the civil and domestic code. Atharvaveda shows a tired and fearful people who after Aryan domination in despair have resorted to magic charms to obtain their goals.[217]

The word Veda means knowledge. Runoko Rashidi tells us that one of the groups of early Black settlers in India were known as Veddas. They lived mostly in the metropolis of Ceylon and are described as short, flat nosed, dark skin, curly haired people.[272] Some scholars think their tribal name Vedda strongly suggest they may have had a hand in the formative writing and publishing of the Veda Scriptures.

Although the Upanishads, one of the principle documents of ancient Hinduism, are a separate literate unto themselves, they are sometimes added to the Vedas. The Upanishads are essays on philosophy and the unity of the one God.

The fundamental doctrine of these writings is the identity of the individual self with the cosmic self, the presence of the Divine Intelligence in all living things which is a Kushite doctrine of great antiquity. Houston says that Indo-European Brahminism

"...claims to be founded upon the Vedas, the sacred books of India, taken over by the Brahmins. They were not the creators of the writings, though today they are the custodians, interpreters and priests. They only attained this place after a bloody struggle with the native races...The Jains, wealthy southern Dravidians, an offshoot from Buddhism, accused the Brahmins of destroying the real historical books of India, wherever they gained ascendency...As time went on Brahmins added to and corrupted the Vedas to confirm their excessive pretensions."[273]

One such being the ominous caste system imposed upon the original Black indigena by Aryan interlopers.

Other outstanding Hindu-Kushite scriptures are the great epic poems Ramayana and the Maha Bharta. The Ramayana tells the story of the hero Rama-Krishna and his Shakti, Sita. It

"...is very ancient. It is an allegory in which good triumphs over evil...This poem is uncontaminated with foreign alloy. It is a picture of Hindu life prior to 1000 B.C. It is also a picture of Cushite civilization at that age. It is the story of the deeds of primitive heroes. The poem contains 2,400 verses and is divided into seven books. It was written about 500 B.C."[274]

In like manner the Maha Bharta "The Great Story" describes events which took place in Kushite India about 1,200 BCE. The most noted section of the work is the Bhagavad-Gita "Song of The Blessed One" a wisdom dialogue on the meaning of life which takes place between Lord Krishna and Prince Arjuna. The entire poem is divided into 18 books containing altogether about 200,000 lines of verse. These and other epic poems of India were originally based on the great deeds of the Hindu-Kushites who preserved and defended the Indus Valley High Culture Civilization founded by the Kushite-Kemetans from Alkebulan (Afrika).

ALKEBULAN: THE SOURCE OF INDUS VALLEY HIGH CULTURE CIVILIZATION

As was previously mentioned the ancient Hindu-Kushites who produced these epic poems were primarily a very peaceful and communal people with high moral standards. Their fervent love of and exalted view of Black Womanhood coupled with a sacred regard for the Divine Power of Sexual Union served as an impetus for the building of their High Culture Civilization.

The science of Yoga, an extension of the Shri-Yantra principle of male and female union, was first brought to the early Indus Valley civilizations by Afrikan giants from Nubia in the Kushite

96

region of east Alkebulan.[275] It is reported that one of the teachers of this science, Aristanemi, lived about 90,000 years ago. Wayne Chandler informs us that:

"The prior Jaina saint, Nami, who preceded Aristanemi, taught and preached the faith fifty thousand years before that. This date extends the lineage to the Eolithic Period [dawn of the Stone Age]. His predecessor, Survata the twentieth Tirthankara, is said to have lived eleven-hundred thousand [1,100,000] years before Nami. The list goes on, down to the earliest Tirthankara [master teacher], who is said to have lived in a period more ancient even than the three and a half million year old Ethiopian female known as Lucy [Denkenesh]...The science of yoga was born out of an antiquity just as mysterious as Jainism...Yoga being related to the mechanical system of the Jainas, which we have seen can be traced back in a partly historical, partly legendary way through the long series of the Tirthankaras, to a remote aboriginal non-Vedic [Harappan] Indian antiquity. Yoga therefore must be immensely old...There is no doubt that this spiritual science was born out of Black Ancestry."[276]

Agricultural science and other basic arts of civilization are said to have been imported to the Indus Valley by Ausaru who headed one of the many successive Kushite-Kemetan colonies there. This particular expedition, either led by Ausaru or someone else under his auspices, may have occurred somewhere between 18,000-10,000 BCE. This is also probably the group that produced an alphabet of 21 signs based on a combination of the Kemetan Medu Netcher (hieroglyphics), and demotic system to be used in HinduKushite writing. Auset the principle wife of Ausaru is credited with having invented the alphabet and writing and decreed it to be disseminated all over the world by her learned priests and priestesses.

The Indus Valley civilization is also known as the Harappan Civilization named so after one of its two great cities, Mohenjo-Daro and Harappa. Each of these metropolises supported populations of approximately 40,000 people. They were built somewhere between 7000-6000 BCE.[277] Every home in Harappa had a graciously appointed courtyard and was equipped with the ancient Kushite version of a trash disposal unit which emptied into a butimen (cement) covered central sewage system tenaciously kept up to very high sanitary standards. Each household also had bathrooms which connected with drainage pipes that ran deep under the main streets

to a central processing location where waste was treated with natron
a very ancient chemical compound made from a mineral alkali with
carbonating properties. Natron was also one of the natural
chemicals used for embalming and purification in the Hapi Valley
civilizations of Kush and Kemet. Dr. John G. Jackson describes the
twin cities and the people who built them thusly:

> "These cities were well constructed. Mohenjo Daro was 2
> square miles in area, with regularly laid-out main and side
> streets, lined with attractive brick houses. Bathrooms were a
> common feature, and they were fitted out with runaway drains
> leading to brick sewers laid under the streets. This culture
> reached its peak about 3000 B.C. These people had
> domesticated cattle, sheep, and elephants; cultivated cotton
> and wheat; built boats and wheeled carts; and became skilled
> workers of bronze and iron. They even discovered a process
> for making iron rust proof...That the Dravidians possessed
> high skill in the fabricating of iron and steel implements is a
> fact not subject to dispute."[278]

At one time the Indus Valley High Culture was spread by the
Black Race through all of India.[279] In fact the ancient Black civilizations of India ruled almost all of Asia. Higgins says, "...a very
great nation of Blacks from India, did rule over almost all Asia in
a very remote era, in fact beyond the reach of history or any of
our records."[280]

THE HEROIC STRUGGLES OF
KUSHITE-BUDDHIST RESISTANCE MOVEMENTS
AGAINST THE ARYAN PLAGUE

Would that our brief recitation of Hindu-Kushite history could
rest here as we focus on the ancient glories of this particular
daughter of Mother Alkebulan, but many things have happened
in India since the time of the Great Indus Valley and Ganges High
Culture Civilizations which endured relatively undisturbed for at
least 8,500 years. Then the Indo-European Aryans came followed
by the Greeks and the Arabs then finally the English. None of these
violent and destructive invaders in their turn brought anything of
real value to the sub-continent of India but rather initiated and
steadily contributed to the debasement and demise of its original
Black populations.

The first wave of foreign invaders were the IndoEuropean Aryans somewhere between 1500-1300 BCE.[281] The great city of Mohenjo Daro was sacked and destroyed about this time causing a shock wave of violent upheaval throughout northern India from the Indus to the Ganges. However, these kinds of incursions did not go unopposed. The indigenous Blacks fought many battles against the invaders and were often victorious. These valiant struggles continued intermittently for about 700 years. Rama Krishna's rocket ship offensive as portrayed in the Maha Bharta was one of them, but Drucilla Houston tells us, "These people were too much addicted to peace to be able to offer prolonged resistance, but they were strong enough to impose many of their ideas and institutions upon their conquerors."[282]

By 800 BCE nomadic Aryans had conquered most of northern India. Nevertheless for over

"...five hundred years the native dynasties waged war against them...From 100 B.C. to 700 A.D. Indian civilization suffered from the inroads of Tartars or Scythians...It was from this element that this cast of [Aryan] Brahmins may have sprung or from earlier invasions, for about 700 A.D. the Brahmins began to gain the upper hand in India."[283]

The barbaric Indo-European Aryan invaders with fiendish abandonment willfully defaced and mutilated many wonderful works of Hindu-Kushite art. That which they did not or could not destroy, they co-opted and claimed as their own.[284]

We have already discussed why Aryan-Brahmins usurped and transformed the original Hindu-Kush deity symbols of natural science. For example, regarding the Indo-European mistranslations and rewriting of the Rig-veda, Houston further informs us:

"Much of the grossness found in these writings cannot be attributed to the creators but to the interpolations of the [Aryan] Brahmins." and that "Buddha-Gautema denied the claims of the Brahmins that they were the divinely appointed teachers of sacred knowledge."[285]

As aforementioned, child marriages, a custom which still exists in parts of India to this day was brought there by Aryan-Brahmins. This practice did not exist among the original Buddhists and adherents to other Hindu-Kushite religious philosophies which had such an exalted reverence for women and children. Drucilla Houston writes:

99

"Barnett speaking of the Aryas or Brahmins in their beginning says of them that, whatever was their inception, their race was vary quarrelsome. They brought no women with them to India but took Dravidian wives...and here...mixed with Cushite blood..."[286]

Buddha-Gautema through the revolutionary protest movement of the Buddhist quest for "enlightenment" openly and fearlessly rejected and opposed the Aryan-Brahmin utter defilement and adulteration of the sacred writings, customs, and religious rites of the Hindu-Kushites of the original "Old Race". Drucilla Houston gives a vivid account of the high morals and quality of life exemplified by these brave Buddhist warriors for justice and righteousness in her fabulous book *The Wonderful Ethiopians of the Ancient Cushite Cushite Empire,* pages 226-228.

THE EVERLASTING JOURNEY

Surely we could extend our spiritual and intellectual journey on the subject of ancient cosmogony to other lands around the world, but in so doing we would never complete the writing of this book. It would take volumes upon volumes to cover such an enormous body of traditions. Yet what we have seen in the ancient lands we have been privileged to visit has clearly made us to understand that the psychopictographic imagery and personifications of celestial and terrestrial natural phenomena as illustrated in the cosmogonical and Astro-Mythological sciences had their beginning in the deep south of Mother Alkebulan, fanned out over the Earth like the multi-colored patterns of a kaleidoscope and produced a rippling effect on the whole ancient world.

From the Nubian-Grimaldi, the world's first artists and scientists, these concepts and ideas were bequeathed to their descendents in the many Nubian nations from the highlands of Uganda to the Khoisan (bushmen) people of the Kalahari Desert and on the Serengeti Plains. At the foot of the Mountains of the Moon, they were astutely refined by the most learned and advanced of the Nubians, the mighty Kushites. Then simultaneously carried down to the Hapi Valley where the symbology was multiplied into various cyclical forms and meanings. While other migrating Afrikan tribes and nations transported these ideas to the shores of the Gambia, Senegal and Niger Rivers where they found expression in the Yoruba, Akan and other west Afrikan cosmological philosophies. Then like the brilliant legend of the flaming firebird, they were taken across the burning sands of the Sahara to be united with the creation stories of the indigenous Blacks in the north. Then exported over the Gibraltar Straits into Kushite-Iberia (ancient Spain and Portugal) and Black Britannica.[287]

Kemetan scientists from the Hapi Valley civilizations transmigrated the age old Astro-Mythological Cosmogonies eastward to Arabia, Mesopotamia, Persia, India and the islands of the Pacific as the Phoenicians who while in the service of the Kemetans circumnavigated the world carrying the same concepts and ideas across the Atlantic Ocean into Meso-America. The Maya, Aztec, Inca and Olmec civilizations being prime examples of this transfusion of ideas.

In the process of this global diffusion, some of the High Culture Science found its way into the Hebrew, Greek and Roman creation stories after having been taught to them by Kemetan master-teachers. Yet because these spiritually underdeveloped nations could not fully grasp or understand the lofty concepts of Kushite-Kemetan thought, they were degenerated into mere fantasies and eventually co-opted and corrupted by Euro-centric Christianity.

The god and goddess symbology of north, south, east, west Alkebulan, Asia and Meso-American civilizations and those of Greece, Rome and western Europe will be examined and analyzed in Volume Four of this series, *Afrikan Genesis: Black Gods and Goddesses in the Land of Eden.*

In the following chapters of this particular work on the study of the Theory of Creationism as set forth in ancient Astro-Mythological Cosmogonies, we will be discussing the creation stories of ancient Babylon, the Hebrew-Israelites and the matrix of all the cosmogonies of the ancient world, the Kemetan High Culture Scientific system of the Memphite Theology.

CHAPTER SEVEN

THE ETERNAL STRUGGLE BETWEEN CHAOS AND WORLD ORDER: THE BABYLONIAN STORY

The "Eternal Struggle" made reference to in the title of this chapter in actuality signifies the on-going controversy between the sedentary generally cooperative and relatively peaceful matriachal induced civilizations of the old Kushite branch of the Afrikan race and the more unsettled, wandering, quarrelsome, aggressive and oft-times cruel tribes and nations variously manifested in Indo-European branches and ad mixtures such as the Turanians, Scythians, Aryans, Eurasians, Kassites, so-called Semetics etc.. In the Enuma elish the Kassite-Babylonian version of a creation epoch, the original Kushite-Sumerian Astro-Mythological Cosmogonical symbols are misappropriated and transformed into monsters and characterized as enemies of cosmic order.

Our primary reason for presenting and analyzing the Babylonian creation story is to observe some of the stages of its translation from an essentially Afrikan-centered philosophical concept to a violent saga which expressed Eurasian patriarchal values. Secondly, the Babylonian and Hebrew versions of Kushite-Kemetan cosmogony are probably the most well known because of the widespread circulation of the Judeo-Christian Bible which inculcates them in its traditions of creation and early civilization. As we have already stated, the Babylonians received their education, culture and Astro-Mythological Cosmogonical science from the High Culture of the old Sumerians who inherited same from Kushite and Kemetan expeditions which migrated there and laid the foundations of the empire of Sumer in the land between the two rivers.

W.E.B. DuBois says that the first Babylonians were Black.[289] Godfrey Higgins regarding the ancient Chaldeans from whom the Babylonian nation derived admits:

"in consequence of the prejudice (for it is really prejudice against the Negro; or I ought rather to say against the possibility of a Negro being learned and scientific arising from an acquaintance with the present Negro character). I admit with *great difficulty* the theory of all the early astromonical knowledge of the Chaldees having been acquired or invented by his race and that the Chaldees were originally Negroes."[290]

103

Dr. John G. Jackson also corroborates the Afrikan origin of the original inhabitants of ancient Sumer in Chaldea referring to them as the "black-faced race".[291] The Sumerian application of the Afrikan constitutional system was, as extensive research has shown, the system of law and government practiced by the early Mesopotamian civilizations. For more information on the Afrikan constitutional system of governence, see *Afrikan People and European Holidays: A Mental Genocide*, Book II, pages 64-65 and Dr. Chancellor Williams' monumental work, *The Destruction of Black Civilization*, page 171-186.

Albert Churchward informs us,

> "the Sumerians, Chaldeans and Babylonians, in fact, obtained all their laws and learning from the Egyptians [Kemetans]. The Code of Hammurabi, the Sumerians copied from the Egyptians [Kemetans] and handed on the Chaldeans...Their history of Creation is a copy of the Egyptian [Kemetan]; also..."[292]

In short, Mesopotamian civilization was not inaugurated by the light skinned so-called Semites but rather by the "black-faced" Kushite-Sumerians.

A NEW CREATION STORY IS BORN

Merlin Stone states that "...the religion of the Sumerians was incorporated into the Babylonian culture and the Sumerian language was used much as Latin was employed in the masses of the Roman Catholic Church all over the world."[293] When the Semetic Kassite took over the original Sumerian cosmogony they rephrased it in the most violent and grotesque terms for the so-called Semetic descendants of the mixed Eurasian races were themselves a wild and violent lot. Their interpretation of Sumerian god and goddess symbols of natural science were recast in the bloodiest imagery i.e. decapitation, castration, mutilation, and dismemberment. The Semetic Kassite Babylonian creation story is called Enuma elish and though it is based on the old Kushite-Sumerian cosmogonical philosophy in many essential aspects it differs from it.[294]

When the Babylonian tablets were first copied, most of the names of the Sumerian deities remained in tact, but the later Semetic transcribers substituted the names of their own deities such as Marduk for Nabu and Mama Aruru. The Queen of the Gods was assigned the role of a monsterous devouring serpent whom patriarchal Marduk in an act of matricide murdered and then created the world and its atmosphere from her slain body. In regards as to how this transmorgrified mythos affected the female population of ancient Babylon, Merlin Stone writes:

> "Despite a loss of status in the position of women in Babylon, compared with their predecessors of Sumer—a loss that was accompanied by the gaining ascendency of male deities such as Marduk, who mythically murdered the Creator Goddess Tiamat to gain and secure his position—the women of Babylon still continued to hold certain rights of independence...

Stone further adds:

> "...One of the most interesting and characteristic features of this early civilization of the Babylonians was the high position of women. The mother here is always represented by a sign which means 'goddess of the house.' Any sin against the mother, any repudiation against the mother was punished by banishment from the community. These are the facts which are evidently indicative of a people who at one time held the law of matriarchal descent...In Hammurabi's time women were free to request divorce, and one Babylonian declared that if a wife did not intend to be responsible for her husband's premarital debts she had to obtain a document from him stating that he had agreed. This assumption of the financial responsibility in marriage suggests that most women may have taken part in business and financial affairs (as they did in Egypt) and perhaps at one time had been economically responsible for the family."[295]

Here in the Semetic Babylonian conquest of the Sumerian Empire we have a case in point wherein the conqueror was in turn conquered by the conquered. That is to say though the Kassites had conquered the Kushite-Sumerians militarily, having no real knowledge and culture of their own to bring to this High Culture civilization, they were in turn conquered by the Sumerians culturally for it was very rare among so-called Semetic tribes and nations for women to have any true rights or independence.

When the Kassite Babylonian priests rewrote the Sumerian creation epoch, they misinterpreted whatever ideas they encountered that were unfamiliar to them and they could not understand. Albert Churchward says:

> "the Semetic Theologians did not know enough of the ancient Sign Language to distinguish the evil serpent from the good, the great Earth-Mother from the chimerical [fantastic imagery

of the] dragon of the deep, or the beneficent spirits of elemental nature from the...fiendish forces of external phenomena. The Semetic versions of the legends, Babylonian, Assyrian, or Hebrew, mainly reproduce the debris of the Astronomical Cult which has often been reduced to the status of the nursery tale. *Their fatal defect is that they are not the original documents and have no first-hand authority.* In these the primitive wisdom of old Egypt [Kemet] has been perverted and the Mythical beginnings, which had their own meaning, have been transmorgrified...as example in the Babylonian legends of creation, the seven associate gods who are the Creators in the Egyptian [Kemetan] Mythos, have been converted into the seven evil spirits of a later theology...Thus the creation of woman is made to be the work of seven evil spirits, who, as the Egyptian [Kemetan] wisdom witnesses, did not originate as wicked spirits or as powers of evil."[296]

Actually in the early Babylon of the Blacks, the seven spirits misinterpreted by the later light skinned Kassites represented the seven planets in our solar system that were visible to Chaldean astronomers at the time. Houston says that the Afro-Chaldean civilizations like other Kushite nations worldwide worshipped the one Divine Intelligence who was made manifest in many forms and symbols which demonstrated the manifold aspects of the Supreme Being commonly known in the English speaking world as God.[297] Again Merlin Stone reports that in Mesopotamia (the land between the 2 rivers) the earlier Afrikoid Akkadians,

"...after a rise in position under Sargon in 2300 B.C., eventually gained supremacy in about 1900 B.C. gradually superseding the Sumerians as the cultural and political leaders of the area. They formed a nation known as Babylonia, installing their capitol in the city of Babylon on the central Euphrates...by 1600 BC the Kassites gained control of Babylon. Linguistic evidence suggests that the Kassites were ruled by the northern invaders, the Indo-Europeans, who had gradually infiltrated into Babylon and Assyria."[298]

Concerning the original Kushite-Sumerian cosmogony, Drucilla Houston writes:

"The fragments of the tablets that tell the story of the creation and the deluge date back to 1900 B.C. and seem to be copies of still more ancient documents. With the later infusions from other races came the gross incantations and beliefs in evil spirits of later days...all the popular supersitions of the Middle Ages regarding demons, witchcraft and magic came from [Kassite] Babylon and to great extent were the cause of her downfall."[299]

Again we think it important to emphasis the historical reality that the Babylonian and Hebrew versions of the creation of the world and humans had one common origin and were not derived from each other. They were the products—by way of Sumer—of Kemetan astronomical observance.[300]

ENUMA ELISH: THE BABYLONIAN EPOCH OF CREATION

The Enuma elish meaning "when above" and which can also be loosely translated "before cosmic order" describes the creation of the existing universe according to the Kassite Babylonian priests of Marduk. It consists of seven clay tablets engraved in cuneiform (wedge-shaped) writing that deals with the struggle between cosmic order and primeval chaos. Enuma elish is infused with violent imagery and figurative pessimism in regard to the purpose for the human race. According to this story men were created to merely be servants of the gods. An ancient version of the adage "ours is not to reason why, but to do or die" a philosophy that was greatly perpetuated and callously used for the benefit and self-aggrandizement of the aristocracy in medival Europe and is still skillfully applied to manipulate the non-thinking elements in many European dominated societies today. The United States of America not withstanding.

The copy of the Enuma elish on display in the British Museum dates back to ca. 1450 BCE and was probably composed at the city of Babylon to celebrate the Indo-European Kassite victory over the Black Akkadian Babylonians. It in many ways allegorically portrays the bloody massacres, wanton destruction of artifacts, crazed demolition of edifices and the polluting desecrations of old Kushite-Sumerian sanctuaries which occurred during the Kassite invasion of Chaldea. According to Churchward the archaic version read thusly:

"On the first of the Tablets of Creation of the Chaldeans it is written: 'At at time when neither the heavens above nor the earth below existed, then was the watery abyss; the first of seed , the mistress of the depths, the Mother of the universe.

107

The waters clung together, no product had ever been gathered, nor was any sprout seen. Ay, the very gods had not yet come into being.'''[301]

This was later changed to

"When the heaven (-gods) above were as yet uncreated, the earth (-gods) below not yet brought into being, alone there existed primordial Apsu who engendered them, only Mummu, and Tiamat who brought all of them forth."[302]

First we will tell an abbreviated version of the story as we capsulize portions of the text from the old stone tablets and commentary as recorded in D. Winton Thomas' treatise *Documents from Old Testament Times*, pages 3-13. This will provide us with a basic understanding of the ideas conveyed in the epic. Then we will do profiles on its symbolic characters.

Tiamat and Mummu the Primordial Seas are United

Tablet I, Their waters could mix together in a single stream

Verse 5   Unrestricted by reed-beds, unimpeded by marsh: For, since none of the gods had at this time appeared, These had not yet been formed, or been with destinies decreed.

Forces (gods) of Nature Created by Uniting Waters

Verse 9   In the depths of their waters the gods were created: there appeared Lahmu and Lahamu, they (first) were given Names; But only to an appointed size did they grow and become large, And Anshar and Kishar were born bigger than they.

Birth of Anu the Sky Who Begets, Ea the Earthly Waters

Verse 13   As lengthen the days and there multiplied the years, Ansar in like size produced Anu, his first born: And as Anu, their son, was equal of his parents, So did Anu beget Ea in the likeness of himself.

The Prominent Role of Ea to Planet Earth

Verse 17   But Ea, Nudimmud was else the master of his parents, More intelligent, wiser, mightier in strength: More powerful he was than his grandfather, Anshar, Nor had he a rival amongst the (many) small gods, his brothers.

The Constant Movement of Chaotic Matter

Commentary The swift action of the epic begins with these 'brothers', the noise of whose continuous dancing and reveling now becomes, in a most human situation, a source of great disturbance to the first parents. Apsu seizes the iniative. He summons his servant Mummu and takes the matter to court with Tiamat. Speaking first, he declares he can neither rest by day nor sleep by night because of the noise, and advocates the total destruction of the gods.

Tiamat Speaks on Behalf of Her Children the Dancing Forces of Chaotic Matter

Verse 41 But Tiamat on hearing this Was furious, and cried out against her husband, Cried in bitterness of spirit..., Broke into an evil storm of temper: 'How can we thus destroy what we have borne! Their ways, for all they are abhorrant, it is our duty to abide'.

Tiamat's husband, Mummu, opposes her before the council and proposes the total destruction of his own sons, the gods who represent cosmic matter in perpetual chaotic motion. Apsu rejoices and embraces his son and ally Mummu. A vote is taken in the council and the decision was made to annihilate these gods. It "was then (officially) told unto the gods, their sons: the gods when they heard moved aimlessly about. They lapsed into silence, sat in speechless despair." Ea, the deity of the rivers, sets into motion a plan to counter the decision of the council. He drew a map of the universe as an effigy of Apsu then composed an incantation which he recited repeatedly while holding the map over running water. The story goes on to proclaim that by reason of Ea's conjuring, Apsu and Mummu fell into a deep sleep. Ea slays Apsu and banished Mummu. At this point the high-gods are horrified and "An embassy of gods, whom we shall know hereafter as the rebel gods, has approached Tiamat and succeeded in persuading her to avenge the death of Apsu. It is a very changed Tiamat who now prepares for battle."

The Reptiles of the Formative Sea and Earth are Created

Verse 133 Then Mother Hubur, who cast every mold of life, Unleashed the Irresistible Weapon, four monster-serpents: Sharp was their teeth and pitiless their find, With poison instead of blood she filled their bodies.

109

Verse 145   So powerful were her decrees they were unopposable,
As thus eleven species did she bring forth: And now from
the gods, her sons, who formed [her army], (As a
twelveth) she exalted Kingu, made him chief among
them.

Commentary   The crisis is staged when Tiamat and the rebel gods,
together with her army of monsters and their rebel com-
mander, Kingu, prepare for total war against the great
gods; it is raised to quite alarming proportions when first
Ea [the rivers] and then Anu [the sky], two of the most
powerful of the great gods, are sent against Tiamat but
yet forced to retire; and then, with total destruction
imminent, the divine Assembly is called.

Earlier the tablets told of the birth of Marbuk who would
become the champion for the high gods who are about to engage
in controversy with Tiamat and her forces which they fear they
cannot win.

The Birth of Marduk

Verse 79   In the Chamber of Destinies, in *Atman usurati*, A god
then engendered the strongest, the 'Sage of the gods':
In the depths of the Apsu the god Marduk was born, In
the depths of the Pure Apsu Marduk was born.

Verse 83   He that begot him was Ea, his father, Damkina, his
mother, was she that did bear him. . .He looked on him,
Ea, his father who begot him, He rejoiced and was glad,
his heart filled with joy.

Commentary   But Marduk, for all his size and strength, is yet
young as a god; and when he is approached by Anshar
to champion the cause of the gods against Tiamat, he
accepts only on the condition that he be legally accorded
that supreme authority which his new responsibility
demands. Lahmu and Lahamu convene the assembly,
and, after a great feast of food and wine, the gods appoint
Marduk as King.

The Exaltation of Marduk

Tablet IV On the throne dais *Rubutum* which they had placed
Verse I in position He sat, facing his fathers, for the
ceremony of Kingship: 'Hereby art thou enrolled within
the number of the great gods, Thine appointment has no
equal, thine authority is absolute. Marduk, thou art
enrolled within the number of the great gods, Thine
appointment has no equal, thine authority is absolute.

Commentary Immediately after the ceremony Marduk arms himself
for the fight with bows, arrows, mace and a net held by
the four winds. Then—

Verse 57 ...Set(s) his course towards the sounds of Tiamat
enraged...

The Battle is On

Verse 93 So they came together—Tiamat, and Marduk, Sage of
the gods: They advanced into conflict, they joined forces
in battle. He spread wide his net, the lord, and enveloped
her, The Evil Wind, the rearmost, unleashed in her face.

Verse 97 As she opened her mouth, Tiamat, to devour him, He
made the Evil Wind to enter that she closed not her lips:
The Storm Winds, the furious, then filling her belly, Her
inwards became distended, she opened fully wide her
mouth.

Verse 101 He shot therethrough an arrow, it pierced her stomach,
Clave through her bowels tore into her womb: Thereat
he strangled her, made her life-breath ebb away, Cast her
body to the ground, standing over it (in triumph).

The Creation of the Zodiac in the Severed Body of Tiamat

Verse 135 He rested, the lord, examining her body: Would divide
up the monster, create a wonder of wonders! He slit in
two like a fish of the drying yard, The one half he posi-
tioned and secured as the sky...

111

Tablet V (Therein) traced he lines for the mighty gods,

Verse 1 Stars, star-groups and constellations he appointed for them: He determined the year, marked out its divisions, For each of the twelve months appointed three rising stars.

Verse 5 Having established the rules for the (astronomical) seasons, He laid down the Crossing-line to make known their limits: And that none should make mistake or in any way lose speed...

Commentary Two further stanzas devoted to the phases of the moon, continue the theme of the establishment of the calendar and the regulation of time. A break in continuity follows, but new text presently resume the narrative and Marduk is then seen reshaping the earth out of the lower half of Tiamat's body. Thus in one act of creation [is formed]...

Mountains and Rivers from the Body of Tiamat

Verrse 53 He placed her head in position, heaped [the mountai]ns upon It...Made the Euphr[ates] and Tigris to flow through her eyes,-

The Babylonian Zodiac

Verse 73 The eleven monster (-species) which Tiamat had created, Whose [weapo]ns he had broken, binding them at his feet, He made of them (stellar) images to wat[ch over] the Apsu, That as signs (of the Zodiac) the group should ne'er be forgotten.

The High Gods Applaud Marduk's Victory

Verse 77 As there saw them [the gods], so their hearts filled with joy, Even Lahmu and Lahamu and all of his fathers: Anshar turned to him and hailed him with a royal address, Anu, Enlil and Ea presented him with gifts.

The Decision to Create Humans

Tablet VI As Marduk acknowledged this appeal of the gods, Verse 1 He decided to create another wonder of wonders: Opening his mouth, he spake forth to Ea, Invited him to comment on the theory he proposed.

Verse 5 'Blood will I compose, bring a skeleton into being, Produce a lowly, primitive creature, "Man" shall be his name: I will create *lullu-amelu-* an earthly "puppet"-man. To him be charged the service that the gods may then have rests...

Commentary With Ea's help he made man from the blood of the god Kingsu, Tiamat's ally and second husband. Seeing what he had done, the delighted gods bestowed on him many titles as their undisputed leader and king.

Marduk Becomes King of the Gods

Verse 105 'Be exalted our Son, even he who avenged us, Let his authority be supreme, be it second to none: And let him act as the shepherd of mankind, his creatures, Who, unforgetting, to later ages shall ever tell of his deeds.'[303]

A rather succinct summation of this story is set forth by Will Durant:

> "In the time when nothing which was called heaven existed above, and when nothing below had yet received the name of earth, Apsu, the Ocean, who first was their father, and Tiamat Chaos, who gave birth to them all, mingled their waters in one. Things slowly began to grow and take form; but suddenly the monster-goddess Tiamat set out to destroy all the other gods, and to make herself— Chaos—supreme. A mighty revolution ensued in which all order was destroyed. Then another god, Marduk, slew Tiamat with her own medicine by casting a hurricane of wind into her mouth as she opened it to swallow him; then he thrust his lance into Tiamat's wind swollen paunch, and the goddess of Chaos blew up. Marduk, 'recovering his calm,' says the legend, split the dead Tiamat into two longitudinal halves, and as one does a fish for drying; 'then he hung up one of the halves on high, which became the heavens; the other half he spread out under his feet to form the earth.'"

Durant goes on to say:

> "This is as much as we yet know about [the Babylonian story of] creation. Perhaps the ancient poet meant that the only creation of which we can know anything is the replacement of chaos with order, for in the end this is the essence of arts

113

and civilization. We should remember, however, that the defeat of Chaos is only a myth."[304]

The main objective of the authors of the Enuma elish seems to have been to make Marduk—originally a relatively obscure and local deity to the city of Babylon—a supreme hero, the creator of the world and of man. Note the tendency to emphasize the violent aspects of nature in this particular version of the story as it was contrived by the later Kassite Babylonians. It is indeed a rather stark contrast to the more peaceful creation story of old Sumer. Some scholars think the Kemetan saga of the dismemberment of Ausuru's body in 14 pieces by Set—which is an allegory for the phases of the moon in its monthly cycle—may be of later Eurasian influence in Kemet after it was invaded. Because in the most ancient text originally Set had been a great hero and benevolent deity. Whatever the case may be, the story though having a violent tinge is not saturated with it and this appears to be the general flavor of the original KushiteSumerian cosmogony.

CHAPTER EIGHT

ANATOMY OF A COSMIC BATTLE

Let us now pursue an Afrikan-centered analysis of Enuma elish symbology. Firstly, it must be kept in mind that Enuma elish is an astronomical poem. At the time of its compostion, the city of Babylon was already one of "the great centers of observational astronomy in Chaldea".[305] In those days the plains of Mesopotamia were dotted with Ziggurat towers which rose in 7 plateaus above the ground. The uppermost level of these grand structures were used as astronomical observatories. Most of these had been erected by the original black civilizations who preceded by thousands of years other races in the area. Though the apparent exaggerations of Babylonion priests, who "assert that they have preserved upon monuments observations [which most certainly must have included the Sumerian records] extending back during an interval of 470,000 years,...still the period at which astronomy had arrived at its perfection with the ancients is *beyond* the reach of modern calculation." Excavated documents show that Babylonian astronomers "...could in the year 1722 B.C., delineate the zodiac with the exact positions of the planets at the time of the autumnal equinox,... [which], proves that they knew the laws that regulate 'carefully verified facts' to perfection, and applied them with as much certainly as our modern astsronomers."[306]

The Kemetans in Alkebulan had perfected this scientific methodology many thousands of years before the Sumerians or Babylonians. In fact, as a matter or record, around 10,000 BCE the Kushite-Kemetans produced a revision of their calendar to synchronize it more accurately with the movement of celestial bodies occuring at the time.[307] Recently Russian scientists digging in Egypt (Kemet) have rediscovered glass lenses dating far back in antiquity that were obviously used by the Kemetans in their telescopes.[308]

One of the objectives of the original version of the Sumerian creation epoch was to illustrate scientific principles of astronomy through metophoric animation of a cosmic battle. Another was to demonstrate the struggle between the forces of nature in the early stages of the Earth's evolutionary process. Some commentators suggest that it signifies the conquest of light and order over darkness and chaos. Gerald Massey says that the later version of the Semetic Babylonians composed after the Kassite conquest of Chaldea is

115

really the story of "...the conflict of the dark and light races" in the region.[309] Barbara Walker explains the significance of the formation of the firmament from the body of Tiamat thusly, "By dividing Tiamat, Marduk established the Diameter (horizon), which was the Greek version of Tiamat's name, meaning Goddess-Mother. We still say diameter divides a whole circle."[310] As a matter of fact the terminology diameter comes from the Latin *Dia Mater* meaning "Goddess Mother".

Walker goes on to show how this allegory directly relates to the traumatic moments of birth.

> "Patriarchal writers forgot that 'The Deep' was a personified womb, a Middle-Eastern version of Kali whose being before creation was 'formless'. Most creation myths incorporated the idea of formlessness, in the darkness before the birth that brought 'light' and the splitting of the Mother's body, so she became both heaven and earth."[311]

Many scholars think that the sublimenal impetus for all the cosmogonies of the ancient world was the deep subsconscious recollection of the struggles of labor and childbirth and the early stages of infant development when a child's mother is the only heaven and earth he or she knows. For she is both nurturer and comforting stabilizer, the first to calm the infant's fears and anxieties, the first to define order in the motley of objects in a young child's environment.

Marduk's vanquishing of the rebel gods who were placed among the stars could be symbolic of the valiant wars wages by the Mother-Goddess' children as exemplified in *Black Sumerian Heroes* who were personified in the 12 signs of the zodiac. These fierce warriors (such as those who fought under the guidance of Prince Gudea) appeared as monsters to the ever quarrelsome patriarchial invaders who in order to defeat the remnants of the Sumerian Empire had to finally and reluctantly organize their city-states under the leadership of the city of Babylon's petty chieftian Bel Marduk. Concerning the Enuma elish version of the creation of humans, Walker writes, "Jealous Marduk not only killed Tiamat; he also disposed, castrated, and killed Kingu, and made the first man on earth out of Kingu's blood—which tends to show that Kingu was once the name of the sacrificed god-king, whose blood had the 'feminine' power to make life. Kingu was identified with the moon.[312]

One translation of the story says that Marduk and Ea used a reaping sickle to decapitate and dismember the body of Kingu. The sickle in ancient symbology represented the cresent signifying the role of the phases of the moon relative to the planting and harvesting of crops. In some of the cruder cultures of the East, stories such as the Kassite Babylonian decapitation of Kingu was often associated with the reaping of crops and the blood spurting from the body of human sacrificial victims was symbolically identified with the blood of afterbirth when a woman has delivered her fruit (child). Even today pregnant women are said to be bearing fruit.

The metaphysical correlation between agriculture, fertility and childbirth was very prevelant in the cosmogonical symbology of the ancient world. As you will recall, the original Sumerian version of the connection of birth and motherhood with the creation of man says that the Mother-Goddess, Aruru, made the first humans from clay. This we shall shortly see was later modified by the Hebrews in their Adam and Eve story.

THE AKKAD-BABYLONIAN INTERPRETATION OF THE SCIENTIFIC SYMBOLS OF SUMERIAN COSMOGONY

Keep in mind that the Akkadian-Babylonians were largely Afrikan in their phsiogomy and consciousness and that even though because of the heavy influence of some of their socalled Semetic allies, they were beginning to lean towards a patriarchal world view. They remained primarily matriarchal in spirit and maintained a reasonable level of respect for the feminine principle. Further along we will be discussing the profiles and symbolic meaning of Tiamat and Marduk. Following is a probable interpretation of the other deity symbols portrayed in the first Babyloniari creation epoch translated from the old Sumerian cosmogony and later distorted by the Enuma elish.

Apsu: "Apsu and Tiamat are two great seas which existed in the beginning when all was water." The two seas consorted together to create other gods (forces of nature) to whom Tiamat gives birth.[313] Erich Neumann points out that:

"In Babylonia the male-female unity of the uroboros [reproductive organs] is constituted by Tiamat and Apsu,

117

who are the primordial chaos of the water. But Tiamat is the actual principle of origination: mother of the gods and possessor of the table of fate. Thus it is written: 'Apsu the oldest of beings, their progenitor, 'Mummu' Tiamat, who bear each and all of them'; and it is taken for granted that Apsu and Mummu should submit their decisions to Tiamat.''[314]

Apsu was the male aspect of the "great ocean".

''. . .the source of lakes—especially a large tidal lake which anciently surrounded the city or Eridu in Southern Babylonia—of marshes, and the waters of the subsoil. The word comes from the Sumerian *Abzu*, the first element being *ab* 'sea'; it appears in Greek as *abussos* (the 'bottomless pit' mentioned in Rev. 20: 1-3, is a familiar translation of it, and the word still survives in the English 'abyss'.[315] It was said that the city of Babylon was commanded by Marduk to be built on the very spot of earth immediately above the subterranean waters of Apsu. "In accordance with the law that decrees the negativization of surpassed powers and gods, both he [Apsu] and Tiamat were regarded in later times as solely 'evil and abysmal.'''[316]

Mummu: Who existed with Tiamat and Apsu before the creation of the gods represented the misty clouds floating over the primordial seas. This may originally have been a female deity though some translations and commentaries speak about Tiamat cohabiting with Mummu.

Lahmu and Lahamu: The first children of Apsu and Tiamat. Many translators refer to them as the Silts. The *Funk & Wagnall Dictionary* defines silt as ''an Earthly sediment consisting of fine particle of rocks and soil suspended in and carried by water''.[319]The perfusion of silt was a primary condition of planet Earth during one of its early geological stages.

Anshar and Kishar: The second set of Apsu's and Tiamat's children representing the horizons in the morning dawn and evening twilight skies. The ideas of gods being created in pairs somewhat reminiscent of the Kemetan Ennead which we will be studying in a succeeding chapter.

118

Anu: Son of Anshar and grandchild of Tiamat and Apsu representing the sky. At one time Anu was the supreme male deity in Mesopotamia, an honor accorded him in remembrance of the colony of Anu people from Kemet who first settled the area and established a civilization there. The scientific deity symbol of Anu is directly drawn from the old Kushite-Sumerian -text. Churchward says for an incredibly long time, Anu was a emblem of stability for the seat of power in Sumer.[320] Professor George Rawlinson's translation of the Babylonian creation epoch reads:

"He (Anu) constructed dwellings for the great gods; he fixed the constellations, whose figures were like animals. He made the year into portions; he divided it; twelve months he established, with their constellations, thereby three. And from among the days of the year he appointed festivals; he made dwellings for the planets, for their rising and for their setting...and on the seventh day a holy day appointing, and commanding on that day a cestation from all business. And he (Anu) set the sun in his place in the horizon of heaven."[321]

Ea: The Earthly waters confined to its surface such as rivers, streams, oceans, seas, etc. The son of Anu and great-grandchild of Tiamat and Apsu who was the exact likeness of his father denoting how the sky is reflected in bodies of water. In Enuma elish Ea is portrayed as the father of Marduk his first born whom he assisted in slaying and dissecting Kingu then creating humans from the blood, but older Sumerian texts say that Nabu was the first born son of Ea.

Nabu: Also known as Nebo:

"'the proclaimer', the Accadian translation of various Sumerian ideograms for the god of wisdom and writing, ...Originally this Sumerian deity seems to have been connected with Dilmun and was often identified with the philosophic principle *mummu*; creative word, form. As such he is the son of the water God Enki (Ea), god of the first principle 'water.' As the god of writing, Nabu has charge of the Tables of Fate on which he inscribes the names of men and decides what their lot is to be."[322]

Later Kassite-Babylonian priests imbued Marduk with authority to arbitrate human fates and diminished Nabu from the prominent position of son of Ea to a subordinate role of Marduk's son, "the scribe and herald of the gods". In spite of this ploy, Nabu's "cult eventually rivaled that of his father in popularity" and far surpassed him in the southern city-states.[323]

The noisy dancing gods: Children of Tiamat and Apsu who represent the movement (motion) of primal matter in the constant storms, volcanos and earthquakes of the Archeozoic (Ancient Life) Age in geological time.

Annunaki: Other children of Apsu and Tiamit who were called the "rebel gods" and depicted as monsters because they had fought on the side of their mother Tiamat against Marduk and the council. The Annunaki represented the huge sea creatures ie. giant turtles and aquatic dinosaurs which dominated the planet during the Mesozoic (Middle Life) Age in geological time. George Rawlinson translates one of the tablets which describe the concept thusly. "In the beginning all was darkness and water, and therein were generated monstrous animals of strange and peculiar form."[324] Neumann refers to them as "Tiamat's helpers ...The star gods, the gods of the night sky, which she created,...her allies;...the constellations of the night sky...the star god and all destiny are the product of her caprice."[325]

Kingu: Tiamat's favorite son to whom she originally gave the Tablets of Destiny and the authority to rule over all the forces of nature. In the Enuma elish Kingu was later slain and dismembered by Babylonia's municipal deity Marduk and his supposed father Ea who is said to have created man from Kingu's blood. In scientific terms Kingu represented the first man on Earth and the cosmic consciousness which the Sumerian and Akkad-Babylobians believe was possessed by early humans. Kingu also symbolizes the reality that it is oft-times through blood, sweat and tears that man coaxes bountiful crops from the bosom of Mother-Earth.

PROFILE AND ANALYSIS OF THE TIAMAT SYMBOL

The name Tiamat comes from the Chaldean *thamte* which is related to the later Greek word *Thalassa* meaning "the Sea". She was also given the title Omorka, loosely translated "Ruler of the Sea and all its creatures".[326] In southern Arabia she was identified with the goddess of love Ishtar. In this aspect Tiamat "...when her fecundity and sexual character are stressed, appears nude with accentuated sexual characteristics.[327] The Kushite-Arabians called this statuary Tehema, another form of her name. In India she was associated with Kali-Ma "representing her state of formlessness between manifested universes".[328] "In Kemet, Tiamat was Temu or Te-Mut, oldest of deities, mother of the archaic Ennead of four dual female elements: Water, Darkness, Night, and Eternity. She was also Nun, [Nuni] Naunet, or Ma-Nu, the great fish who gave birth to the universe and the gods."[329] The Kemetans also referred to her as "tyu-ma'at" to denote the connection between water and wisdom as demonstrated in the ritual of baptizing initiates after they had attained a certain level of knowledge.

The concept of water transferring the wisdom of the Mother-Goddess was widely circulated in the ancient world. The early Christians adopted it into their mythology with the story of Jesus receiving the Holy Ghost during his baptism by John the Baptist. In the Akkadian-Babylonian myth it was said that "Tiamat alone produced the fluid of creation". The Arabians believed "its great reservoir was the Red Sea... the eastern shore of which is still called Tihamat by the Arabs".

> [Kassite] "Babylonians said their god Marduk divided his mother Tiamat into two parts, upper waters and lower waters. Likewise, the Jewish god 'divided the waters which were under the firmament from the waters which were above the firmament.' (Genesis 1-7) the Jewish God also divided the Red Sea, which was likened to Tiamat herself.
>
> The idea of dividing waters was not original with the Jews. Goddesses did it before gods. The Hindu Goddess Bindumati, 'Mother of Life', divided the waters of the Ganges. The Goddess Isis [Auset] divided the waters of the river Phaedrus to cross dry-sod."[330]

Tiamat's original status in black Akkadian mythology attribute her with the power to alter night and day and set the processions of the months, seasons, and years. Neumann says of her aspect as the symbol of the night sky:

"...that is why, not only as the Mesopotamian Tiamat, but throughout the world, she holds the Tables of Fate, the all determining constellations of heaven, which is herself. And accordingly the Great Mother, adorned with the moon and the starry claok of night, is the goddess of destiny weaving life as she waves fate.[331]

Of the Semetic version of the Tiamat symbol, Merlin Stone says:

"Tiamat was described in this myth as a dragon or serpent. The actual association of the serpent with the female deity, all through the texts and inscriptions of Sumer and Babylon, was probably the very reason this symbolism was used in the [later] Indo-European myths."[332]

Notwithstanding the fact that the name of the Hebrew sacerdotal tribe of Levi meant "son of Leviathan"[333] an Old Testament text asserts, "In that day the Lord with his sore and great and strong sword shall punish leviathan the piercing serpent, even leviathan that crooked serpent' and he shall slay the dragon that is in the sea."[334]

Harper's Bible Dictionary elicuates this passage of scripture in the following manner:

"Biblical allusions to leviathan are part of an almost universal mythology in which a monster, symbolic of evil, is contending against but ultimately defeated by the power of good. Isaiah, possibly influenced by the Babylonion Creation epoch, uses the ancient mythological idea of the destroyed leviathan (27:1) to symbolize the triumphant Day of Judgment,...."[335]

The designation leviathan means "the wiggly one" or "twisting serpent". The poetic imagery of leviathan is a Semetic depiction of the crocodile from the Hapi River which was originally a symbol of the Primal Ocean.[336] Marduk's and Yahweh's symbolic destruction of leviathan in essence expressed the desire of the Kassite-Babylonian and other very small patriarchal nations to supplant the world power and universal cultural influence of the Kushite-Kemetan Maternal-centered spiritual philosophy and Astro-Mythological Cosmogony. The later European's psychological dismay with dragon symbolism as allegorized in the fire spitting dragon in the King Arthur and St. George legends is a subconscious throw back to the first invasion of paleolithic (Old Stone Age) Europe by the Afrikoid Nubian-Grimaldis. This subject will further be discussed in Volume Two, *Afrikan Genesis: An Historial Reality*, in the chapter entitled The Original Black Race: First Wonder of the World. The villification of the dragon (crocodile) and condemnation of the serpent as a purveyor of evil is a chauvinistic distortion based on the white male's fear of the female principle in natural phenomena. One of the many aspects of this principle is graphically depicted in ancient Astro-Mythological Cosmogony in the scientific symbol of the benevolent maternal serpent coiled around the cosmic egg in the same manner as Earthly reptiles surround their eggs with warmth and protection.

According to Barbara Walker:

"Modern scholars tend to ignore Tiamat's maternal creatress nature, describing her as nothing more than a 'dragon of chaos' slain by Marduk. It is seldom emphasized that this was a myth of matricide, or that the Goddess was the one who created the world. Some traditions indicate that Marduk's murder of his mother may have been motivated by jealousy, like Cain's murder of Abel. Mother Tiamat had overlooked Marduk and chosen another of her sons, Kingu to be...the universe."[337]

Neumann adds:

"Therefore Tiamat is far from being only the abyssmal nocturnal monster that the later patriarchal world of the victorious Marduk saw in her. She is not only the genetrix but also the true mother of her creatures. She is filled with wrath when Apsu and Mummu decide to kill the gods, her children; and it is only when the gods have slain Apsu, her husband, the primordial father, that she takes up the battle of vengence against them and becomes destructive."[338]

And Merlin Stone says, "Even in the Babylonian-Kassite myth, Tiamat was recorded as the first divine being. According to this legend, Tiamat originally possessed the Tablets of Destiny, which after Her murder, were claimed as the property of Marduk." Stone goes on to inform us that "the female faith was a most complex theological structure, affecting many aspects of the lives of those who paid Her homage. It had developed over thousands of years and its symbolism was rich and intricate."[339] Semetic, Babylonian and misogynistic Hebrew priests "...biased proclamation for its ending, had actually been designed to be used in the continuous

Levite battle to suppress the female religion. It was, perhaps, a more updated version of the dragon or serpent myth whose vestiges are found in the biblical Psalms and the book of Job."[340]

The paranoid tradition of Indo-European and so-called Semetic mythologists, to translate many of the high culture scientific symbols for the lifegiving and sustaining principles of nature into symbols of evil, was carried forward into European fairy tales wherein any representation of the original Black Race was made out to be some type of monster ie, the bears in *Goldilocks and the Three Bears*, the witch of *Hansel and Gretal* and the giant of *Jack and the Beanstalk*. In each of these instances, the heroes of the story were morally wrong and criminally liable by civilized standards. Goldilocks should be charged with breaking and entering and vandalism; Hansel and Gretal with the destruction of private property and stealing; Jack could rightly be convicted of trespassing, robbery and murder for after all he did kill the giant who was only trying to retreive his property. Many of these fairy tales will be discussed and analyzed in Volume Four of the series *Afrikan Genesis: Black Gods and Goddesses in the Land of Eden*.

MARDUK AND THE "STOLEN LEGACY" OF KUSHITE-SUMER

Marduk's prominence as a deity symbol was the result of "sheer political good fortune" when the city of Babylon was made the capitol of the new empire. As its Chaldean name Bab-ili suggests it was the city of many small gods and goddesses. Legend has it that the city was built by these gods. At the beginning of this period, Marduk was a relatively obscure deity, a god among many of the other city-gods. Though he was known to the sixth king of the first Babylonian dynasty, the Kushite Hammurabi (c. 2300 BCE), the myth claiming Marduk's supremacy did not actually appear until after the Kassites had conquered Babylonia ca. 1700-1600 BCE. But accordinging to George Rawlinson "it is in Babylon, and especially in the latter Babylonian Empire under Nebuchadnezzar and Neriglissar, that his worship culminates. It is then that all the epithets of highest honor are accumulated upon him and that he becomes an almost exclusive object of worship;...."[341]

The consecutive reigns of Nebuchadnezzar and Neriglissar were from 605-556 BCE. The priests of later Babylonia assigned to Marduk attributes that belonged to the older and more significant High Culture scientific Sumerian deity symbols. The Enuma elish portrays Marduk not only as the champion of the gods and conqueror of Tiamat, but also presumes him to be the creator of the universe as well, a glory which they had no historical and cultural right to appropriate to him other than the fact that Babylon had then become politically the most important city in the land. The Sumerian cities of southern Chaldea never accepted this usurped status of Marduk. To them he was still an inferior water deity, a tribal god who had only played a minor and relatively unimportant role in the religious life of the land prior to the Kassite Babylonian conquest of Chaldea.

> "To cite only two outstanding examples, it was the military success and political drive of the Semetic Amorites that made the city of Babylon the religious and cultural center of the land and that gave the Amorite god Marduk preeminence in the Babylonian pantheon. Nevertheless the Babylonian theologians found it necessary to justify Marduk's newly acquired exalted position by the legal fiction that his Sumerian predecessors, the gods An and Enlil, had themselves officially transferred their powers to him."[342]

Walker says that legends of the Babylonian municipal god:

> "...strongly influenced Jewish ideas of Yahweh. Marduk claimed to have created the world by seperating the celestial and the abyssal waters, as Yahweh did (Genesis 1:7); actually, Marduk did it by cleaving the body of his mother Tiamat, who personified all 'Waters.'...Marduk also inherited the tablets of sacred law that the Mother Goddess had given her elder, favorite son [Kingu]."[343]

In the Enuma elish Marduk's confiscation of the sacred laws of the Tablet of Destiny is a similitude of the Kushite god Ras Shamra dictating the laws for the Code of Hammurabi as depicted in earlier Babylonian iconography and later assumed by the Israelites in their story of Moses receiving the Tablets of the Decalogue (Ten Commandments) from Yahweh on Mt. Sinai. The Enuma elish antagonist view of the dividing of Tiamat's body by Marduk to create the firmament is also based upon the rather more peaceful Kushite-Kemetan scientific symboloty of Shu (the air) seperating Geb (the Earth) and Nuit (the sky) to establish the firmament. At least in the Kemetan cosmogony the two entities are permitted to reunite on occasion when the sky covers the Earth

125

with its rain, but in the Kassite Babylonian story, the sky is violently torn asunder from the Earth forever and the cooperative spirit of sexual union is completely obliterated as the male deities become supreme.

The classical Sumerian name for Marduk, long befoe the city of Babylon was founded, was Asaru signifying his title as the son of Ea (Enki), the god of rivers and streams (cp. Ausaru the deity of the Hapi River in Kemet. Shortly after Babylon was built he became Enbilulu—a god of thunderstorms. The later designation Marduk assigns to him a solar aspect for it means "the son of the sun". The *Encyclopedia Britannica* says "So completely did Marduk finally dominate the religion of Babylonia that he is chiefly known as Bel Marduk, the Lord Marduk."[344] The patriarchal Semitic manifestation of Marduk as a sun god continued to expand astronomically to where he was eventually identified with one of the planets in our solar system. Of this George Rawlinson writes, "In his stellar character, Merodach [Marduk] represented the planet Jupiter, with which he was supposed to have a very intimate connection."[345]

The *Random House Encyclopedia* sums him up thusly, "Marduk, the supreme deity in the Babylonian pantheon of gods, originally an earth deity who personified waters fertilizing quality, he acquired the attributes of local deities as the power of Babylon grew."[346] Many scholars think the story of the dismemberment of Tiamat by Marduk may be based on an actual incident of a man—probably a ruler of some sorts—who had in fact murdered his mother and the Kassite-Babylonians incorporated this shocking event into their creation epoch to accentuate the violent nature of the Enuma elish.

Understanding that the Babylonian creation epoch is a symbolic illustration of scientific principles which date so far back in antiquity they cannot be accurately chronocalized and that these basic principles were translated and misinterpreted many times throughout the ancient world, we can confidently conclude this chapter by stating that the initial scientific perception of the Akkadian (Black) Babylonian priests was rooted in the old Kushite-Sumerian records and though grossly distorted by the later Kassite Enuma elish, glimpses of its pristine Afrikan-centered wisdom still manages to flash through the violence and controversy.

CHAPTER NINE

MOSAIC CREATION STORIES IN THE HEBREW-KUSHITE TRADITION

HOW THE HEBREW VERSION OF CREATION CAME TO BE

Many similarities are at once observed between the Babylonian epoch and the early chapters of the book of Genesis in the Hebrew Old Testament. This should not be surprising for the Hebrew and the original Akkadian Babylonian people were allied branches of the same Kushite racial stock. It was natural that their ideas respecting the origin of the world and their traditions as to its primitive history should have much in common. Not withstanding the diverse adaptations of the symbology, they were both inspired by a common creator, the Kushite branch of the original Black Race that once dominated the globe.

Normally, people who live in the same region or geographical location, especially those of the same racial stock, share primarily the same ideas about things although they may have some variants in their expressions of them. Yet the Israelite story of creation is far more serene than the ultra-violent Enuma elish. Though the Hebrews worshipped the oft-times violent male deity, Yahweh, whom they conceived of as a god who could be jealous and angered to the point of destroying the world by flood and annihilating cities with fire as well as also striking down certain human beings in their tracks and who scared the sandals off everyone gathered at the foot of Mt. Sinai as he roared from the thundering clouds. They also sometimes spoke of Yahweh as a loving and merciful father.

The limited knowledge of the so-called "chosen people" retained in their creation stories of the Astro-Mythological Cosmogony of the High Science of the Kushites and Kemetans is tantamount to dwarfs nibbling at the heels of sleeping giants by comparison. However, the Genesis record of the Hebrews is one of the most familiar to many people the world over, specially Afrikan people. It appears that just about all Black folks, at least in the western hemisphere, have a Bible in their homes and/or have been influenced by the JudeoChristian Church's interpretation of same. Therefore, we deem it fitting at this juncture to present an overview of the Hebrew myth of creation. In Volume Three of this series, we will provide a verse-by-verse Afrikan-centered commentary on the Hebrew-Israelite story of creation as recorded in the book of Genesis.

The title Genesis is a Greek word meaning "of origin". It is a transliteration of the Hebrew *B-Reshith* which provided the opening words of the book "in the beginning" For a long time the fact that a great portion of this scroll was a translation of the *Kemetan Book of the Coming Forth By Day and By Night* misnomered the *Egyptian Book of the Dead* was lost to general scholarship; then as a result of mid to late 19th Century investigations and archaeological finds:

> "...not only was the key to hieroglyphic writing [Medu Netcher] found, unlocking the Egyptian [Kemetan] past, but the long-standing puzzle of cuneiform script was finally solved—a remarkable feat of scholarship that brought to life lost languages, peoples, and cultures and added some 2,000 years of human history to the meager Greek and Biblical sources that alone were available until then.[347]

Archaeologists, through their recent finds, have also demonstrated that the early Bible writers used current ideas about the origin and organization of the world and how they shared in some ways though not in others the cultures of their time. The Fifth Century BCE is the period generally ascribed to the initial penning of the book of Genesis and this may explain the parallels in the Genesis story of creation, the Garden of Eden and the flood with similar traditions in Babylonian literature; which during their exile there, the Hebrew scribes became very familiar with. What we are saying here is that the Hebrew-Israelites, a small nation of one of the branches of Afrikoid Kushite racial stock, who eventually settled and lived in the kingdom of Judea on the Palestinian strip, really did not begin to shape and formulate their stories of an event that all other peoples in the region who possessed a script had written about until after they were captured and subjugated by the Babylonians in the year 538 BCE.

When the Babylonians under Nebuchadnezzar had made an end of utterly demolishing the capitol city of Jerusalem, they took what was left of the Israelite tribes of Judea and Benjamin into bondage for 70 years. While there in Babylon, the Israelite priests set about creating and recording a history of the Hebrew people in the context of a world cosmogony with the hope that the reading of these scrolls would help to restore the future generations of their subjugated nation to soverign independence. There were also other reasons why the Israelite priests undertook this new vocation. For discussion of same, see *Afrikan Woman: The Original Guardian Angel*, pages 6-8 by this author.

The Hebrew scribes recorded their concept of the beginning of the world and the creation of man in a traditional mythological legendary manner after the fashion of other Afrikan nations. These Kushite-Kemetan civilizations were the only ones who produced paper, pen and ink and published most of the writings that were in circulation for thousands of years in Mesopotamia. For the art of writing was first invented in the Hapi Valley.

The writing, editing and rewriting of the Hebrew creation story continued on from early fragments possibly penned ca. 800 BCE through the most intensive period of Babylonian captivity (ca. 500 BCE) to the literary projects of Ptolemy Philadelphus during the Greek domination of Palestine (ca. 200 BC) then finally it was refined by the Rabbis at Jaminia (ca. 90 CE). The *Encyclopedia Britannica* states:

> "That the records of the pre-historic ages in Genesis 1-11 are at complete variance with modern science and archaeological research is unquestionable. But although it is impossible to regard them any longer as genuine history or as subjects for an allegorical interpretation (which would prove the accuracy of *any* record) they   are of distinct value as human documents."[348]

Gerald Massey further elucidates this point as recorded by Dr. Charles Finch in *The Journal of Afrikan Civilization:*

> "The Hebrew Books of the Genesis, Exodus, Numbers, Joshua, and Judges are invaluable as a virgin mine of mythology; they are of utmost importance as an aid in recovering the primeval types of Egyptian [Kemetan] thought...For the Hebrews who collected and preserved so much, have explained nothing. There is evidence enough to prove the texts are Egyptian [Kemetan] and the people who brought them out of Egypt [Kemet] must have been more or less Egyptian [Kemetan] in race, and of a religion that was Egyptian [Kemetan] of the earliest and oldest kind."[349]

At this point we would assure our readers that this overview of the book of Genesis is presented as a scientific study. It is not intended to proselytize anyone to a particular religion or as an attack on anyone's personal system of belief. Having said that, let

129

us examine the historical reality of the fact that the Genesis record is one of the many expressions of the Theory of Creationism.

We must emphasize the fact that it is a theory because beyond one's faith or belief which we do not wish to argue here, it cannot really be proven. Any attempts to prove its historical and scientific validity by simply quoting from the text itself is like trying to settle a dubious matter before a court of law without the benefit of corroborating testimony of reliable witnesses. Surely, this would not be an intelligent manner in which to go about finding the truth. Although as we have said, it is not our intent to speak disparingly about whatever a person may believe. We do, however, stress the fact that one must clearly understand that the difference between what is in the realm of belief and what is in the realm of verifiable historical reality may be somewhat opposed to each other.

However, there is no need for there to be any consternation or struggle about this. For when you come to realize that many times what you are reading in the Bible is a story which is simply depicting a particular principle. One observes that even a cursory knowledge of history reveals that all people in the world who had a script and could write set down in their sacred books a history of the world according to their particular cultural view of the world at the time of their writing. And you will also find that each of these nations and cultures claimed that when the Creator made the world and the human race, he began right in the area in which they were presently residing. In antiquity it was the tendency of the sacred literature of most any nation to assert that creation started in their land. For example, in Mexico in their ancient traditions, they will tell you that humanity began there. In west Alkebulan they will say man started in Nigeria or Ghana or one of the other nations in that region of the world. This is a universal practice because it is natural for people to think that way. It expresses their personal relationship as a tribe or nation to the Creative Force in the universe. Yet no one can prove these assumptions; the only thing we do know for certain is that no matter who is telling the story or which of the theories is being espoused, it is an irrefutable historical and scientific fact that humans first appeared somewhere on the Mother Continent of Alkebulan (Afrika) probably as recent anthropological rediscoveries have shown to date in the heartland of Afrika in the equatorial zones at the foot of the Mountains of the Moon.

The Afrikan genesis of humanity we know for certain and this we are satisfied has been proven over and over again with an impressive array of "hard evidence". For more information on this author's view on the subject of Afrikan genesis, see Volume Two of this series and the forthcoming work *Afrikan Origin of the Human Species: Another Study in Grass Roots Anthropology.*

THE BOOK OF GENESIS
AS MYTH AND LEGEND

Professor Buckner B. Trawick informs us the biblical mythologies:

> "...transmitted as oral tradition, were repeatedly reinterpreted and supplemented until the composite   work...was complete in its final form. The various   authors of this comprehensive history drew on many different sources. For information about the earliest centuries (before c. 1000 BC), the historographers had to rely almost entirely on oral tradition—myths, legends, accounts of famous battles, scraps of folk songs, and the like— all handed down by word of mouth, perhaps for many generations."[350]

As many people read the story of Genesis and other books in the Bible, they tend to think this is exactly the way they were first conceived and written. Factually speaking this was not so. The stories had been told from generation to generation to generation by way of oral tradition and when the priests decided to record them, they had to pull from a lot of different sources and of course in writing them down, they used their own contemporary interpretations of the available data. Albert Churchward says "Hebrew ancient books...only converted the genuine into a spurious species and passed it off on the ignorant and unsuspecting as a brand new issue direct from God."[351] In reference to the later European editorial translations of Hebrew texts, Barbara Walker adds:

> "Obviously the Bible was full of myths and legends, but most orthodox theologians had no idea of their meaning. One reason was that they didn't study the corresponding myths and legends of other cultures...Christian missionaries thought theirs was the only pipeline to divinity, the deities of all other people throughout the world were devils, and the myths of the Bible were absolutely true whereas all other myths were absolutely false. Nowadays such crude beliefs seem no less superstitious...".[352]

The biblical book of Genesis is a mythological method of describing events which took place thousands, maybe millions of years before the writer began to set them down on paper. Therefore, the stories you read in the Bible, if you take them literally, can sometimes have you a bit confused. One for instance, which we will be covering in detail in Volume Three of this series, is how Noah could take every animal in the world two-by-two of some and seven of others and put them on a boat that wasn't even a good block long. Stay on that vessel, not only for forty days and forty nights of thunderstorms and rain, but for a little over eleven months after the storm was over. Now the question arises, just how do you fit pairs and sevens of all the animals in the world in a sea craft that is less than a city block in length. Why you have over 800,000 species of insects alone. One can well imagine that the people on this mythological vessel were in a whole lot of trouble having to feed this mega-menagerie, not to mention the fact that every living Earthly creature has to go to the bathroom. For it is a law of nature. Any creature which consumes food must at some time eliminate it. This story says there were only eight people aboard Noah's ark. Needless to say, this must have been quite a job for a crew of this size to keep up with all of their chores. No wonder Noah got drunk after it was over.

We will find as we study and analyze this story in Volume Three of this series that there are many other traditions about people who took sailing vessels and loaded them up with samples of all the different animals in the world. To date many of the legends of this type have been recovered and we will be discussing them in the aforementioned work.

Taking under consideration the criterion of historical reality, we must conclude that what we are looking at in the Genesis record is not an actual fact but rather a concept or principle being conveyed through the attention getting method of mythic storytelling. Some analyze this psychological phenomena thusly:

> "This curious mythological idea, and the still more curious fact that for two thousand years it was accepted throughout the Western World as the absolutely dependable account of an event that was supposed to have taken place about a fortnight after the creation of the universe, poses forcefully the highly interesting question of the influence of conspicuously contrived counterfeit mythologies and the inflections of mythology upon the structure of human belief and the consequent course of civilization."[353]

So what we are dealing with here is primarily Hebrew mythology. Now. Just who were the Hebrews? As far as we know the name Hebrew comes from the word haribu meaning "people who crossed over" signifying the journey of Abraham from Ur of Chaldea across the Euphrates River and into the then Kemetan ruled Palestinian Strip ca. 1675 BCE. They were originally an Afrikan people who were a composite of the Kemetans, old Sumerians, other Chaldeans and Canaanites. They were sometimes known as the red-purple that is to say mahogany people. The Bible says in reference to their racial stock in Amos 9:7, "Are ye not as children of the Ethiopians unto me, oh children of Israel? saith the Lord...". Thus scriptually verifying their ancestry.[354]

What was the intent of biblical mythology? Why was Genesis written in the manner in which it was? The answer probably lies in the general consensus that it is important for all people to know their cultural and ethnic history as well as their particular role in the history of the world. Yet it also seems to be even more important for them to perceive their own contributions to world civilization in extraordinary terms. This attitude can of course, when carried to extreme, cause some peoples and cultures to over exaggerate their significance and/or to appropriate unto themselves the real achievements of others.

Trawick, though somewhat subjective, gives a pretty good assessment of the primary intent of biblical mythologists. He says that their objective "...was to present each religious truth as they saw it (often as miraculous truth governed by divine intervention) and to bring that truth home to the reader by any literary means that came to hand. They thought and wrote emotionally and figuratively. Hence some of their writings may contain more of *poetic* truth than statistical or historical evidence."[355]

Some of the questions which seem to have always been on the minds of humans from remotest times are; how did I get here; how did the Earth come into being; why am I here; why is there an apparent difference between good and evil? These are things that have always stirred the minds of humans throughout the ages. Some other questions that have continually troubled man are; why do people sometimes act so bad; why can't folks behave? Thus all people as a result of trying to understand life's mysteries develop traditions and/or literature to express their particular ideas and answers to these and similar questions. The Judeo-Christian Bible is just one such effort. The book of Genesis is the Hebrew approach to many of the questions which have been so prevalent in the minds of humans from time immemorial.

Again we must emphasize the reality that in the process of writing the book of Genesis, the Israelite scribes', unlike the Kemetan and other Kushite High Culture priests/scientists' primary interest was religious, not scientific. This must be kept in mind; so if there seems to be some conflict between the approach of scientific investigation to the origin of things and that of the Genesis record, it is because the objective of the Hebrew religious leaders and editors of various sources of cosmogonical ideas in vogue during different periods of its composition is probably totally different from what our approach to the study of the origin of things might be today. Most clergymen are reluctant to admit to the inaccuracy of biblical mythology because it might impact upon their livelihood. On this point Barbara Walker says:

"The real point was that organized religions had an economic interest in maintaining literal interpretations of biblical myth. Guignebert says, 'the doctrine of the inerrancy of the Bible... necessarily placed theology in an attitude of surly and sanguinary [blood thirsty] hostility towards the exact and experimental sciences, which it will not abandon save most reluctantly and after as much delay as possible... [M]ethods have changed, the illusion still current have decreased, but its spirit is scarcely altered.' When the theologians began to give in, they complained that viewing the Bible as myth would destroy the whole structure that their livelihood and self-respect depended on."[356]

Today being so far removed from the actual happenings and events recorded in the book of Genesis and the fact that we as a people have been relatively separated from the true "knowledge of self" and the historical reality that our Afrikan ancestors were the first to write and produce a Bible (the Hebrew one included), there is a general tendency to believe more emphatically in the fantastic elements of myths than we do in scientific reality and the principles the myths were intended to convey. Actually, many religious dogmatists become embroiled in heated disputes over different aspects of the myth, even though the very fighting over the myth is a denying of the actual divine principle that it is supposed to be representing because such asinine squabbling defies good logic and common sense.

Devotees of the Bible and the Qu'ran say that these "holy books" teach humanity to love one another. Yet many of the demoninations of Christianity and the "isms" and "schisms" of Islam are still antagonistically intolerant on one another. Surely, this is not the true characteristic of the original Afrikans who first recorded the symbology of these myths as a part of the technical language of their High Culture science. Reflecting on this great legacy should help us to overcome the pathology of internecine struggle over whose point of view is the absolute and only truth. Divesting ourselves of such a burden will greatly contribute to relieving some of the stresses and tensions which assault the nervous system of all too many Black People in today's world. Therefore, to redeem our rightful place in the sun, we suggest that the wisest rule for this or any other issue is to be tolerant and allow for salubrious diversity remembering that first and foremost we are an Afrikan people with "one God, one Aim, one Destiny".[357]

THE BIBLICAL GENESIS: JUST ANOTHER STORY

Godfrey Higgins declares:

" When I find learned men believing Genesis literally, which the ancients, with all their failings, had too much sense to receive except allegorically, I am tempted to doubt the reality of the improvement of the human mind. What says the celebrated St. Augustin? 'That there is no way of preserving the literal sense of the first chapters of Genesis, without impiety, and attributing things to God unworthy of him.' But St. Augustin has only followed the learned Origen who has maintained that the literal sense of the history of the creation in Genesis is *absurd and contradictory,...*"[358]

Sts. Origen (c. 185-254 CE) and Augustine (354-430 CE) respectively were indigenous Afrikan bishops of the early Christian church.[359]

It appears the book of Genesis originally had a dual meaning; one for the learned initiated priests and the other for the common folks. Therefore, Higgins says, "...its allegorical nature may perhaps be safely assumed, notwithstanding the nonsense of modern devotees...". Then this bold scholar adds:

"Although it is clear from the works of Philo and others, that the learned in all ancient times acknowledged an allegorical sense in the account of Genesis; it is equally clear from the works of that learned man, that in his time its meaning was in a great degree lost. The most celebrated of the Christian fathers equally admitted it to be allegorical, but the moderns have a difficulty to contend with,...their fanaticism...".[360]

Philo was a Hebrew philosopher who lived between 20 BCE and 50 CE.

The narratives in Genesis Chapters 1 through 11:9 is the record of ancient Israel's reflections on what is generally considered to be prehistoric times blended with a compendium of traditions handed down by the elders from generation to generation.

Hebrew scribes, as did many other Afrikans in those days, utilized the storytelling method to set forth the ideas in Genesis Chapters 1 through 11:9 because it effectively arrested the attention and stimulated the memory. These early fragments of divers sources were used to introduce the basic themes of the whole biblical drama which can be summarized thusly; first, there was a beginning, the world began at sometime, somewhere; secondly, the world did not come into being by chance, there was a preeminent Creative Force which brought it to fruition through an orderly progressive development; thirdly, man and woman is the crowning act of creation for whom all else on planet Earth beforehand was made; fourthly, through disobedience of a Divine prohibition, humanity's original parents fell out of harmony with the laws of nature thus causing discord and chaos on the Earth; and finally, man must strive to return to his original upright state through ritual observance of the priestly code and unswerving obedience to the laws of Yahweh (God) as interpreted by the Israelite priesthood.

In contrast to the cosmogonies of their neighbors, the Kemetans, the Phoenicians, the Sumerians and the Babylonians, the Israelite creation story first began to be written at a time (ca. 800 BCE) when Hebrew culture as such was in its infancy. These initial literary efforts were probably based on fragments of Mosiac writings which may have survived the days of their early wilderness wanderings and uneasy settlement in the land of Canaan.

In the early stages of Hebrew literature, their primary concerns was with that which affected them as a small and vulnerable nomadic people. Later as they became more sedentary and relatively established as a nation, the priestly scribes began to view the Israelites in relationship to the rest of the world and they figured, like all the other more advanced nations which surrounded them that they had better adapt a mythology and a legend built around their place in the origin of things and as a result they inaugurated the recordings of a prehistoric account of things from a Hebrew frame of reference. Therefore, in essence, what you are looking at in the book of Genesis is what Dr. John Henrik Clarke refers to as a "Jewish survival book" and although it started out as a collection of ideas and documents complied over a extended period of time by a rather small and insignificant nation among the Afrikan world powers of that day, it was effectually like many another Black creations co-opted and grossly misinterpreted by later Asian mixtures and European groups who intermittently invaded Palestine. Especially the mixed multitude offshoot descendants from the original Afrikoid Hebrews who were scattered to diaspora after the Roman army besieged and destroyed their capitol city, Jerusalem in 70 CE.

THE PRODUCT OF MANY NATIONS

In past ages of antiquity, there was a kind of universality in all the creation myths. Thus, the mythology of the Bible is a by-product from other more original sources. Barbara Walker stresses that:

"...all peoples, nearly everywhere in the world, shared the same fables of the creation, the flood, the magic garden with its tree of life and its primal couple, the wise serpent, the heaven-piercing tower, the divided waters, the chosen people, the virgin mothers, the saviors, and all the rest. It has been said both testaments of the Bible are only recent and relatively corrupt derivations from a world-wide cycle of archetypal myths."[361]

J.R. Dummelow's *One Volume Bible Commentary* informs us that "it is now widely admitted that the Genesis account of creation contains elements of belief which existed perhaps thousands of years before the book of Genesis was written." Though we have stated it before, for some of our readers, there still may be the need to re-emphasize the fact that the collection of stories, myths and legends designed to illustrate great pivotal events in world history such as the beginning of the world and the creation of humans had

137

existed long before the recording of the book of Genesis. Therefore, it is a fact incontestable that the theology of the book is based on extremely ancient traditions. Higgins admonishes:

> "We ought never to lose sight of this fact, that, whether mere mythos or matter of fact, the doctrine of Genesis has been the moving cause of the conduct of almost all the world from the very earliest times. It was not a book confined to the Jews, but a book of the secret mysteries of the whole world, which appears to us to be confined to the Jews, because their secret books are those only which have been preserved."[362]

Though Higgins makes a very valid point here, we must add that although the Hebrew Genesis is the most widely known, it by no means the only writings of this idiom to survive. There is *The Book of the Coming Forth By Day and By Night* and other early Afrikan literature which served as the matrix for the Hebrew and all the other creation stories in the ancient world. We will be demonstrating this historical reality further on in Chapter Eleven.

The Hebrews looked to other people with whom they had ideas in common about the world even though they did not necessarily venerate the same deity. The biblical authors held many views similar to those of neighboring people who did not worship their tribal gods. Buckner Trawick notes, "The earliest Hebrews thought of Yahweh as a tribal God who was interested particularly in them, and who had made with them (that is with Abraham) a Covenant to the effect that he would prosper them as his Chosen People if they would worship only him and obey his commandments."[363]

Initially the Hebrews, contrary to what we are told, acknowledged that other people had the right to worship the Creator according to their understanding and by other names until the time came when the Israelites set out to claim and aggressively take for themselves land which rightfully belonged to the Canaanite tribes and nations in Palestine. Then to justify the genocidal acts being committed against these people to acquire their lands, the Hebrew priests declared it was a mandate from the one true God, Yahweh, and all other gods, at least of the Canaanites, were his diabolical enemies and their devotees had to be put to the sword.

Walker comments on how the spirit and attitude of arrogant intolerance of the old Israelite priests was incorporated into the many Judeo-Christian mistranslations of the ancient texts by mentioning that "Bible revisions tended to erase earlier deities, especially female ones. After the centuries of chosing and revising canonical books, nearly every trace of female divinity had been eliminated from Christian literature."[364]

Drucilla Houston elucidates, "We know Hebrews while in captivity in Babylon secured the authentic genealogies of the first children of men...Babylonian tablets tell of an original race of black men called Admi, the Adites of the Cushite Arabian traditions."[365] Churchward emphasizes:

> "Modern research discovers in the Hebrew writings a composite work, not as the autogram of the Hebrew legislator, but as the editorial patchwork of mingling Semetic legends with cosmopolitan myth, which were copied from the Egyptians [Kemetans], either directly or indirectly but without the gnosis [wisdom]..."[366]

The term Semetic as applied by Churchward in reference to the Hebrews is a bit of a misnomer. Though their language is generally classified as a Semetic tongue, they themselves were primarily of Afrikoid racial stock.

AN ARTIFICIAL BLEND OF DOCUMENTS

Somewhere between 250-100 BCE when the Hebrew priests were trying desperately to hold on to their ancestral traditions in the face of Greek Hellenism, an unknown editor or editors who had access to documents containing the traditions and early records of the Israelites clumsily fused them together into a whole. To accomplish this task, several classifications of documents had to be integrated. A close examination of Genesis Chapters 1 through 2:3 and Chapters 2:4 through 4:25 reveals two of them, the J and E documents. Biblical scholars refer to these two main threads of the narrative in the Hebrew creation story as primitive (the J document) possibly written ca. 850 BCE and priestly (the E document) written ca. 700 BCE.

The primitive and priestly versions of creation are supposed to have been based on older written accounts compiled from oral traditions. An attempt at blending these documents into what would eventually become their present form was made during the Persian domination of Palestine in the days of Ezra, the scribe ca. 444 BCE. Regarding the Hebrew scribes use of Kemetan documents in the Genesis record, Churchward says:

"The translators of the Memphian text point out that there were evidently two originally independent texts which have been artificially blended to produce a deceptive appearance of unity which agrees with the fundamental difference betwixt the Elohistic and Jehovistic versions in the Book of Genesis, ...in which two accounts of the creation have been run into one."[367]

Barbara Walker outlines the contradictions inherent in the J and E documents as they were employed in the Genesis creation story. We have employed the corresponding text so those of our readers who wish to can do a first-hand comparative study.

E: birds and beasts created before man. (1:20-25)
J: man created before birds and beasts. (2:18-19)
E: birds made of water, along with fishes. (1:20)
J: birds made of earth, along with beasts. (2:29)
E: man given dominion over the whole earth. (1:26)
J: man placed only in the garden, 'to dress it and keep it,' like the men created to be farmer-slaves in the [Enuma elish]. (2:8,15.)
E: man and woman created together, after the beast: 'male and female created he (they) them, and God (*elohim*, the deities) blessed them.' (1:27)
J: man created alone, before beasts and birds; woman made from his rib. (2:7,19-20,21-24)
E: creation took place in six days. (1:31-2:1)
J: creation took place in one day. (2:4)[368]

Note how the more recent E (priestly) document creation story was placed first (Genesis Chapters 1 through 2:3) and the J (primitive) document of the creation story was edited as a kind of afterthought or post script (Genesis 2:4-25) in the composite narrative of the priestly scribes ca. 500 BCE. The reasons for this switch will be explained shortly.

Sometime between 500-450 BCE:

"...after the return from the Babylonian Exile, the priests at Jerusalem felt the need to consolidate and systematize Jewish religious law and history, to provide a unified constitution or manifesto for the restored Hebrew nation. They felt obligated to preserve the sacred material of the J, E, D, and H documents, but they rewrote some of it and added new portions of their own."[369]

The J, E, D and H documents were rewritten successively. J, the primitive document, uses the appellation Yahweh (the Self Sufficient one) in reference to the Creator, translated Lord God in the King James Version and Jehovah in other English versions. The authors of the E (priestly) document used the plural terminology Elohim (the Strong Ones) as a designation for the Creator, translated God in the English versions. The content of the D document, the Deuteronomic Code, ca. 621 BCE, "...consists of rules for religious practices and its emphasis is on purification of worship by recognizing the Temple at Jerusalem as the only sanctuary of God".[370] The composite of this document was edited from the Deuteronomy scroll and the scroll of Joshua. The H document, ca. 570 BCE, is known as the "Holiness Code" and is the work of an unidentified scribe or priest who compiled it as a book of rules for ethical and ceremonial guidance.[371] These writings are now referred to as the book of Leviticus in most translations of the Old Testament scriptures. Both the scroll of Deuteronomy and the scroll of Leviticus were once thought to be the works of Moses (ca. 1240 BCE) but internal examinations of these books prove quite the contrary. More in depth information on this subject will be provided in a forthcoming work by this author entitled *The Afrikan Origin of the Bible*. Presently supportive evidence and a clear detailed discussion on these points can be heard on the cassette tape Seminar Series, *Amazing Black Facts of the Bible Study Course*. See the catalog section in the back of this book for details.

The blending of the J, E, D, and H documents in the Hebrew Old Testament scriptures have come to be known as the P (priestly) document because of its methodical and prosaic style with a heavy· emphasis on dates, measurements, genealogies, ceremonies, and covenants and its exaltation of the patriarchal deity, Yahweh, while defaming the universally revered female deities of the ancient High Culture Civilization. At the time of the compilation and editing of the P document, the male dominance attitude among the Hebrew-Israelites had reached its zenith. Examples of the P document can be found in Genesis such as the E document creation story in Chapters 1 through 2:4, Exodus, Leviticus, Numbers and Joshua. The J, E, D and H documents amalgamated into the P document was probably the set of scrolls used in the Ezra addition of the Old Testament scriptures, ca. 444 BCE.

The P document scrolls were again revised in the Septuagint, the version of the 70 around 270 BCE under the auspices of Ptolemy Philadelphus, a Eurasian Greek ruling in what was called Egypt at the time. Ptolemy, in a grandiose design to establish the Greeks as world class thinkers after they had stolen and destroyed much of the recorded High Culture scientific knowledge of ancient Kemet, proposed to collect the various literatures of the then known world, translate them into the Greek language and deposit them in the Alexandrian library. During the course of this undertaking, the Greeks managed to acquire through the work efforts of the Kemetan scholars under their domination some 500,000 books which the Greeks promptly proclaimed as being their own creation.

This dishonest action taken on the part of the Greeks was a major step in the stolen legacy of ancient Afrikan knowledge so today universities and educational institutions in the western world espouse a non-existent body of knowledge called Greek Philosophy which should be more properly referred to as the Greek Lie. Because there was no such thing as Greek philosophy in the ancient world, what came to be misnomered as such was actually Afrikan theology plagiarized by the Greeks. In fact, there is absolutely no verifiable historical account of the existence of many of the so-called early Greek philosophers. Herein is one of the most bodacious European hoaxes ever perpetrated in the academic world. This historical reality is so very clearly and beautifully presented in *Stolen Legacy* by Dr. George G.M. James. We recommend that the reading of this treatise is a must for all seekers of truth everywhere.

It is against this background that the Greek (Septuagint) version of the Hebrew Old Testament scriptures was translated and editorialized. Then somewhere between 250-100 BCE these scrolls were further revised and synthesized within the form and content of the ultrapatriarchal P document.

CHAPTER TEN

AN AFRIKAN-CENTERED SYNOPSIS OF THE HEBREW CREATION STORY

We begin this chapter with another statement by Albert Churchward. "It is the making of the secret earth of Amenta by Ptah and his associate gods [forces of nature] that has been converted into a creation of the heavens and the Earth in the Book of Genesis."[372] The term Amenta comes from two Kemetan words *Amen* meaning "secret" or "hidden" and *ta-*"land", literally "the secret land". Amenta was an "ideograph" symbolically representing the evening sun setting behind the mountains. Churchward illustrates the concept in this manner. "...As the sun went down in the west at night and rose again in the east in the morning, so this symbolically represented the soul traveling throughout the Tuat and Amenta until it finally accomplished its journey and joined the Divine source again."[373] Amenta is also identified with the

> "two earths, or the 'double earth,'...the upper earth of Seb and the lower earth of Ptah-tatanan Lord of Eternity...The two earths meet in Annu, for it is the border of the two earths. In this there is a shifting of boundaries from South to North, to East and West, in the union that is now established."[374]

In this aspect it is called the Garden of Amenta and paradise, "the beautiful earth of eternity." These are enormously ancient and complex concepts which can be rather difficult for contemporary minds to comprehend as they seem to have been for the Hebrew scribes who transmorgrified them into the mythology of their creation story. Many Afrikan-centered scholars associate Amenta with the Continental Drift Theory of planet Earth's land mass. This particular interpretation of the Amenta symbol of ancient Kemetan scientific language is probably the closest one to its most likely meaning:

> The two earths—represent the giant continents of Gondwanaland and Lurasia which existed during the Mesozoic Period in geologic time, ca. 200 million years ago.

> The union of the double earth into the paradisiacal Amenta— the welding of Gondwanaland and Lurasia into the Megacontinent Ptah-taten (Greek: Pangaea)when the two giant continental plates collided as a result of the planet's tectonic action.

143

Such a rendering is not by any means far fetched because it is a known fact that Kemetan scientists possessed a profound knowledge of the planet's geological history. In fact, "the half has never been told". The subject of the various geological periods in Earth's development and their relationship to the ancient Afrikan High Culture Science is discussed in Volume Two of this series which is a study in common sense geology and grass roots anthropology.

There is also an astronomical explanation of the Amenta principle. Churchward cites the Memphite Texts. "When Ptah had build his mansion in the double earth, the two horizons were united, or, as it is said, the double earth becomes united, 'the union is in the house of Ptah,' and the two pillars in the gateway in the House of Ptah are Horus [the day] and Set [the night] the united ones made peace."[375] The union of the "Two Horizons" signifies the cosmic harmony of the universe as seen in the starry heavens of the night sky when daylight is for a time reunited with the primordial womb of darkness. Thus the ancients created the esoteric imagery of the two brothers, Sut and Heru (Set and Horus), making peace with one another upon the lap of their mother.

Another Amenta symbol with intricate nuances of meaning is the Tat, cross of Ptah. The Tat was a sign of the four quarters of the Earth; south, north, east and west. When planted in the earth on one of the great hills of Ptah at the winter solstice, it served as an instrument to measure and record time as its shadow was cast at the first sunrise. Being ever mindful of the fact that the scientists in the ancient High Culture civilizations of our Afrikan ancestors were some "heavy" brothers and sisters, let it suffice us to say that Professor Albert Churchward's view as to the Hebrew's incomplete translation of the complex scientific symbology of the Memphite theology is just one of the many such learned opinions on the initial sources of the Israelite creation story.

The diverse metaphoric implications in the Genesis record will be meticulously explored in Volume Three of this series. Unfortunately, though we have raised the subject, we are unable to give a complete discussion and interpret the details of the Amenta symbology in this work; however, we will do so as we explain the meaning of the mystic deity symbols of the ancient world in Volume Four.

Barbara Walker points out the fact that, "the Bible brought plants into being before the sun on which planet life depends;

[Genesis 1:11-13, 16-19.] made... birds before 'creeping things' on land which was hardly the case; [Genesis 1:20, 24] and produced 'light' before the only sources of light, sun and moon. [Genesis 1:3-5]"[376] Godfrey Higgins suggests, "The words of our Bible [Genesis Chapters 1 and 2] as here used, 'without form and void' have not any meaning." They came from the Hebrew "teu-u-beu" denoting "matter effete, unproductive, unprolific, ungenerating..."[377] The application of this phraseology by Hebrew priests and scribes was of patriarchal influence. All the other cosmogonies they borrowed from spoke of a primeval ocean of energy abounding in lifegiving matter as the first cause maternal unction of all living things, even the Kassite Enuma elish placed the cosmic sea of Tiamat at the beginning of creation although it had Marduk murder her later and create "the heavens and the Earth" from her severed body.

The all pervading core of cosmic logic in the ancient world with the exception of a few nations was the eminent role of the female energy in the creation of life. In the book *Afrikan Woman: The Original Guardian Angel*, this author poses the question, "Why did woman become the dominant symbology of life-giving elements in the ancient world?" Then answers:

"No doubt because then, as now, all men knew that it was their mother's loving care which carried them for 40 weeks, birthed them and kept them alive in their early stages of introduction to life. That is why they developed such a wide variety of expressions of her manifold attributes... in ancient Kemetan High Science symbology, the matter of primal Earth called Ptah emerged as the cosmic egg in the form of a great mountain from the primeval ocean called Nun or Nuni. Originally, this symbol in part represented the sea water-like chemical composition of the female womb. Nun is said to have contained within it the male and female energies and united them to create all other things and creatures...this was a universal symbolic formula for early man because the first and most profound world that a human ever knew was that of his/her mother's womb. Then once delivered into the temporal world by her, his/her early life experience was overshadowed by her maternal protection, nurturing, instruction and discipline...this was the first of all mysteries."[378]

ADAM AND EVE AS
MYTHOLOGICAL SYMBOLS

The Theory of Creationism as set forth in the early chapters of Genesis teaches that "God" created Adam and Eve as mature adults in a fully formed world abounding in plants and animals which appeared to be decades and even hundreds of thousands of years old. Trawick says "some commentators have suggested that the accounts of Creation in Genesis are mythological and that Adam and Eve symbolized mankind and womankind but were never intended to be regarded as a particular man or a particular woman."[389] The *Encyclopedia Britannica* adds "the narrative of Genesis I in giving an account of the 'creation' of man does not necessarily imply that a single pair only was thus formed at the first." Then the article makes the observation, "...though it [Genesis] is probably a revision of a very ancient tradition, going far back behind the earliest appearance of Israel as a nation...the narrative is naive in its detail and elementary in its theology."[380]

The name Eve is originally from the Hindu-Kush *Adita Eva*-the very beginning and *Hava*-life and was translated into the Hebrew *chawwah* meaning "mother of all living" [381]Adam is from the Hebrew *Adamah* and the Akkadian *Adumah* originally meaning "child of black mud",[382] later modified to a designation for "man" when the Hebrew scriptures were translated into Greek (ca. 270 BCE). The term was then made to commiserate with "genus" and then the Latin *homo* (ca. 400 CE) and finally the English equivalent "man". Merlin Stone reflects:

> "As I began to read other myths that explained the creation of life, stories that attributed the event to Nut or Hathor [Het Heru] in Egypt [Kemet], Nammu or Ninhursag in Sumer, Mami, Tiamat or Aruru in other parts of Mesopotamia and Mawu in Africa, I began to view the legend of Adam and Eve as just another fable, an innocent attempt to explain what happened at the very beginning of existence. But it was not long afterward that I began to understand how specifically contrived the details of this particular myth were...The lessons learned in the Garden of Eden were impressed upon us over and over again. Man was created first. Woman was made for man. Only man was made in God's image. According to the Bible, and those who accepted it as the divine word, the male god favored men and had indeed designed them as naturally superior."[383]

Concerning the exaggerated superiority status of Adam pro-liferated by Rabbinic and Islamic traditions, *Encyclopedia Britannica* informs us:

"Later thinkers and writers greatly expanded the story, and drew from it conclusions which were originally foreign to it. Rabbinic thought ascribed to Adam before the Fall a super human grandeur. One legend indeed, followed in the Koran, relates that all the angels were ordered to fall down and wor-ship Adam, and that Satan refusèd, on the ground that he was made of fire and the man of clay."[384]

The first claim of male preeminence in creation recorded in Hebrew literature was promulgated in an essentially male dominated environment during the middle period of the Israelite monarchy ca. 850-700 BCE. This was the J document referred to as the "primitive narrative" by biblical scholars because it was the Israelite's earliest attempt at developing a creation story. The J docu-ment in general expresses an extremely insecure patriarchal attitude. First, defying all biological reality, it tells us that Eve was created from the rib of Adam (Genesis 2:21-22); second, it assigns to Eve the second-class status of Adam's subordinate "help-meet" to keep him from being lonely since he had not been able to find a suitable "beast" to fill this role. Let us examine the text and take careful note of the language.

"And the Lord God said, it is not good that the man should be alone; I will make him an help meet for him. And out of the ground the Lord God formed every beast of the field, and every fowl of the air; and brought them unto Adam to see what he would call them: and whatsoever Adam called every living creature, that was the name thereof. And Adam gave names to all cattle, and to the fowl of the air, and to every beast of the field; but for Adam there was not *found* an help-meet for him."[385]

Now let us logically analyze the text.

Verse 18 states the man was lonely and needed help,

Verse 19 implies that to solve this problem, Yahweh (the Lord God) formed animals and brought them to Adam.

Verse 20 in essence, this verse says, though it is not clear what method he used while searching the animals for a mate, that Adam could not find a suitable one among them,

Verses 21 & 22 as though it was an afterthought, Yahweh (the Lord God) anesthetized Adam, performed supernatural surgery on his torso and made-for Adam his very own woman, thus solving the problem of finding a "help-meet".

The story does have its touching moments in Verses 23-25 when Adam awakens and declares the woman to be an essential part of his being and expresses a passionate desire to "cleave unto" her as they being "not ashamed" became "one flesh". But in light of the fact that in the creation legends of Kemet, Sumer, Persia, India and Kushite-Babylon, men and women had been created simultaneously and in pairs and generally portrayed as friendly, affectionate, and ofttimes tenderly erotic couples. The J document in the Hebrew story leaves a lot to be desired and is surely lacking in scientific and historical reality. This primitive narrative is preoccupied with the idea of projecting Adam as the crowning act of creation made in the express image of a male deity (Yahweh/the Lord God) and with relegating to Eve a role of secondary importance in that she was made in the image of Adam. The J document further solidifies Eve's subordinate role in Genesis Chapter 3 where she is accused of being the primary reason why sin came into the world. In this story she is ultimately doomed, through all her Earthly female descendants, to be eternally obedient to the male of the species. Stone says:

"It is then, perhaps, not overly speculative to suggest that the myth of Adam and Eve, the myth which Professor Chiera tells us shows evidence of having been 'produced in scholarly circles,' may have been intentionally written and included in the creation story of the Bible as yet another assault upon the Goddess religion."

Then Stone goes on to suggest:

"We may indeed find that the seemingly innocent myth of paradise and how the world began was actually carefully constructed and propagated to 'keep women in their place,' the place assigned to them by the Levite tribe of biblical Canaan."[386]

The Eve symbol as depicted in the "temptation and fall" portion of the Hebrew creation myth is reduced to a gullible woman in need of the constant guardianship and guidance of her husband,

148

Adam. She is so simple minded that she cannot be left alone, not even for a moment. The first time she wandered out of Adam's sight, she was conned by a serpent who robbed her and her future family of immortality and caused her and her husband to lose their luxurious estate in the Garden of Eden. This whole idea is reflective of Levite priests' misogynistic attitude toward women in general. *Encyclopedia Britannica* says, "Here, then, we have certain theories about human nature, held by the Israelite of the middle monarchy. Though the view of God is crude and anthropomorphic, yet it is clear that He is the author on man's being...and the subordination of woman is generally recognized."[387]

Reverend Theodore Allen known affectionately to many Black Liberation theologians in the Banneker City (Washington, DC) area as the "country preacher" says that the story of the temptation of Eve as recorded in Genesis Chapter 3 could be morally classified as entrapment and if taken literally would be tantamount to a "sting operation" staged by today's police departments.

At the time when the primitive narratives of the J documents were being composed, the Mother-Goddess religions of the surrounding nations were giving the Israelite priests fierce competition, even among their own rank and file. The reaction of the sacerdotal class in Israel to the strong influence of goddess veneration among the Hebrews, especially females, was to foster the subjugation of women to such an extreme degree that according to Merlin Stone their judiciary system, during certain periods of their history, demanded the death sentence for any married woman who had been raped.[388] Then they set about on a defamation of character campaign against the Mother-Goddess principle by hurling scathing epithets through their vagabond prophets at this awesome force they could not adequately reckon with and accusing her acolytes of the most debased and degenerate rites. In spite of this type of hostility expressed towards the feminine principle in J documents and the political climate during this period in the small nation of Judea's history, Mother-Goddess veneration continued to blossom, prosper and gain in status among the rank and file of the Hebrews reaching even unto the highest offices of government including the monarchy itself. After the fall of the capitol, Jerusalem on August 5, 87 BCE, an assembly of Judean Hebrews who had fled to Kemet responded to an address vehemently delivered by the Prophet Jeremiah with the following rebuff.

"At this, all the men who knew that their wives offered incense to alien gods, and all the women who were standing there, a large assembly (with all the people living in Pathros in the land of Egypt), answered Jeremiah as follows, ' we have no intention of listening to this word you have spoken to us in-Yahweh's name, but intend to go on doing all we have vowed to do: offering incense to the Queen of Heaven and pouring libations in her honor, as we used to do, we and our fathers, our kings and our leaders, and in the towns of Judea and in the streets of Jerusalem: we had food and plenty then, we lived well, we suffered no disasters. But since we gave up offering incense to the Queen of Heaven and pouring libations in her honor, we have been destitute and have perished either by sword or by famine.' The women added, 'When we offer incense to the Queen of Heaven and pour libations in her honor, do you think we make cakes for her with her features on them, and pour libations to her, without our husbands' knowledge?'"[389]

During the composition of the E document, ca. 700 BCE, many of the Hebrew priests were relaxing their stringent attitude towards the Mother-Force because of its steadily growing popularity among the masses of their people. Due to international trade and exchange and a more tolerant foreign policy on the part of their monarchs, they were being reintroduced to the maternal elements of the cosmopolitan cosmogonies in vogue at the time, especially in Canaan. That is why the early priestly narratives (E document) reads "male and female created he them" and was placed forward in the sequence of the Hebrew creation stories.

The gradual upgrading of the female status in their literature was later reinforced by Hebrew scribes who had access to the old Sumerian records while they were in exile in Babylon and under the Persian domination, but these concepts were later submerged again by the Greek and Roman subjugation of Judea and the Israelite rabbis of the diaspora from the First to the Fifth Centuries CE.

In spite of its many discrepancies, the Genesis record and other books of the Hebrew Old Testament can be of great value to us for many of our people may never have even heard of ancient Kush (Ethiopia), Kemet (Egypt), or Babylon or other such places without first having been introduced to them via the Bible. Most of us will probably not be able to travel to these lands where the ancient

Afrikan High Culture civilizations once existed and see the viable evidences of their former glory first-hand or visit the British, French, German and other museums where exhibits of our "stolen legacy" are on display. Yet you can use the Bible right in your own home as a gateway to the rediscovery of the true knowledge of yourself. For the Bible is, after all, an Afrikan history book. How to utilize it most effectively for this purpose will be demonstrated in Volume Three of this series and the forthcoming works, *The Bible: An Ancient Afrikan History Book* and *The Afrikan Origin of the Bible.* In the meantime, we suggest you acquire and listen to many of the audio cassette tapes on the subject presented by this author. The various titles are listed in the Fourth Dynasty Publishing Company catalog in the back of this book.

CHAPTER ELEVEN

AN INTRODUCTION TO MEMPHITE THEOLOGY—THE ORIGINAL COSMIC SCIENCE OF DIVINE BALANCE

THE MEMPHITE DRAMA: AN ORIGINAL AFRIKAN GENESIS

We shall now examine the basic philosophy which provided the impetus for the whole High Culture system of ancient Kemet. It is known as the Memphite Theology or the Memphite Drama. George G.M. James informs us that "The Memphite Theology is an inscription on a stone, now kept in the British Museum. It contains the theological, cosmological and philosophical views of the Egyptians [Kemetans]." He further states that it is "the source of modern scientific knowledge".[390] Let us stop here for a moment and define the terms Dr. James has set forth in the preceding quote.

Theological—from *theo* meaning "god" and *logia* meaning "study of", literally the study of the concept or idea of God.

Theology in its proper and original context was designed to lift man to the heights of consciousness, to inspire the human brain and expand the mind beyond the confinements of the external world.

Cosmology—from the Greek *cosmos* meaning "the universe" and *logia* meaning "to study", literally the study and philosophy of how the universe phenomena.

That is the remarkable appearance of the cosmic scheme of things as manifested in the myriad forces of natural law. The totality of life interacting on planet Earth; in the air on the land, in the sea, and the synchronization of Earth with the other planets in our solar system and the very core of the universe itself. In essence, the Memphite Drama demonstrates the interrelationship and balance of the whole cosmic scheme.

Philosophy—from the Greek work *philio* meaning "love" and *sophia*-"wisdom", literally the love of wisdom.

Philosophy bespeaks an individual's or people's view of life. That is the frame of reference for their outlook or worldview. The Memphite Theology contains the ideology and conceptualization

153

of the Creative Force (God) in the universe which also includes the study of the origin of the universe and how it functions, evolves and grows.

The intellectual and spiritual philosophical discipline expressed in the Memphite Theology generated the drive for "bigness" as evidenced in the achievements of the ancient Kemetans whose wise sages created and developed the 47 year study of the Mystery System wherein the High Priest attained 360.4 degrees through the mastering of various stages of enlightenment and by memorizing the 42 books of Tehuti.

The mindset which produced the gargantuan buildings, temples, pyramids and statuary that were created by these intellectual giants as well as the other magnificent elements of Hapi Valley High Culture civilization was to a large degree inspired by the Memphite Drama which embodies the conceptualization of the Divine Intelligence, the understanding of the universe and how it works and the general cosmic scope of the Kemetan worldview. These three basic concepts form the foundation and core of the Memphite Theology.

There were many other cosmogonical systems in circulation throughout the long dynastic periods of the Kemetan Empire. Each of them centered on legendary rulers or heroes who were uniquely identified with some force/forces of nature and posthumously endowed with special powers and attributed certain acts in creation by the High Culture priests-scientists of ancient Kemet. This aspect of the Kemetan Astro-Mythological methodology was a very effective and practical way of teaching complex scientific concepts to their students and imprinting the principles of natural law and the interrelated workings of the universe in all its manifestations upon the minds of the Kemetic people.

The four main cosmogonies our scholars have presently been able to ascertain from their research and rediscovery thus far are the Hermopolitan, the Heliopolitan, the Memphite and the Theban. These are Greek terms and we are only using them here because of their general familiarity. Further on the correct names are parenthesized. Each of these creation legends were the products of powerful city-states that variously existed throughout Kemet's long history which according to ancient traditions and modern archaeological rediscovery began somewhere between 18,000-17,500 BCE, the time of the inauguration of agricultural science in the Hapi Valley.

- Hermopolitan System (the City of Wisdom)—based on the legend of Tehuti, the learned scribe and author of the 42 books of Kemetan knowledge, wisdom and science.

- Heliopolitan System (Sun City)—based on the legend of Ra its chief deity who represented the rays of the sun.

- Memphite System (Menefer)—the capitol city of Aha Menes the pharaoh who united upper and lower Egypt and was symbolically identified with Ptah the deity who united Amenta (the two great continents of Gonwanaland and Lurasia into the mega-continent Ptah-taten/Pangaea).

- Theban System (Wo'se, the Eternal City of 100 Gates) — centered on the legend of Amon/Amen, which means "so be it" or "so it is", its chief deity symbol which represented the hidden knowledge manifested in the physical/spiritual duality in all things in nature; the secret self of inner being.

After the unifications of the two lands and all their city-states into one great nation under Aha Menes—which according to the indigenous historian Manetho occurred ca. 5500 BCE, the Memphite Drama became the predominant cosmogony in the Kemetan Empire. It appears that the Memphite Drama was composed or either in a state of revision during the first dynasty in celebration of the founding of the city of Menefer also known as Hikuptah "House of the god Ptah" which the Greeks later corrupted into "Egypt" as a designation for the whole land of Kemet because they could not pronounce the Kemetic word Hikuptah.

The Memphite Drama was also composed or revised to commemorate the unification of upper and lower Kemet when Pharaoh Aha Menes turned the tide and drove Eurasian political forces out of the land. This event occurred some 4000 years before the Hebrews and at least 5000 years before the Greeks began to become civilized. The historical record shows that the Memphite Theology was published again ca. 700 BCE on a slab of basalt by Pharaoh Shabako of the 25th Dynasty. At a time when the Nubians from upper Kemet were once again regaining power in all the land while driving the foreign Eurasian rulers from the delta region in lower Kemet. Many Afrikan-centered scholars refer to this inscription as

155

the King Shabako Version of the Bible because it was a form of a bible for it contained the ethics and theology of the Kemetan people. Concerning this, Professor Joel A. Rogers writes:

"Ethiopians [Kushites], that is Negroes, gave to the world the first idea of right and wrong, and thus laid the basis of religion and all true culture and civilization. The earliest exposition of this yet found is in the so-called Memphite Drama, which is known only through a copy on a slab of basalt made by order of an Ethiopian [Kushite] king in 700 BC..."[391]

To our Afrikan ancestors the concept of right and wrong was based on the cosmic order of the universe. This is something we must clearly come to understand in our day. In the beginning Black People arrived at a concept of what was right and what was wrong by observing the order of the universe and by striving to live in harmony and achieve balance with the cosmic scheme of things. Actually the word sin as used in the English language today means "imbalance". Therefore, a thing or a deed is wrong if it throws you out of harmony with yourself, your natural environment, the universe in general and causes you to stir up discord with those around you. Such actions indicate that one is out of harmony and not attuned with the Creator. Therein is the basis for determining right and wrong and it is predicated upon one's understanding of and attitude towards how natural law operates in the universe.

Now why are we putting such great emphasis on this? Because all too many of our people have been made to think on a mundane level for much too long. Many of us do not look above and beyond a given situation but only see what is immediately before us; however, when you can look with cosmic understanding at the world around us in its many aspects, manifestations and moods, then you will be able to transcend the mundane adversities in your path and attain victory through intelligent and disciplined efforts. With this state of consciousness, you will not feel the need to indulge in inharmonious discord within yourself or through interaction with your people. This age old principle of harmony and balance is the foundation for communal brotherly love which has always been the philosophy of true Afrikans throughout the ages as demonstrated in the words "Do unto others as you would have them do unto you" which were engraved on the walls and pillars of temples and monuments throughout ancient Kush and Kemet.

THE AFRIKAN PHILOSOPHY
OF DIVINE BALANCE

It was in the Hapi Valley that philosophy, the love of wisdom, originated with the ancient Kushites and then was embraced by the Kemetans. This occurred at a period so remote in history that it cannot be dated. Thus far no one knows when the original Black Race began to systematize complex concepts of natural law into a theosophical worldview and codified body of knowledge. We simply know that when the enigmatic global Kushite Empire appeared on the scene, such philosophy was already firmly in place. And at the time of the founding of the Hapi Valley civilization, c. 18,000 BCE, it was ancient and during the 1st Dynasty period when the two lands were united, c. 5500 BCE, it was in a state of revision.

From the many documented evidences of this historical reality—many of which are emblazoned in stone—we can unequivocally state that there was no such thing as Greek Philosophy but rather Afrikan theology transmogrified. For the lofty ideas and principles which came to be misnomered Greek Philosophy existed and were taught by Afrikan scholars to their students many, many millenia before the feuding Greek city-states violently emerged on the scene in the Ionian Islands of the Kemetan (Mediterranean) Sea ca. 1400 BCE.

Ancient Afrikan philosophy as it was manifestly expressed in the Memphite Theology was centered in three cardinal ideas.

1) "The universe was created in an equilibrium and it is the subtle and complex interplay between the light and dark that gives our universe its form and its reality. In the Deified Man, the paragon of Egyptian [Kemetan] soul science, the opposites are united and transcended."[392]

Dr. Charles Finch as quoted above stated that the ancient High Culture scientists of Kemet believed "the universe was created in an equilibrium". That is to say, a balance and that balance according to them was best shown forth on the Earthly plane by humanity's lifestyle when it becomes one with the Creator and strives to carry forward the destiny of man on planet Earth which is to change things from what they are to what they ought to be. Therefore, if you are not in the process of creating better, then you are in the process of contributing to worse. That was and is a basic tenet of the Memphite Theology which is succinctly stated today

157

in the New Afrikan Creed, Article 9. "Therefore, I pledge to struggle without cease, until We have won sovereignty. I pledge to struggle without fail until We have built a better condition than man has yet known."[393]

As pertaining to the phrase "deified man", in the language of the ancients this denoted a person who was spiritually attuned to the Divine Will of the cosmos. For as pointed out in the book *Stolen Legacy*, the object of all learning was to bring man to a godlike state, to motivate men and women to become gods and goddesses. That is to make them godlike in mind, body and spirit, to elevate them to being one with the Creator moving in harmony with the Divine Will and being ever cognizant of the fact that they were moving within the realm of Omnipresent power.

2) "...Creation proceeds from chaos to order, by definite and gradual steps, showing design and purpose in nature, and suggesting that it must be the work of a divine Intelligence."[394]

Ancient Afrikan High Culture scientists taught that there is an Intelligent Power which permeates the universe and created order out of cosmic chaos. In the context of today's limited understanding, many people generally think of the Creative Force or God as an entity residing in one special location (heaven, etc.) or that one must go to a particular house of worship to make contact with "The One". By so doing, those who have been conditioned to think this way are ignorantly seeking to limit the Supreme Divine Energy which is everywhere and in everything. This way of thinking also places restrictions on one's access to the Creative Force. The Muslims refer to this Force as Allah which means All and in All. This is a prime example of how Islam, like all the other religions, reaches back to this and other philosophical principles of the Memphite Drama.

The concept of creating order out of chaos was also projected on a personal level which suggested that one could accomplish this by rightly applying the principles of natural law and that this is the only way in which humans can maintain an environment where people can grow and accomplish great things thus attaining true peace of mind.

3) The Creator (God) is the sum total of the universe, the Universal Mind who is self-created and fills a limitless space and who is the *core* of that boundlessness. The forces of nature revealed

in the lesser deities (gods) compose the manifold revelations of the Cosmic God who endowed matter with dynamic will backed by perfect intelligence. In Kemetan philosophy, this force was variously known as Neter-Nu, The One, and Om-Um.

The philosophical principle of Almighty God as the sum total of the universe denotes this, if you really want to know the Creator, go within yourself, your secret self and go out and get in tune and commune with the forces of nature. If you want to know the Lord, go to the delivery room and watch a woman deliver a child. Let us hasten to say here that we are by no means suggesting that one should not attend services at houses of worship but simply stating the reality that communion with Mother Nature and your inner being.is the quickest way to make contact with the Divine Force.

The self-created dynamic of Divine Intelligence in the universe was known to the ancient Kemetans as Neter-Nu which symbolized perfect will in the sum total of the cosmos which has existed from eternity to eternity. This concept of cosmic order begins with the Afrikan and no where else. Most other people's efforts to conceive of a universal God has always seemed to end with them trying to conform the universal Divine Intelligence to their narrow concepts and views on life, often to the point wherein many who foster such dogmas will resort to subjugating and/or killing other people/peoples who will not accept their banal conceptualizations of the Creator. Afrikan people, before their encounter with Eurasians and Europeans, generally had no such problems because they had a highly enlightened view of the Creative Force commonly referred to in the world today as God. To the ancients a cosmic understanding of Neter-Nu, Almighty God, was true religion and constituted sincere worship of the Creative Force.

The Neter-Nu principle was also called ''The One'' and was symbolically represented by a circle with a black dot in the middle. The Afrikan understanding of Neter-Nu, The One, in the science of life was as the all governing Intelligence, the all absorbing Divine Mind in the universe. We will be returning to a discussion of the Neter-Nu principle shortly; however, at this juncture, let us observe the general outline of the form and structure of the Memphite Theology.

159

ANATOMY OF THE MEMPHITE DRAMA

Now let us discuss the basic outline of the Memphite Theology. Dr. James wrote:

"The Egyptian [Kemetan] cosmology must be presented in three parts; each part being supplementary to the other, and presenting a complete philosophy by their combination. Part (I) deals with the Gods of chaos, part (II) deals with the Gods of order and arrangement in creation, and part (III) deals with the Primate of the Gods, through whose *Logos* creation was accomplished."[395]

The terminology "gods" as it is being used here means forces or powers of nature and signifies the manifold manifestations of the Neter-Nu, "The One"—the sum total of the universe. This is an ageless complex concept which is difficult for many people in today's world to comprehend especially those who have lived or are still living under the shadow of white-supremist domination and/or influence. Some may ask, How do you believe in the One God and still show reverence for lesser deities? The answer is very simple. The One Supreme Divine Intelligence in the cosmos is manifested in myriad ways. One could live many lifetimes and never know them totally and that is what the deity symbols represented in the ancient world; the fact that the presence of Almighty God can be found in every living thing.

One example of this percept can be found in the New Testament Scripture, John 10:31. "Jesus answered them, Is it not written in your law, I said, Ye are gods?" This is a direct quote from the Hebrew Old Testament (law) as recorded in Psalms 82:6. "I have said, Ye are gods; and all of you are children of the most High." Why would Jesus tell his disciples and the Israelites they were gods? Because in those days the designation gods meant lords or forces that govern which denotes the fact that there are different levels of perfection and stages of understanding of how the Creator is made manifest in all areas of life. Only when one limits himself/herself to one particular way of thinking does confusion set in and foster intolerance of others who have reached different levels of understanding.

The appellation *Logos* is a Greek word that means uttered intellect. That is intelligence and thought as it is exemplified through

160

the spoken word. For example, in John 1:1 we read, "In the beginning was the Word and the Word was with God, and the Word was God."

Self-indulgent seminarians who are philosophical masturbaters like to make a big deal of this terminology *Logos* although half the time they do not know what it really means. We will give more attention to this topic and the original meaning of the word further along in this study.

THE NETER-NU PRINCIPLE
IN KEMETAN COSMOGONY

We return now to our discussion of Neter-Nu which denoted the Kemetan persistent belief in the unity of Almighty God. Churchward reminds us that the great thinkers of ancient Kemet used "different types to depict the various attributes they associated and believed 'The One Great God possessed';..."[396] Wallace Budge refers to this methodology as "a pure monotheism manifested externally by symbolic polytheism" and further informs us that the Kemetans "believed in One infinite and eternal God who was without a second,...From a number of passages drawn from texts of all periods it is clear that the form in which God made himself manifest to man upon Earth was the sun, which the Egyptians [Kemetans] called *Ra*...His visible emblem...and that all other gods and goddesses were forms of him." Budge then goes on to cite some of the passages from the ancient texts which expounded this precept:

> "God [Neter-Nu] is one and alone, and none other existeth with Him—God is the One, the One who hath made all things—God is a spirit, a hidden spirit, the spirit of spirits,...He hath existed from old and was when nothing else had being. He existed when nothing else existed and what existeth He created after He had come into being,...God is father and mother, the father of fathers, and the mother of mothers. He begetteth, but was never begotten; He produceth, but was never produced; ...He createth, but was never created; He is the maker of his own form, and the fashioner of His own body—God Himself is existence...His names [manifestations] are innumerable, they are manifold and none knoweth their number...He fashioned men and formed the gods..."[397]

161

To the ancients the body of God was understood as the universe itself and they expressed this idea by stating, "he multiplies himself millions of times." This passage gives us a master key to understanding the concept of "a pure monotheism manifested externally by symbolic polytheism". This was/is the sublime philosophical worldview of the conscious Afrikan that there are so many ways to come to know and understand the Creator who is manifold in forms and numbers.

It should be remembered that these passages of Kemetan scriptures quoted above predate the Hebrew Old Testament and the Judeo-Christian Bible by some 10,000 or more years.

CHAPTER TWELVE

THE MEMPHITE DRAMA AND THE PTAH PRINCIPLE OF RATIONAL INTELLIGENCE IN EARTH'S CREATIVE PROCESS

SCIENCE OF THE PRIMEVAL WATERS

We have previously talked about the Memphite Drama as containing all of the theology—God concepts, cosmology—study of how the universe functions and philosophy— worldview. Now we will get into the elements which spell out the cosmogony of the Memphite System. As we have studied, cosmogony is from the Greek *kosmos* which means "world or universe" and *gonia*—"to be born", literally "how the universe was born". A cosmogony is generally an explanation of the origin of the material universe as it relates to planet Earth and is usually set forth in the imagery of a people's cultural and historical experience.

The ancient Afrikan High Culture Scientists never thought of Earth in a singular context. They always conceived of our planet as being part of a total whole. From this we learn the vital lesson that if one does not understand the whole universe as a sum total of its parts, then one is out of tune with nature and cannot truly understand his/her place in it. This is a preponderant principle of Afrikan High Culture Science which comes down to us from very ancient times.

The Bible says in Genesis 1:1-2, "In the beginning God created the heaven and the earth. And the earth was without form, and void; and darkness was upon the face of the *deep*. And the Spirit of God moved upon the face of the *waters*." This idea is borrowed from the Memphite Theology which says too that in the beginning all things were born of water. John G. Jackson puts it in modern scientific terms relevant to the formation of life on planet Earth.

"...life can only occur within a very restricted zone of temperature...Thus life must have originated when the earth developed a temperature that was neither too hot nor too cold, for life cannot survive where it is either roasted or frozen. Of the one hundred-odd elements of which the stuff of the universe is composed, only a very few show any affinity for life. Living matter consists mainly of atoms which possess the property of forming large molecules,...The atoms of hydrogen, oxygen, nitrogen, and carbon combine to form molecules consisting of hundreds, even thousands, of atoms. Carbon is of prime importance in the chemistry of life. So life first arose in the warm primeval ocean, beginning with the evolution of chemicals capable of assimilating carbon."[398]

Everything needed to sustain life can be found in the sea. Thus nearly all the ancient stories of creation spoke of the beginning of this solar system particularly our planet as emerging from the nothingness of nebulous billowing waters and pictographically portrayed all material things coming from a chaotic condition of potential energy that through the spoken word of Divine Intelligence was gradually brought into order. The book of Genesis in the Hebrew Old Testament uses the phrase "and God said" nine times to describe the primal act of creation. In this the Israelite scribes were merely following the tradition of the Memphite Theology and other cosmogonies that were in circulation at the time.

Dr. Cheikh Anta Diop cites a Phoenician example of this.

"Phoenician cosmogony is revealed in fragments of *Sanchonia-tion*...According to these texts, in the beginning there was uncreated, chaotic matter, in perpetual disorder (*Boho*); Breath (*Rouah*) hung over Chaos. The union of these two principles was called *Chephets*, Desire, which is at the origin of all creation. What impresses us here is the similarity between this cosmic trinity and that found in Egypt [Kemet]...Henceforth the thread would be unbroken until the advent of Osiris [Ausaru], Isis [Auset], and Horus [Heru], ancestors of the Egyptians [Kemetans]. The primitive Trinity then moved from the scale of the universe to that of man, as it did later in Christianity... Phoenician cosmogony reveals once again the kinship of Egyptians [Kemetans] and Phoenicians, both of Kushite (Negro) origin."[399]

Albert Churchward explains why the idea of "the face of the deep" was so germane to the old creation stories.

"The Egyptian [Kemetan] phrase for creation was 'Of the first time,' and mainly limited to the bringing forth of life. The beginning in 'the first time' described in the Ritual was with birth from the abyss, the birthplace of water within the earth...Thus we have the Deep, the darkness of the face of the Deep, the light breaking out of darkness, the waters and the light springing forth from the waters in the eatable plants. Water had revealed the secret of creation in the life which came as food by water from the Mother-Earth in the unfathomable deep. The secret of water as the source of life was the primal mystery to the Egyptians [Kemetans]...".[400]

Returning to the matrix of all the creation stories, the Memphite Drama, let us analyze the element of the primal waters, the source of everything called Nun or Nuni.

The Memphite symbology of the primeval waters represented basic matter as it exists in water which is the source of all life. In the primeval water of Nuni was contained the male and female germ of everything which was to be created on planet Earth. This is the way in which the Memphite Drama portrays the beginning of our solar system and the origin of life on this terrestrial ball.

The ancient Afrikan High Culture Scientists also perceived this cosmic reality as it was reflected on the earthly plane through their careful and disciplined study of the cycle of procreation; observing that once the spermatozoon of the male reaches the divine egg in the womb of woman, it later becomes an embryo where it is suspended in a liquid solution which is very similar in its chemical composition to sea water. This is a major aspect of Nuni, the primeval waters which existed at the beginning of "the heavens and the earth" and is manifested on the human plane in a mother's womb.

The human experience of procreation also exemplifies the cosmic phrase "and darkness covered the face of the deep" because a child is conceived in the darkness of a mother's womb where it develops and is nurtured for forty weeks of gestation, then brought forth to the light at the time of birth.

THE SCIENTIFIC PRINCIPLE OF PTAH-TJENEN "THE OPENER"

While we are still focusing on the creation of this solar system and planet Earth, let us now examine another element of natural phenomena depicted in the Memphite Cosmogony which tells us that the Earth's land mass, as signified in the mighty hill of Ptah, sprang up with an awesome whoosh out of the element of life from which came all terrestrial things, the primeval waters of Nuni. The deity symbol Ptah came to be known as the god of gods, that is the force of the earthly forces. Ptah represents the geological separation of land and sea which is stated another way in the Old Testament scriptures wherein the emergence of Ptah is portrayed thusly:

165

"And God said, Let the waters under the heaven be gathered together unto one place, and let the dry land appear: and it was so. And God called the dry land Earth; and the gathering together of the waters called he Seas: and God saw that it was good."[401]

As we have previously mentioned, the designation Egypt is a Greek term derived from *Hi-ku-ptah-*"the mansion of Ptah". The scientific principle, Ptah, was variously known to the Kemetans as "the opener" who causes to be an act of creation which gives form and identity to that which previously has not been known. And Ta-tjenen "the risen land" which denoted the planet Earth as an embodied microcosm of the macrocosm.

Regarding Ptah giving "form and identity to that which had no form", the Bible says God spoke and the land appeared and implied that first there was no form. There was only "the face of the deep" suspended in space. Then the word (Logos) went forth and the land and seas were separated. What we are talking about here, whether it be in the language of the Memphite Drama or the Bible or any other cosmogony, is a massive gigantic series of geological events which the learned authors of the Memphite Theology uniquely convey to us in terms of spiritual principles consciously at work in the creation of life. Not only does this graphic mental visualization symbolize the Ptah force in the physical realm of nature, but it also is emblematic of the spiritual nature of the original Black Race and their descendants, who are an extension of the earth as signified in Ptah.

Therefore, this principle dwells in each and every one of us, and like the mighty hill of Ta-tjenen that laid dormant in the midst of the primeval waters of Nuni until the unction of Neter-Nu, the Divine Intelligence caused it to rise up with epic magnificence, so too can the Ptah principle in every Black man, woman and child alive today be lifted to higher and higher levels of mental and spiritual consciousness, enlightenment and physical well-being through a conscious connection with the creative force as manifested within your "secret-self", that is your innermost being.

Jesus the Black Messiah put it so beautifully when he declared:

"Ye are the light of the world. A city that is set on a hill cannot be hid. Neither do men light a candle, and put it under a bushel, but on a candlestick; and it giveth light unto all that are in the house. Let your light so shine before men, that they

166

might see your good works, and glorify your father which is in heaven."[402]

Ptah-tjenen as an embodied microcosm of the macrocosm denotes the philosophical principle that what exists in the celestial cosmos is also reflected in some form or fashion on planet Earth. For example, the study of an ant hill or the cocoon of a butterfly reveals in microcosm what happens in the macrocosm on the larger scale of the universe just as the human brain, through its workings, reveals the order of the pattern in which the universe functions. For all things in the cosmic scheme are related.

Again a clear understanding of the Ptah principle demonstrates why Afrikan people everywhere must be free and independent on their own land; so they may govern themselves according to the principles of natural law and Divine Intelligence and not be subjugated by or under the control of those who historically have never been able to live in harmony with the world around them. For either they must control or destroy it. This is not the way humans were meant to live. That is why Jesus told the masses of Black People who were gathered about him in his day, "Fear not, little flock; for it is your Father's good pleasure to give you the kingdom." In another scripture one of the prophets of the ancient Kushite-Hebrews wrote, "And the Lord shall make thee the head, and not the tail; and thou shalt be above only and thou shalt not be beneath;..."[403]

THE MANIFOLD ATTRIBUTES OF PTAH

Now let's discuss some of the attributes of the Ptah principle of natural science. The first attribute of Ptah as set forth in the Memphite Theology describes him as "the first principle". The "first principle" — symbolizing rational intelligence — as it is related to planet Earth — which is the underlying permeating unction of the universe as revealed in the creation of this solar system and planet Earth. What this states in essence is that the pervailing intelligence of the cosmos has now been systhesized through the creation of Earth and its atmosphere for practical use on this planet.

The narrative illustrates that Neter-Nu moves through Ptah, the risen land, to make the "first principle" comprehensible to the inhabitants of planet Earth. Because all that man needs to know in this world, he can learn by returning to the land and observing

167

the laws of nature. For instance, everything which keeps modern technology in motion whether it be electrical equipment, motor cars, airplanes, spaceships or computer chips is a product of the land. For as Mr. Muhammad taught, land is the basic fundamental of wealth. Therefore, the raw materials needed to maintain today's technology are extracted from the bosom of the earth.

The second attribute of the scientific principle of Ptah is "Intelligent Cause". That is the manifestation of universal Divine Intelligence as expressed through the law of karma which is the scientific principle of cause and effect. That is to say for every action there is a consequence or reaction. The Bible states it thusly, "As a man soweth so shall he reap." The wise elders in our Afrikan communities refer to this precept as "what goes around, comes around". In other words, what you put into the earth is what you redeem from the earth. What you diligently and sincerely put into life determines how life will reward you.

The third attribute of Ptah is the "Divine Nous", a Greek reference which means "Divine Mind". It symbolizes the limitless realm of thought and demonstrates that though Ptah as the earth may be confined in this aspect to the four corners of the globe, still the earth receives its energies and its powers from cosmic thought. Thus germinated within its soil is the Divine Intelligence of the universe which imbues everything. Thus the Ptah principle is revealed in the Memphite Drama as the limitless realm of thought in the Divine Mind.

Everything in the world was first a thought. As experienced on the plane of human activity, before anything can become a visible, tangible reality, it must first be conceived in the mind. Therefore, any rational thing conceived in the mind can eventually be achieved. You just have to find a way to do it. The Divine Nous aspect of Ptah is a symbol of that reality; an eternal symbol to the original Black Man that thought precedes everything and if your thoughts are properly attuned, if your visualization is correct, you will surely find a way to achieve that which you have conceived. But you must be as constant as the everlasting earth.

Jesus, an Afrikan, who himself was an initiate in the Kemetan Mystery System,[404] taught that "any man who puts his hand to the plow and looks back is not worthy of the kingdom". From this parabolic saying alone we can ascertain that the brother was about freeing some land from the white Roman power structure that was holding his people in subjugation on their own territory.

Persistent optimistic thought is the key to the success of any endeavor. So if you learn the right lessons from negative experiences and maintain a positive state of mind and move in a positive way, you will never really be hampered by adversity. You can observe this principle as it is carried out in the life of the little ant. No matter what obstacle you put in his way, he will keep on moving. He will either go under it, around it or over it, but he keeps going forward to reach his goal and destination. That is because brother ant is governed by Nous, the Divine Mind of Ptah.

The totemic symbol of Ptah in ancient Kemet was the scarab, a kind of beetle because no matter what you put in the beetle's path, he will keep of going. The sign of the Ptah scarab is known in today's zodiac of astrological symbols as the sign of Cancer, the crab because like the crab, the dung beetle of ancient Kemet can move forward, backward, side-to-side or anyway he wants to go because to his way of thinking "ain't no mountain high enough, ain't no river wide enough, ain't no valley low enough" to keep him from meeting his destiny. So my beloved Brothers and Sisters, when life's adversities get in your path, think of the Ptah principle of the Divine Mind as manifested in the scarab, beetle, the crab and the ant.

The story is told of the New Afrikan genius, Dr. George Washington Carver. On one occasion he was invited to a scientific conference because through his agricultural acumen this man had helped save the south from starvation. The land had virtually been ruined as a result of the Civil War. White folks in the scientific community invited him to the conference thinking they could pick his brain and co-opt his knowledge. Carver being a great humanitarian decided to accept the invitation. After an arduous and dusty journey, he drove his horse and buggy up to the front door of the building in which the conference was being held. The Black man serving as the doorman was apparently a person who lacked a true knowledge of himself and respect for his people. So this mentally dead Negro accosted Dr. Carver with the words "Nigger, who do you think you are? You can't go in this building through the front door. Carry your dusty raggedy behind around the back where you belong." Dr. Carver didn't say a word. He just quietly walked his horse and buggy around the back of the building. As time went on the conferees started to become concerned because Carver was a man known for his punctuality. They wondered if he had been in a fatal accident or maybe some ignorant red-neck Cracker not knowing who he was may have dealt him some harm. Lo and behold, one of them looked out the window and there was Dr. Carver out back on his hands and knees contentedly lost in the wonder of observing the complex organization of an ant hill and making a record of their movements. This was a man who was truly in harmony with the Ptah principle of Divine Mind. The foolishness of the external world didn't really bother him because he was determined to follow the path of enlightenment. That is a good example of the sum total of the diligent pursuit of the limitless realm of thought in the Divine Mind as it can be manifested in the human experience.

The Ptah principle of the Divine Nous as recorded in the Memphite Drama also projected the superconscious mind as a reflection of the subconscious mind which can be the limitless mode of spiritual revelation. For example, the superconscious minds forgets things. The subconscious mind forgets nothing. Everything you ever saw, everything you ever heard is recorded in there somewhere. You just have to know how to go into your subconscious mind and retrieve it. That is why under hypnosis when your mind is not encumbered with external distractions, you can recall things you thought you had previously forgotten.

One can, with sincere effort, spiritually induce a mild form of self-hypnosis which can assist you in recalling information from the subconscious storehouse of your mind. This can usually be accomplished through concentration and meditation on positive affirmations relative to your particular objective. This was just one of the superior methods used by the learned scholars of the ancient Kemetan High Culture System to enlighten themselves and to transfer knowledge to their students. This subject along with some practical suggestions for applying these techniques will be discussed in a forthcoming work by this author entitled *Awake O' Sleeping Afrikan Giants* under the topic Mind Science and Meditation.

The Ptah principle of the Divine Mind also teaches that it is through the subconscious mind that the Eternal Mind influences the superconscious which is usually preoccupied with the external world. Through meditation, one can make contact with the Limitless Mind, and the Divine Intelligence can become the regulating factor in your thought processes. In this way, you and the Divine Mind become one. Everything one needs to know exists in some form of knowledge in the cosmos. Therefore, you must keep returning to the Universal library and draw from the boundless wellsprings of its illumination.

All the knowledge that the world and man knows and immeasurable information that has long been forgotten on the superconscious level was once known by various representations of our Afrikan ancestors and many of the atoms and molecules which constituted their manifested substance still live on and are lying dormant in our minds. That is why it is so important for our people to come to a light of understanding which will put us in touch with the Divine Mind.

In his fourth attribute Ptah is portrayed as "the God of order"—the force that governs order and form and is responsible for creating order out of chaos. According to the Memphite Theology, the primeval waters were in a chaotic state. Then Neter-Nu, the One, through the power of wisdom brought forth Ptah, the earth, from Nuni, the waters to give form and shape to the planet. So in this aspect, Ta-jenen represents order and form. Thus Kemetan scientists taught that the study of the earth and its environment as well as striving to live one's life in harmony with it helps to establish order in the world.

Generally people who are agrarian and live close to the land are people who are peaceful in nature and function in a communal way. They are usually very spiritual in their outlook because they are close to the earth. In fact, you are not really cultured unless you are close to Mother Earth because the word culture comes from the Latin *cultura* which originally meant "cultivation of the soil." Those who do not live close to the land and spend their lives nomadishly wandering about have a tendency to be antagonistic and abrasive, hard on their women and lean towards war and the enslaving of others.

Of course these are generalizations. However, in *The Cultural Unity of Black Afrika*, Dr. Cheikh Anta Diop outlines the basic difference between the historical attitudes and philosophical worldview of the Afrikan and the Caucasian. The careful and conscientious scholarship of Dr. Diop demonstrates that the path that was taken by the Afrikan led them in the direction of zenophilia (the love of humans) because originally Afrikan people lived close to the earth and their High Culture societies were developed from the ancient agrarian principles laid down by the Mother Force as manifested in the Afrikan woman who established agricultural science and therefore the basis for all civilization. Thus Afrikans and other peoples of color who are indigenous to a land base tend to demonstrate love for all humanity and a fervent reverence for the earth and its creatures.

171

On the other hand, a careful study of archaic Caucasian European history reveals that originally they had to eke out their living in the cold and harsh environments of the far recesses of the north left behind by the receding ice sheets of the Wurm Glaciation ca. 20,000 BP. These albino people known as Cro-Magnon—who had to fight wild dogs before they could inhabit the caves—and their Caucasian descendants generally had a shorter life span than most people of color during the early periods of world civilization because their diet consisted mostly of raw meat which is probably one of the reasons why their nature was so violent and aggressive.

Even in the modern world, after many years of encounter with the civilizing hand of the Afrikan, all too many Caucasians tend to manifest—however subtly it may sometimes appear—extreme aggression and hostility towards people of color, especially Black People in the United States and throughout the world while at the same time hypocritically proclaiming "liberty and justice for all". This is not intended as an indictment of the entire 13 percent Caucasian population in the world or as a statement of what some may unwittingly misnomer "reverse racism"; however, we cannot omit what a sound observation and analysis of history reveals. All you have to do is take a good look at the present state of the planet which is still and has been for much too long largely, whether overtly or covertly, dominated by the zenophobic (fear of other humans) philosophy of white supremacy. Nevertheless as one of the old New Afrikan spirituals says "I'm so glad that trouble don't last always." Therefore, we are, on every level of human activity, beginning to reclaim our rightful place in the sun.

For further discussion on this subject, read *Afrikan People and European Holidays: A Mental Genocide*, Book Two, chapter three by this author.

"The Preserver" is the fifth attribute of Ptah who maintains order and form through his connection with the principle of Ma'at, a female deity symbol representing wisdom and justice, the hallmark of order who gave Ptah the power to rule the earth. In ancient Kemetan High Culture Science there could be no activation of the masculine principle unless it was united with the feminine principle. This was/is the philosophical worldview of the conscious Afrikan. It was the come lately Eurasian and European who came up with the idea of a male god who has a son by himself. Due to the pathological disorder of their ambiguous sexual dimorphism and psycho-sexual maladjustment. See Michael Bradley's *The Iceman Inheritance*

172

Concerning the wisdom principle Ma'at, one of the scriptures of the Hebrew-Israelites who received their first philosophical worldview from the Kemetans says:

"All that is hidden, all that is plain, I have come to know, instructed by Wisdom who designed them. For within her is a spirit intelligent, holy, unique, manifold...for Wisdom is quicker to move than any motion; she is so pure, she pervades and permeates all things. She is a breath of the power of God, pure emanation of the glory of the Almighty...She is a reflection of the eternal light, untarnished mirror of God's active power...She employs her strength from one end of the earth to the other, ordering all things for good."[405]

Kemetan wise men described this principle thusly: "Ma'at is the right path before him who knows nothing...Ma'at is great and her effectiveness is everlasting."[406] Her emblem was a feather on the scales of justice (judgement). Walker says, "Egyptian [Kemetan] priests drew the Feather of Ma'at on their tongues in green dye, to give their words a Logos-like power of Truth so their verbal magic could create reality.[407] The biblical book of Proverbs which borrowed most of its saying from Kemetan scrolls describes Ma'at in her aspect as wisdom in the following manner:

"Can't you hear the voice of wisdom? She is standing at the city gates and at every fork in the road, and at the door of every house. Listen to what she says...Listen to me! For I have important information for you. Everything I say is right and true, for I hate lies and every kind of deception. My advice is wholesome and good...my instruction is far more valuable than silver or gold. For the value of wisdom is far above rubies; nothing can be compared with it. Wisdom and good judgement live together, for Wisdom knows where to discover knowledge and understanding...I, Wisdom, give good advice and common sense, because of my strength, kings reign in power. I show the judges who is right and who is wrong. Rulers rule well with my help...my paths are those of justice and right. Those who love and follow me are indeed wealthy. I fill their treasuries. The Lord formed me in the beginning, before he created anything else. From ages past, I am. I existed before the earth began. I lived before the oceans were created, before the springs bubbled forth their waters onto the earth; before the mountains and the *hills* were made. Yes, I was born before God made the earth and fields, and high plateaus...

And so, young men, listen to me, for how happy are all who follow my instruction. . .For whoever finds me finds life and wins approval from the Lord."[408]

The word wisdom as used in the above text comes from the Hebrew *chokmah* and means skillful application of knowledge. That is what wisdom is, the correct application of knowledge. This idea ties in well with the Ptah symbol of the earth because man learns the ways of life from studying the forces of nature as manifested in the earth and as he grows in the light of understanding of that knowledge, he also learns how to apply it to the benefit of and in cooperation with other humans. In this way humanity exhibits wisdom and wisdom is Ma'at, the motivator of Ptah for as Ptah-tjenen came up out of the waters of Nun, Ma'at was by his side. Divine Wisdom was always there. This is one of the legacies of the Memphite Theology bequeathed to Afrikan people from time immemorial.

THE EVERLASTING POWERS OF PTAH-TJENEN

To insure that we have a clear understanding of this principle in the context of today's language, let us once again reflect on the Ptah principle in ancient Kemetan natural science.

Ptah signifies, among other things, the spiritual principle of creative and controlling Divine Intelligence that fashioned the phenomena of nature whose secrets are to be found in the soil of the earth and is exemplified in modern physics as uranium and other raw materials used to generate atomic energy. He also represents the resources that are used to construct airplanes, spaceships and all other modes of transportation. In fact, most everything utilized or consumed by the world's population has to come from the soil, rocks, gasses, and subterranean fluids of the earth.

One small but eloquent example of how the Ptah principle applies to mechanical devises is the lens of the microscope and telescope which magnifies man's visual capacity many times over enabling us to see and observe things we would otherwise not be able to see. The raw materials used to create such lenses is sand, an element of the soil of the earth.

In the area of human health, one of the main ways in which well-being can be reasonably assured is through the proper consumption of food produced from the bosom of Mother Earth. These are just a few instances of how the Ptah principle is constantly at work in our daily lives.

Ptah also denotes the active matter of which the earth is formed. It was said that in him all earthly things lived, moved and had their being. For he transmits power and energy to all agencies and controls the life force of all material things including the physical aspects of animals and humans through his thought and command. Thus, through our communication with nature and the correct answering of its call, we are moving in harmony with the thought and command of Ptah. This particular philosophical view of the Memphite Theology stresses to us the importance of being attuned to and in harmony with the earth.

Now let us talk about the powers of Ptah. The Bible speaks of Ptah's everlasting power thusly, "One generation passeth away, and another generation cometh; but the earth abideth forever."[409] The word power as used in the English language comes from the Greek *dynamos* which means the ability to make things happen. Because of their prodigious possession of this "ability to make things happen" and their fervent belief in the principle of divine order and rationale, the ancient Kushites and Kemetans' witnessed to and verified the Ptah power by building like giants. For this philosophy of life inspired them to think on a grand and majestic scale. Here was a people who knew they were supposed to be and do the best and they did it. For they were ever striving to become one in thought and action with "The One". We, their descendents, would do well to emulate them in our time.

We will now discuss how the power which Ptah "the Risen Land" received from Neter-Nu in the form of Ma'at (wisdom) was transferred to another principle force of nature, Atum, the atom which is a component of all material things. The Memphite Theology said all that exists on the terrestrial plane came into being by way of the uttered thought of Ptah revealed in the spoken word of the Logos, in the person of Atum. It illustrates how Ptah absorbed the Divine Intelligence of the cosmos into the material substance of the earth. This made Ptah-tjenen the manifestation of the creative force as thought and wisdom in the earth. Atum, to whom Ptah transmits active power, becomes his speech and utterance. Keep in mind here we are discussing complex scientific principles as they were espoused in the Astro-Mythological symbology of the Memphite Drama which was used by Kemetan High Culture scholars to teach and graphically illustrate these principles.

A good example that will aid us in understanding Ptah's transference or power to Atum can be found in today's mechanical world. For instance, radios and other types of electronic equipment could not transmit sound without their components which are made from the raw materials of the earth which the Memphite Theology personifies in the Ptah symbol. The cosmic intelligence inherent—as in all things—in these inanimate materials is given active life through the right combination of relative elements which enable them to attract energy from the atmosphere and transmit it into the vibrations of audible sound which can be experienced by the human ear.

The same principles are at work in video equipment which projects images as well as sound. This is a modern day expression of Ptah-tjenen (the materials of the earth) transferring power to Atum (condensed sight and sound). Let us go over this again as it is laid out in the Memphite Theology. Ptah, the thought, the will, the desire to bring the earthly elements into active practical relationships was present in the beginning after being brought forth from the watery womb of Nuni by the wisdom of Ma'at, but the visible and tangible reality of that desire did not manifest on the functional material plane until a vibration went forth which was the spoken word, Atum. In John 1:1-3 we read about this same Atum principle. "In the beginning was the Word, and the Word was with God, and the Word was God. The same was in the beginning with God. All things were made by him; and without him was not anything made that was made."

The designation the "Word" as applied in this scripture is translated from the Greek *logos* which simply means the intelligence of the universe in spoken form which brings things to life. Whenever a word goes forth, vibrations are set in motion and it causes a reaction of some kind. Even if that reaction is not readily discernable, there is a reaction taking place if only in someone's mind. Viewing this in the light of day-to-day living, if what is being spoken is negative, you can be sure it will at some point cause a negative reaction particularly in your bodily chemistry because when you get caught up in negative thoughts and actions, you release poisons in your system that rob you of some of your life force. On the other hand, when you practice the habit of thinking and acting in a positive manner—which many times is a struggle in this present world, you release lifegiving and life sustaining energies. For whatsoever you speak out of your mouth will eventually bring back to you that which you sent forth. So always remember every endeavor to maintain a positive state of mind and being is indeed worth the effort.

When Black People meet, instead of feeding more energy into the negative forces of the external environment by constantly talking about adverse circumstances, affirm goodness by appealing to the power of the Divine Intelligence in the cosmos that is made manifest in you. The psalmist put it so beautifully when he wrote, "I had fainted, unless I had believed to see the goodness of the Lord in the land of the living."[410]So my beloved, Brothers and Sisters, when you first wake in the morning assume as Sister Patti Labelle sings "I got a new attitude", a happy spirit and affirm a positive state of mind. When Brothers and Sisters greet you with "What's happening" answer "Black Folks on the rise". When you lie down on your bed at night, give thanks for the many lessons learned from the day's activities and let yourself drift off to sleep focusing on your life as you really desire it to be. Hold only the visions of the beauty of life and you may be surprised by some of the wonderful things that will happen in your dreams. In fact, a consistent positive mental attitude, awake or sleeping, can bring great changes for good in one's quality of life.

The relationship of the scientific principle(s) Ptah/Atum (Logos) also signifies that what you say should have a solid foundation and be grounded in reality. In the psycho-pictography of the Memphite Drama, Atum the "Logos" principle we have just been discussing also emerged from the primeval waters of Nun through energy emanations that was activated by the "mighty hill" of Ptah. Atum (Atom) attached himself to Ptah by sitting upon the top of the "mighty hill" and becomes the "Unmoved Mover". We will discuss this activity in terms of modern nuclear physics further along in this study but for the moment let us focus on the inter-relationships of the Ptah and Atum principles relative to energy emanation and vibration. To this purpose we draw from the *New English Translation* of the gospel according to Mark 5:25-34 which records the story of a woman who had been suffering for a long time from a chronic physical disorder and who was trying desperately to meet Jesus and ask him for help. The crowd gathered about him was so great she could not gain direct access to this master teacher. Nevertheless when all else failed, the poor

177

unfortunate woman drew upon her inner strength to make the connection through energy emanation and vibration. This is how the story goes:

> "Among them was a woman who had suffered from haemorrhages for twelve years; and in spite of long treatment by many doctors, on which she had spent all she had, there had been no improvement; on the contrary, she had grown worse. She had heard what people were saying about Jesus so she came up from behind in the crowd and touched his cloak; for she said to herself, 'If I touch even his clothes, I shall be cured.' and there and then the source of her hemorrhages dried up and she knew in herself that she was cured of her troubles. At the same time Jesus, aware that power had gone out of him, turned around in the crowd and asked, 'Who touched my clothes'. His disciples said to him, 'You see the crowd pressing upon you and yet you ask, "Who touched me"'. Meanwhile he was looking round to see who had done it. And the woman, trembling with fear when she grasped what had happened to her, came and fell at his feet and told him the whole story. He said to her, 'My daughter, your faith has cured you. Go in peace, free forever from this trouble.'"

The words *"your faith* has cured you" are very significant. Now this woman was in bad shape. She had reached a point of exasperation because she had spent her last dime on doctors and none of them could help her. At this point her attitude was "all or nothing at all". "I have nothing else to lose and everything to gain." So she, at that moment of touching Jesus' garment, released her mental anxieties about the sickness. Some physicians think one reason a disease or sickness can stay in our bodies for extended periods of time is because we accept and allow it to exist there often aiding and abetting it through bad health practices. But if one can arrive at a level of thinking and consciousness wherein you strongly beleive that ill health is not supposed to be a part of your life then one's chances of recovering from sickness and disease is far greater. There are many documented cases of this which remain an enigma to the medical profession, but it should come as no surprise to us. After all every organ in the entire human body is governed by the brain which is the seat of the mind.

Whether this story is true or not, it does illustrate certain cosmic principles;

1) The instance where Jesus became aware that "power had gone out of him" demonstrates how energy can be transferred from one person to another.

2) The fact of the woman's faith being so strong because she was in tune with the possibility of sound health which enabled her to mentally let go of the malady.

We hasten to add it is doubtful this New Testament narrative was intended to be used to justify the rip-off artistry of the so-called faith healers such as overrated television evangelists and the like. We have simply cited this story to show there is a precedent in the scriptures for the transferencè of energy emanation and vibration as set forth in the Memphite Drama's rendering of the scientific principles of Ptah and Atum.

The Greeks called this type of phenomena magic from *magikos* meaning "Magi (wise men)''—those who are able to do that which is beyond the known forces of nature giving the appearance of having control over natural forces through supernatural agents. Europeans refer to this as magic because what they tried to do through brute force, the Kemetan priests achieved by way of spiritual means. For the Afrikan's objective was not to conquer nature but rather to learn her secrets and be at one with her. This gave them the power to offset many of nature's adverse aspects.

In ancient times Black People were very, very proud of their color and felt that because Mother Nature had given them melanin and the sun had blessed them with a rich dark hue, she was a friend instead of a foe which had to be conquered and subdued.

One observer of psychic phenomenon noted that what appears to be magic:

"...is simply an unexplored power of the mind...the purpose of ritual magic is to direct the will, to focus the 'true will'. In his everyday life, man scarcely makes use of his will; he seldom wants anything sufficiently long or sufficiently intensely to summon his 'true will'. For when a man wants something deeply, and believes he can achieve it, he directs all his will towards it; this is the basic act of summoning 'magical' powers."[411]

Because of their profound understanding of this reality:

"according to Herodotus, the Egyptian [Kemetan] Priests possessed super-natural powers, for they had been trained in the esoteric philosophy of the Greater Mysteries, and were experts in Magic. They had the power of controlling the minds of men (hypnosis), the power of predicting the future (prophesy) and the power over nature, (i.e., the power of

Gods) by giving commands in the name of the Divinity and accomplishing great deeds...here it might be well to mention that the Egyptian [Kemetan] Priests were the first genuine Priests of history, who exercised control over the laws of nature...it must also be noted that Magic was applied religion or primitive scientific method."[412]

Again let us emphasize here, when you do not understand what is taking place, it is supernatural to you. Once you understand a principle at work it is no longer perceived as supernatural; for in your new and illuminated understanding, it becomes part of the total scheme of things. I once saw a demonstration of this by a group of Black Folks in Banneker City (District of Columbia) who had been studying the principles of vibration and energy emanation. They came together and formed a circle around a rather large brother sitting on a chair. Each of them simultaneously touched the chair with just the index finger and thumb of each hand joined in the shape of a pyramid. As they moved in unison, they were able to lift it straight up in the air and hold it there with the brother still sitting unstirred upon it. Then with a collective state of mind, they gently returned the chair to solid ground. This was an excellent example of the combined application of psychokinesis and aura power.

Everyone is surrounded by an aura which is the energy field that emits from them in the same manner in which the sun emits energy. This fact has been proven by the use of the Kermean camera which has even photographed the auras of missing limbs of mummified bodies in Cairo, Egypt. For instance, even though the hand of the person was disconnected from the body, the outlining aura was still present after hundreds, sometimes thousands of years. Even in today's world if a person's aura is positively charged by their mental state, they will emit positive energy that will generally be welcomed by those whom they may encounter, but if, as the saying goes, "the vibe is funky", they will let off a negative energy which most likely will drive people away and/or draw adversity. Animals are usually keenly sensitive to people's auras and will react accordingly especially if the vibration is not right. Therefore, it behooves us to learn how to harness and practice using our mental vibrations and aura emanations to help enhance our personal quality of life as well as those of our loved ones, friends, community, nation and race.

Let us stop for a moment and reflect on what life would be like for Afrikan people everywhere if we all practiced this simple aspect of a positive lifestyle. That is what Dr. George G.M. James was talking about when he wrote that for the Afrikans of the ancient High Culture System, the object of all learning was to enable humans "to become godlike and...experience...the liberation of the mind from its finite consciousness, when it becomes one and is identified with the Infinite."

SUMMARY OF THE
PTAH SCIENTIFIC PRINCIPLE

What we have learned thus far in our study of the Memphite Theology is of great importance to us because it involves us in the search for the understanding of the Supreme Principle-the Intelligence underlying the whole universe as made manifest in the earth through the scientific principle of Ptah. Of course we have only begun to scratch the surface of a knowledge and wisdom that was so vast it defies modern man's imagination and stretches so far back in the remote mist of time that its origin is enigmatic. The Memphite Drama is but a fraction of the great body of knowledge that once inspired the entire world and engendered mighty Black civilizations all around the globe. Our contemplation of the Memphite Theology as laid out in these several chapters is designed to further spur the consciousness of our readers to ever evolving levels of illumination and enlightenment with the prayer that it will help us collectively to "create a better condition and a better world".

Concerning the Ptah principle, one of the ancient Kemetan texts reads, "And so it comes to pass that it is said of Ptah: 'He who made everything and brought the gods into being.'... So Ptah was satisfied, after he had made everything, as well as the divine order."[413] According to the Memphite Theology, Ptah did all this but he did not do it alone because Ptah is merely carrying out the will of Divine Intelligence as revealed in the earth. He in turn was assisted in this process by Atum as we shall see. Both Ptah and Atum are revelations of Neter-Nu who each have separate and distinct functions in the creation and maintenance of things relative to planet Earth.

So in summing up Ptah or Ptah-tjenen, he represents the source of all material wealth, prosperity, physical and spiritual well being, boundless substance, endless supply as it is manifested through

181

the soil, rocks, gasses and subterranean liquids of the earth. Ptah, like the other deity symbols of the Memphite Theology we will be discussing, is a particular manifestation of the total whole, the Neter-Nu. Now in order for this divine intelligence of the Neter-Nu to be known and understood by humans on a earthly plane, there are certain principles of science which we need to know and study.

The Memphite Drama tells us that Ptah is the principle of science denoting the awesome power of the Earth's landmass through which the Divine Intelligence reveals itself in and works for the sustenance and use of this planet's inhabitants. In a word the scientific principle of Ptah represents the source of all the earth's material resources. For as previously stated "land is the basic fundamental for all wealth". Therefore, the Provisional Government of the Republic of New Afrika sends forth the challenge to all Afrikan people in the western hemisphere, "Free the Land."

The idea of Ptah rising as a primeval hill out of the waters of Nuni was probably inspired by the many hillets which appeared as though they were emerging from the receding waters of the plains at the end of the annual Hapi (Nile) River innundations. This would naturally have made a strong impression on the creative minds of the Kemetans because the abundance of produce from the rich soil created by this natural phenomena made their nation the richest and the most powerful in the then known world. The copious supplies of food harvested from the black soil of the Hapi Valley also conferred upon ancient Kemet the status of being the breadbasket of the fertile crescent.

CHAPTER THIRTEEN

THE MEMPHITE THEOLOGY AND THE UNMOVED MOVER PRINCIPLE IN ANCIENT AFRIKAN ATOMIC SCIENCE

ATUM: THE ALL AND NOT YET BEING

In the Memphite Drama the deity symbol of Atum is used to describe many aspects and levels of natural science, among them astronomy, physics and atomic energy and of the academic sciences; logic, rhetoric and elocution. In the area of the esoteric sciences, psychokinesis and aura vibrations. In *Stolen Legacy* we read, "The Egyptian [Kemetan] God Atum (Atom) means self created; everything and nothing; a combination of positive and negative principles: all-inclusiveness and emptyness; a Demiurge, possessing creative powers; the Creator Sun."[414] The attributes of Atum cited above such as the "self-created" are various manifestations of the Neter-Nu, The One who actually created all and was not created. When these aspects of the Divine Intelligence are revealed in Atum, he becomes the "Unmoved Mover". Of this Dr. James wrote:

> "I shall now discuss the doctrine of the Unmoved Mover as based upon the same act of creation. According to the Memphite Theology of the Egyptians [Kemetans], Atum created Eight Gods [forces] who proceeded from eight parts of his own body. He was seated upon Ptah the Hill [uranium] and was unmoved. In this act of creation Atum (Atom) became the Unmoved Mover."[415]

In addition, James mentions that Atum is the atom of science and that he also represents the sun in our solar system. Keep that in mind. We will return to this thought later. The Memphite Theology tells us that this same Atum created eight forces who proceeded from eight parts of his body. He was seated upon Ptah the Hill, which in this instance represents uranium, when he did this and was unmoved. In this act of creation, Atum assumes the role of the Unmoved Mover. He created these eight gods which also symbolized certain scientific principles, but they did not create him. So, therefore, in that regard, he is the Unmoved Mover.

As we have just mentioned, Atum is not in and of himself the Unmoved Mover but rather he is acting as an agent receiving energy

183

through Ptah from the true self-created "One" who is the Neter-Nu to accomplish this act. What the Memphite Drama is stressing here is that the Atum principle of the Divine Intelligence, through the act of creating these eight forces out of his own being, is replicating that which was in the very beginning done on the higher level of the Supreme Cosmic Energy which permeates everything and created all things out of its movement and utterance. This concept will become clearer and clearer to us as we continue our progression in this study.

Putting it on a personal level, as the practical aspects of the mystery of the Atum principle unfolds before us, the reader will be able to ascertain as to how we can internalize this principle to become "unmoved movers" in our daily lives.

In his aspect as the "Unmoved Mover" creator of the eight gods (forces), Atum is also known as the "Demiurge". Dr. James says, "It was the function of the Demiurge to create the universe; and in so doing his first act was the creation of the Gods [earthly forces], who accordingly became the first creatures."[416] Demiurge means the intermediate driving force which constitutes, stimulates and gives locomotion to the elements of matter. As an intermediate force it is the avenue through which the Divine Intelligence brought about active living matter on the Earth (Ptah) and also represents the agency through which the creative force sustains active living matter on planet Earth which is Atum in his aspect as the sun. Step-by-step we are getting there. For those who may find the interchanging of Atum's roles a little confusing, stay with me. We will understand it better in just a little while.

THE THERMONUCLEAR POWER OF THE UNMOVED MOVER

Now let us deal with the Atum principle as it applies to modern science. "The atom of science is really the name of the Egyptian [Kemetan] Sun God that has come down to modern times...and carries identical attributes, with the Sun God."[417] All material things on the Earth consist of matter. Matter occupies a given space, but when matter is altered by radiant energy i.e., intense heat or cold, as in the instances when iron ore is melted into a liquid state by intense heat and the flowing liquidity of water can become a hard block of ice if frozen by extremely cold temperatures.

184

Matter is composed of molecules. The same is true of all the atmospheric elements known as energy such as air, heat, cold, moisture, electricity, etc.. Molecules in turn are constructed of atoms. For example, one tiny drop of water contains billions of molecules made up of three atoms each; a total of three billion atoms. Atoms are composed of the smallest unit of matter known as particles. The major three are protons, neutrons and electrons. The protons and neutrons reside in the nucleus which is the heart and center of the atom. The electrons orbit the nucleus in much the same manner as the planets in our solar system orbit the sun. The path traveled by the orbiting electrons are known as energy levels. A speck of dust barely perceptible to the human eye may contain nearly a billion atoms. Everything on this planet and in its atmosphere contains atoms and molecules. That is why the ancient Afrikan High Culture Scientists described the atom (Atum) as the Unmoved Mover who created all things because atoms are everywhere and in everything.

Let us stop here and reflect for a moment. Just imagine! This kind of knowledge was known to our Afrikan ancestors thousands of years ago; many millenia before the Greek, Roman or any other type of civilization other than those founded by the Kushites existed. In other words, Black People were the first and only people to possess this knowledge for thousands upon thousands of years. This is clearly evident in the Memphite Drama which was in a state of revision at the founding of the First Dynasty by Pharaoh Aha Menes ca. 5500 BCE.

In the interest of clarity, we will stop here for a moment and interject some factual reasons as to why this author prefers to use 5500 BCE as the date for the uniting and upper and lower Kemet.

Euro-centric Egyptologists generally set the date for this event between 3400-3100 BCE because many of them cannot entertain the thought of an Afrikan Civilization being some 5,000 or more years antecedent to Greece—the first Caucasian civilization. However, some European scholars such as Petrie, Unger, MacNaughton and Champollion-Figeac base their dynastic charts on the calculations of Manetho, an indigenous Kemetan of the 3rd Century BCE, who developed the dynastic system for recording the various periods of pharaohic rule from the time of the uniting of the many kingdoms and city/states of upper and lower Kemet into one great nation. Manetho received his information directly from the Kemetan priests/scientists who had been keeping the records of their people's long history bequeathed to them from generation-togeneration.

Resuming our contemplation of atomic science as revealed in the principle of Atum, we observe that by sitting on the pinnacle of "the Mighty Hill" Atum/Atom enables the matter of earth (Ptah) which may be confined in a particular space to become radiant energy which moves beyond the boundaries of that space. This is known as atomic power. One of the methods of obtaining atomic energy is by splitting the atom. This is called nuclear fission. Uranium, a radioactive metallic ore, is the main catalyst used in this process. For example, "the fission of one gram of uranium yields about 23,000 kilowatt-hours of energy, enough to light a medium-sized apartment building for a month."[418]

Let us reiterate this concept again as it is stated in the Memphite Theology and correlate it with today's scientific language. What enables the atom to be split; what is the element you have to utilize to split the atom? Uranium. Where does uranium come from? From Ptah. And what is Ptah? A symbol of the earth's resources. So when Atum/Atom sits of the hill of Ptah, he becomes the Unmoved Mover because the force of Ptah in his aspect as uranium splits Atum the atom and he sends forth energy. The energy of this nuclear fission creates new forms of life. The eight gods (forces of nature) which we will investigate a little later on. Also with this action a great explosion occurred and the awesome utterance of Atum was heard.

Obviously the Kemetan High Culture Scientists who set down the principles of the Memphite Drama were very well acquainted with the science of atomic energy and knew that "Atomic energy originates from water and earth, since water, H20, and uranium, an indispensable ingredient in atomic energy is found in the bowels of the Earth." They noted "that both Atom and the Hill came out of the primeval Waters."[419] Just think, water and the earth produces the forces you need to split the atom to bring forth nuclear energy in the world was a fact known by the Afrikan at least 7,500 or maybe even as much as 20,000 years ago. Wow! The knowledge of this historical reality alone does wonders for the mind.

Atomic fission and fusion is much too engaging a subject for us to go into any further here. However, we have cited these few basic facts about the creation of atomic energy to show the correlation between "modern science" and the High Culture Science of ancient Kemet as illustrated by the Ptah and Atum scientific symbols of the Memphite Drama.

186

As you may recall, we started out being informed by Dr. George G.M. James that "the Memphite Theology is the source of modern scientific knowledge" and that "the atom of science is Atum the Kemetan sun god". In fact, most encyclopedias render the phonetic spelling of atom, AT-um. "Atum (Atom) also means the all and the not yet Being." Because an atom possesses the potential to become more than what it is. Once uranium (Ptah) unites in thermolysis with the atom (Atum) and the atom is split, it therefore creates another force or other forces by reproducing itself.

Because of their profound understanding of this scientific reality, our wise Afrikan ancestors believed that for us there was no such thing as death, only the last rite of passage from the Earthly plane to the realm of everlasting cosmic energy. This idea was based in part on their familiarity with the fact that the atoms and molecules which constitute our total being—mentally, physically and spiritually are indestructible because they are a part of the Eternal energy that has always existed. Thus at the time of our physical departure from this life, our atoms and molecules are released and live on in the atmosphere to become one with the incalculable zillions of ancestral atoms in the cosmos and are in some fashion manifested in other forms and substances i.e., our children, grandchildren and other members of our posterity. In this sense Afrikan people are eternal because this process goes all the way back to the first humans who emerged on planet Earth some two or more million years ago.

The original Black Race also thought of this concept in terms of the sacred act of procreation which perpetuates the human species making it "eternal". Thus establishing our mystic bond with the neverending cycle of life. For just as within the atom, interaction between protons and electrons, under certain conditions, can cause an alteration of the nuclei resulting in a tremendous release of energy which creates new forms of molecules, so it is with the dynamic bonding of the masculine and feminine energies of the Black Man and Woman which can create new life on a spiritual as well as a physical level.

Dr. James says in the Memphite Theology the atom of science also "...represents the principle of opposites, and shows the identity between the Egyptian [Kemetans] Sun God and the substratum of matter." The principle of opposites is demonstrated by the atom (Atum) through the interrelationship of its latent and active powers; protons, positive electrical charges and electrons,

187

negative electrical charges which brings us back to the cosmic reality that everything in the universe functions on two basic underlying principles. The interplay between feminine and masculine energies. That is why many traditional Afrikans began their prayers and meditations with the invocation "Mother/Father God" because they recognized the opposite principles of the masculine and feminine operating in harmony in the "Creative Force". Let me hasten to say—in case some might misconstrue—that the unity of the masculine and feminine principles on the cosmic level does not in any way whatsoever condone homosexuality in the human experience. I am stating this so emphatically here because some who are inclined in the direction of such a lifestyle have attempted to read into the spiritual/scientific function of male/female unity in the spiritual realm a validation for their unsavory acts. But there is no basis for this in the historical reality of ancient Afrikan High Culture civilizations. For as Dr. Yosef ben Jochannon says, "In these societies, faggots were not tolerated." Again we emphasize the two DISTINCT principles of female and male energies meet in the Divine Intelligence to PRODUCE new life and ever reoccurring cycles.

Now we will discuss "the identity between the [Kemetan] sun god and the substratum of matter". Why is Atum the atom identified with the sun? Because the sun's power that is generated to planet Earth is the result of atomic power. The extremely high temperatures of the sun's surface causes thermonuclear fusion changing the nuclei within the atoms that make up the sun and the atomic reaction sends forth light and heat ninety-three million miles from its surface to the surface of our planet penetrating the earth and energizing its substratum. Without this atomic power from the sun, few, if any, life forms could exist on planet Earth. That is why the sun was such an important deity symbol in ancient Kemetan High Culture Science because it exemplifies, like no other physical entity in our solar system, the sustaining power of the Creative Force in the entire universe. Our ancestors did not worship the sun; they merely reverenced it. They worshipped Almighty God, yet they reverenced the sun as a conduit for the power and energy of the Divine Intelligence as it relates to planet Earth. To them it was the most obvious way that the Supreme Being reveals itself to this world.

Another reason why Atum was identified with the sun is because just like the atom, the sun has three basic components;

188

1) the substance of the sun that is its mass, similar to the nucleus of the atom, 2) the light of the sun which emanates from the million mile wide circumference of its corona, an equivalent of the atom's proton(s), 3) the heat of the sun which is created by thermonuclear fission on its surface and travels ninety-three million miles through space to warm planet Earth, a type of the electrons in an atom which journey freely in their orbital paths of energy levels. In another instance:

> "the structure of an atom can be compared with that of the solar system. In the sun's position, the atom has a tiny, dense nucleus made up of protons and neutrons. In place of the planets, it has electrons that orbit (whirl) unceasingly around the nucleus. Like the solar system, the atom is mostly space. The extremely small nucleus contains all but a tiny fraction of the atom's mass."[420]

THE ATOMIC POWER OF
THE SPOKEN WORD

The creative power of speech is demonstrated thusly in an ancient Kemetan scripture.

> "It is the heart [mind] which causes every completed concept to come forth, and it is the tongue which announces what the heart [mind] thinks. Thus all the gods [forces] were formed... indeed, all the divine order came into being through what the heart [mind] thought and the tongue commanded...Thus were made all work, and all crafts, the action of the arms, the movement of the legs, and the activity of every member of the body, in conformance with the command which the heart [mind] thought, which came forth through the tongue, and which gives the value of everything."[421]

Dr. James elucidates:

> "It is now clear that by making contact with Ptah, Atum immediately received the attributes of Ptah's
> creative thought and speech and omnipotence and became the instrument and the Logos and the Demiurge, through whom the task of creation was undertaken and completed...The qualities or attributes of entities [energies], human or divine, are distributed throughout their various parts, and contact with such entities [energies], releases those qualities."[422]

Let us briefly analyze this concept of the Logos once again. Everything in the world began as a thought then became a word defining the thought because a thought has no real power in the creative process unless it sends forth its vibration which is the power of the spoken word. The word defines the thought and eventually it becomes a tangible reality. Consequently, the ancients believed the utterance of a name which has never before been spoken was in and of itself an act of creation which evoked atomic energy in the ethers causing all things and beings to be brought into existence because they knew and clearly understood speaking a word brings forth certain vibrations which causes energies to be put into motion. That is why correct and orderly speech was so important to them as demonstrated in the Kemetan Mystery System curriculum i.e., grammar, rhetoric, logic, etc. It was understood then even as it should be understood now that what is said out of your mouth can determine your state of being and set the stage for what goes on around you. That is why artifacts of the three monkeys, hear, speak and see no evil motif, has become a very popular curio in many cultures. This ancient Kemetan scientific principle of commanding utterance is revised and expressed in the psalms thusly.

"Praise the Lord, O heavens! Praise him from the skies! Praise him, all his angels, all the armies of heaven. Praise him, sun and moon, and all you twinkling stars. Praise him, skies above. Praise him, vapors high above the clouds. Let everything he has made give praise to him. For he issued his command, and they came into being;..."[423]

This text illustrates the principle of the power of the word bringing life into being as demonstrated through Atum in the Memphite Theology. Note how celestial objects such as clouds, the sun, moon and stars are accorded the gift of speech which indicates that everything in the cosmos has an audible sound vibration. This is also portrayed in Psalms 19:1-3. "The heavens declare the glory of God; and the firmament showeth his handiwork. Day unto day uttereth speech, and night unto night showeth knowledge. There is no speech nor language, where their voice is not heard."[424]

Now we will examine one of the many manifestations of the scientific principle of Atum of the Memphite Theology as revised and expressed in Christian theology.

"Even the mystery which hath been hid from ages and from generations, but now is made manifest to his saints...For by him were all things created, that are in heaven, and that are in earth...all things were created by him, and for him...Who is the image of the invisible God, the first born of ever creature...and he is before all things, and by him all things consist."[425]

Here the writer is speaking of the Christianized concept of Jesus in the same context that we have read about Atum/Atom who is the image of the invisible God, the revelation of the Divine Intelligence made visible through the movement of the Demiurge, the Unmoved Mover as demonstrated in the force of the atom and the lifegiving energy of the sun. Atum/Atom is in all things in the earth, visible and invisible, carrying out the will of Neter-Nu the One. The portion of the New Testament text which reads "Even the mystery which hath been hid from ages and from generations" is an admission of the fact that the principle of the Unmoved Mover the Demiurge, the atom, the atomic force which moves in all matter and energy as described in this scripture has been taken directly out of the Mystery System of ancient Kemetan High Culture Science. Dr. Alvin Boyd Kuhn makes this even plainer by observing the fact that the mysteries transmitted to the Bible were not fully understood by the Judaic and Christian scribes attempting to translate:

"...from the scrolls of papyri five thousand to ten thousand years old...Long after Egypt's [Kemet's] voice expressed through the inscribed hieroglyphics [Medu Netcher] was hushed and silenced, the perpetuated relics of Hamitic [Kushite] wisdom, with their cryptic message utterly lost, were brought forth and presented to the world by parties of ignorant zealots as a new body of truth..."[426]

Dr. George G.M. James explains to us how and why the original philosophy of the Kemetan priests/scientists, as recorded in the Memphite Theology was co-opted and corrupted by early Christian theologians:

"And now we come to the third actor, and that is Ancient Rome, who through the edicts of her Emperors Theodosius in the 4th Century A.D. [CE] and Justinian in the 6th Century A.D. [CE] abolished the Mysteries of the African Continent; that is the ancient culture system of the world. The higher metaphysical doctrines of those Mysteries could not be comprehended; the spiritual powers of the priests were so unsurpassed; the magic of the rites and ceremonies filled the people with awe; Egypt [Kemet] was the holy land of the ancient world; and the Mysteries were the one, ancient and holy catholic [universal] religion, whose power was supreme. This lofty culture system of the Black people filled Rome with envy, and consequently she legalized Christianity which she had persecuted for five long centuries, and set it up as a state religion and as a rival of the Mysteries its own mother. This is why the Mysteries have been despised; this is why other ancient religions of the Black people are despised; because they are all offspring of the African Mysteries which have never been clearly understood by Europeans... The result of this was (a) misrepresentation and erroneous opinion that the Afrikan Continent and people are backward in culture and have made no contribution to civilization and (b) the establishment of Christianity as a rival against the Mysteries of the African System of Culture, in order to perpetuate this erroneous opinion."[427]

The main point that Dr. James keeps emphasizing in his brilliant and illuminating book, *Stolen Legacy*, is that the ancient scientific knowledge which was created by the Black Race and eventually given to the world was co-opted by a people who did not understand it. Europeans simply could not, then and even today cannot, comprehend the true meaning of the symbolism of Afrikan philosophy and religion and even though through underhandedness, betrayal and military conquests, they stole it; they caused the world to lose sight of the deep significance of the scientific principles it represented. Dr. John G. Jackson cites a very good example of this during the days when the Kemetans taught the Greeks.

"...the Greeks got many of their gods from the Egyptians [Kemetans]; but neither the Romans nor the Greeks really understood the symbolism or mythology of the Egyptians [Kemetans]. These Europeans turned the gods into men, and the esoteric meaning of the old religion was lost; and hence the ancient beliefs finally passed into a state of innocuous desuetude. The old gods after being humanized became objects of ridicule rather than adoration."[428]

Concerning the eight gods (forces of nature) created by Atum, we have already described them in Chapter Two. The Kemetan Cosmogonical Sphere in the Ancient World. At this juncture we shall briefly reintroduce them and what they represented in terms of ancient Afrikan Astro-Mythological scientific symbology and then

192

explore their combined aspects in relationship to the scientific disciplines of astronomy and physics.

The eight primary forces of nature created by Atum the Atom are collectively referred to as the Ennead. This designation also includes Atum, their inaugurator making a total of nine gods.

THE ANCIENT COMPUTER SYMBOLS
OF THE ENNEAD

The act of creation which took place while Atum remained unmoved as he embraced Ptah—which we have already discussed from the standpoints of astronomy, physics, logic and esoterics— produced the family of nine gods which included Atum himself who came to be known as the Ennead, a Greek word which means "a group of nine".

The cosmic universal principles as symbolized by Ptah, Atum, the Ennead, and other deity symbols of the forces of nature are constant and they remain unchanged in the universe. Yet because of the manifold concerns of the human experience, they are progressively made manifest in various dimensions. What we are saying here—based upon the philosophy of the High Culture science and religion created by our ancient Afrikan ancestors—is that which existed from the beginning and even before there was a beginning in terms of this world, the Divine Intelligence of the universe which permeates all things is a constant unchanged Supreme Principle, but is made manifest to planet Earth in a variety of ways. So when we talk about Ptah, we are talking about a dimension of The One, The First Cause, the Supreme Being. When we speak of Atum, the Ennead or any other gods or goddesses, we are speaking about specific dimensions of Neter-Nu, the one Almighty God.

As we established at the onset of our investigation of the Memphite Theology *Afrikans worshipped the One Supreme God Force in an absolute monotheism* expressed externally through the manifold manifestations of that Eternal Force which they graphically projected through the use of many signs and symbols. This Astro-Mythological Scientific Symbolism was an essential ingredient of their High Culture civilizations. Dr. Asa Hilliard, III tells us that in ancient Kemet, science preceded religion because both were founded on the observation and study of the laws of nature. Consequently, the priests were also scientists.[429] To the Afrikan way of thinking, there was no real difference between the two. Religion has only been at odds with science since Eurasians and Europeans, after many unsuccessful attempts, finally invaded and militarily subdued ancient Kemet. It is with this understanding that Dr. James wrote, "It is quite clear that the concept of the 'Unmoved Mover' is derived from the Egyptian [Kemetan] theological or mystery system, and not from Aristotle [the Greek], as the modern world has been made to believe."[430]

The scientific symbols of the Ennead as depicted in the Memphite Theology functionally served the ancient Afrikan High Culture priests/scientists and their students in much the same manner as computer symbols are employed in modern technology and science today.

CHAPTER FOURTEEN

DESCRIPTION AND FUNCTION OF THE NINE POWERS OF ANCIENT AFRIKAN ASTRO-ATOMIC SCIENCE

We will now briefly delineate the descriptions of these nine gods and their areas of function. These are the forces of order and arrangement in the cosmos and they are represented in one godhead called the Ennead. As stated Atum is the immediate source of eight of them which he sends forth from his own body as four pairs, male and female. Thus creating eight god forces who together with himself becomes nine. The Memphite Drama describes these eight forces of nature as Shu and Tefnut (Air and Moisture), Geb and Nut (Earth and Sky), Ausaru and Auset—whom the Greeks called Osiris and Isis—(the Hapi River and the rich soil of its banks), Set and Nepthys (the darkness of night and its tranquility). Here is the manner in which each of them functioned:

Shu—portrayed as a masculine force which denotes the atmosphere which surrounds planet Earth and the air we live and breathe in. This personification of a natural force in the Memphite Drama is characterized in the Genesis record thusly. ''And God said, Let there be a firmament [atmosphere] in the midst of the waters, and let it divide the waters from the waters. And God made the firmament [atmosphere], and divided the waters which were under the firmament [atmosphere] from the waters which were above the firmament [atmosphere]: and it was so.''[431]

Tefnut—his feminine consort is the moisture in organic things which keeps them from drying up and dying. When a living breathing thing dehydrates it is because the power of Tefnut is no longer with them.

Geb—a masculine force which in this particular manifestation is localized earth. That is a certain territory or parcel of land. As you will recall the symbol for the whole Earth and its resources is Ptah. Ptah-tgenen is the world. Geb is a place in it.

195

Nut or Nuit—the sky over that earth which is a feminine force. Nuit is the heaven wherein dwells the sun, moon and stars to whom she gives birth each day and night and every month.

Ausaru (Osiris)—the Hapi River which fertilizes the soil during its annual innundations. He also represents the masculine aspect of the moon.

Auset (Isis)—the alluvial deposits along the shores of the Hapi River who absorbs the potency of the Hapi's (Ausaru's) waters into her earthly womb and brings forth new life in the form of the Hapi Valley's abundant crops. She is the nourisher, the mother-force of nature at its best. She also represents the feminine qualities of the moon.

Set or Sut Nashi—Although this was not always his role, in this instance he represents the dry desert darkness and man's primitive fear of the darkness.

Nephthys or Nebthet—is the female principle in the unseen world. She is the tranquil ethers which makes the darkness of night peaceful and serene. Nebthet takes the fear out of darkness.

Ausaru and Auset later had a son, Heru (Horus), who represented the light of Atum in his aspect as the sun and thus brought light out of darkness. The Hebrew scribes recorded it this way:

"In the beginning God created the heaven and the earth. And the earth was without form, and void; and darkness was upon the face of the deep. And the Spirit of God moved upon the face of the waters. And God said, Let there be light: and there was light. And God saw the light, that it was good: and God divided the light from the darkness. And God called the light Day, and the darkness he called Night, and the evening and the morning was the first day."[432]

In scientific terms what is being conveyed here is the geological fact that this terrestrial ball, Earth, was in darkness for millions of years before the light of the sun began to penetrate its atmosphere and generate life in the seas and landmass on this planet. How all of this relates to the geological evolution of Planet Earth will be discussed in Volume Two of this series, *Afrikan Genesis: An Historical Reality* which is a study in common sense geology and grass roots anthropology. We believe our readers will really enjoy the way the subjects are handled in this work. For it sets forth these sciences in the language most of us can understand.

Note how all the elements of nature represented by eight of the scientific symbols of the Ennead, each of them being portions of energy and matter consisting of atoms (Atum), are influenced by Atum the sun which governs this solar system. For a more detailed description of the various members of the Ennead, godhead, see Chapter Two.

THE HELIO-CENTRIC
SYSTEM OF THE
NEBULAR HYPOTHESIS

In all that we have been talking about so far, we have been dealing with science in its various dimensions of the physical, the spiritual and the mental. Now we come to view a synthesis of the Ennead which brings it home to our understanding of science today. It is called the Heliocentric Philosophy or the Nebular Hypothesis. Helio-centric means "sun centered" and signifies the sun as the center and focal point of our solar system. Nebular Hypothesis denotes a supposition supported by seemingly probable known data.

"According to the nebular hypothesis our present solar system was once a molten gaseous nebular [luminous cloud] this nebular rotated at an enormous speed as the mass cooled down it also contracted and developed greater speed. The result was a bulging at the equator and a gradual breaking off of gaseous rings, which formed themselves into planets. These planets in turn threw off gaseous rings, which formed themselves into smaller bodies, until at last the sun was left as the remnant of the original parent Nebular. From this context it is clear that the original parent nebular was fire or the Sun, and that by throwing off parts of itself, it created some planets, which in

197

turn threw off parts of themselves and created others. According to the context of the Memphite Theology, the creator God was the Sun God or fire God Atum (Atom), who named four pairs of parts of his own body, from which Gods came forth."[433]

In our day we understand there are nine planets which revolve around the sun, but in the Memphite Theology Atum was the sun and at the same time one of the planets that orbited with the other eight around the sun. It appears the objective of the Kemetan High Culture scientists was to state this; planet Earth—naturally being the one we live on—was the one that contained more of the sun's elements and power, that special part of Atum. What we are looking at in the Memphite Theology in regards to the tradition of the creation of the Ennead is a scientific and esoteric expression of the creation of the nine major planets in this solar system. In this we get a glimpse of the enormous and incalculable intelligence of the Kemetan High Culture scientists who also observed and recorded the fact there are nine oraficial openings in the human body, seven of them in the head and that it takes an average of nine months gestation to bring forth a child. All of this and so much more was a part of ancient Afrikan cosmic science.

Again Dr. James cites:

" . . . in this story of the created Gods by Atum the Sun God into a family of nine i.e., the Ennead, we have the original source of two important scientific hypotheses of modern times: (1) There are nine major planets and (2) The Sun is the parent of the other planets (This latter being supported by the Nebular Hypothesis)...At any rate, the entire setting of the Memphite Theology is astronomical, and what could be more natural, than to expect an astronomical interpretation?"[434]

What we have been observing here in the Memphite Drama is the study of the science of the world's beginnings in all its dimensions as perceived by the High Culture priests/scientists of ancient Kemet; the essence of which is Creation was accomplished by the will of the Divine Intelligence Neter-Nu through the harmony and balance of two creative principles the unity of the Mind with the Logos, creative utterance.

THE MEMPHITE THEOLOGY
A KEY TO SUCCESSFUL
SCIENTIFIC RESEARCH

In summation, the Memphite Drama sets forth the basic cosmogonical (origin of the world) philosophy of Hapi Valley High Culture civilization in mainly the scientific symbol language of astronomy and nuclear physics among other sciences. Being the world's earliest scientists and among the first original Afrikan nations to observe the heavens and record the orbital paths of their celestial bodies and whose priests understood and documented the laws of physics, the Kemetans would naturally project the psycho-pictographic images of their creation stories in this manner. As was said the Memphite Theology was the matrix and set the basic pattern and philosophy of all succeeding cosmogonies i.e., the creation stories of Sumer, Arabia, Persia, India, Babylon, Judea and many other nations.

Note, the language of the Memphite Drama, though written in simular astro-mythological terms, is somewhat "heavier" in scientific disciplines than the others which as time went on—though maintaining the same basic principles— became more and more personified and allegorical. This may have been due to the fact the further the original Kushite civilizations moved from their centers of operation in the heartland of Alkebulan (Afrika) where the knowledge transference systems were first invented, the various local geographical differences and cultural nuances of their multiplicity of global civilizations required an alteration of language and style in the psycho-pictographic projection of their many creation stories. It should also be understood that in the ancient cosmogonies we are dealing with ideas that have been in existence for an extremely long time. In the case of the Kemetan civilization alone, they may have been transmitted from generation to generation for eighteen thousand or more years.

The reason why some of these concepts may appear to be so complex to us today is because these brilliant Afrikans were able to take the same scientific principle and make it represent a variety of aspects and nuances of natural phenomena. They could take one god or goddess symbol and apply it a "thousand different ways". That is why their knowledge and achievements were so awesome. George G.M. James says:

"What science knows about (a) the number of major planets (b) how these major planets were created by the Sun and (c) the attributes of the atom has been traced to the Cosmology of the Memphite Theology, which suggests that (d) science knows only 1/5 of the secrets of creation and therefore 4/5 of such secrets yet remains to be discovered (e) consequently The Memphite Theology offers great possibilities for modern scientific research."[453]

Imagine this. Today's world of modern science and technology has hardly touched the surface of the infinite knowledge and wisdom of the cosmos as it was understood by the original Black Race. The rediscovery and reclaiming of that knowledge presents a great opportunity for Afrikan People in particular and the world in general to enhance the quality of life on planet Earth and get back to, among other things, the business of solving the mystery of life and death. Dr. James wrote in the year 1954, "I believe that the time has come, within which man will be able to unlock most of the secrets of nature hitherto hidden and unknown." This extraordinary scholar further stated:

"Successful scientific research in the principles and secrets of nature lies in the study of the Memphite Theology, whose symbology requires the key of magical [spiritual] principles for its interpretation. With this approach our men of science should be able to unlock the doors of the secrets of nature and become the custodian of unlimited knowledge."[436]

Yes, my beloved Brothers and Sisters, we can once again become the "custodians of unlimited knowledge" through the rediscovery, recovery and redemption of the ancient Afrikan High Culture Science. This sacred mission requires diligent and disciplined study and investigation; however, it is a joyful task filled with wonder and excitement at each renewed revelation of our true place in world history, culture and science. Yet simply gaining this "accurate information" as illuminating as it may be is not enough to re-establish us as "the custodians of unlimited knowledge". We must also embrace this resurrected knowledge as did the Kemetan priests of old with the power of *magikos*. The tern "magic" as applied here is in reference to those spiritual principles which will enable us to transcend the limited knowledge of this present world and infuse us with cosmic consciousness through our collective and

200

individual efforts of attunement and oneness with The One, the Supreme Divine Intelligence which permeates everything in the universe. The Bible describes this state of being as:

"...the peace of God, which passeth all understanding...Finally, bretheren, whatsoever things are true, whatsoever things are honest, whatsoever things are just, whatsoever things are pure, whatsoever things are lovely, whatsoever things are of good report; if there be any virtue and if there be any praise think on these things."[437]

"Whatsoever things are of good report...think on these things", that is to say even though one may have to sometimes acknowledge the negative in order to find ways of correcting a given situation as it relates to quality of life, you should still at all times maintain a positive attitude towards yourself and Black People and the world in general. Even when it is necessary for you to commit a harsh or violent act in self-defense or the defense of those in your care and keeping such as children, elders, etc.—which is the divinely ordained right of all creatures. In such instances, in order to insure that you do not become consumed by bitterness, intense hatred and bloodlust, you must remain balanced within through a positive mental attitude. This was the way of the mighty Afrikan warriors of antiquity and is the generally the attitude of our freedom fighters today. "Do what you gotta do, but don't let it do you." This is "the peace of God, which passeth all understanding."

When you have reached the place where you are able to walk around in a chaotic world at peace with yourself, a large part of that attitude is probably the result of knowing you are a part of a people who —despite the fact that many of them might not know it — are the eternal force of the godpower in the universe manifested on the Earth itself. If ever there were a chosen people in the history of the world, surely the rediscovery of this ancient knowledge points to the original Black Man and Woman. For no other people have ever taken the time to systematically record and embody this great knowledge of the universe into such a magnificent system as the Memphite Drama and the ancient Mystery System of High Culture education of which we in our time have only begun to scratch the surface. This is the legacy that your and my ancestors bequeathed to us and today, with that knowledge, we can now go into the Bible or any other record or institution and recognize and extract from it the knowledge that was once stolen from us,

201

then take that knowledge and use it both for personal and collective empowerment.

As we bring this chapter and this study to a close, it is fitting that Dr. George G.M. James, from whose work we have been drawing so heavily, should have the last word:

> "This is the legacy of the African Continent to the nations of the world. She has laid the cultural foundations of modern progress and therefore she and her people deserve the honor and praise which for centuries has been falsely given to the Greeks."[438]

EPILOGUE

AWAKENING THE SLEEPING GIANT WITHIN

It is our hope that the information we have been sharing with our readers in Volume One, *Afrikan Genesis: Amazing Stories of Man's Beginning* will not only be beneficial in terms of the personal and collective enrichment which liberated knowledge of this sort can bring to a people but, will also be of practical use to our readers in their daily walks of life. Therefore, in keeping with this thought, we will now consider how we can internalize the information we have been discussing throughout this book especially the last three chapters.

At this juncture let us re-emphasize the historical reality that in these various creation stories, our wise ancient Afrikan ancestors clearly understood the deity symbols of Astro-Mythological Cosmogony they employed in them. Every symbol, every god and goddess was just another way of expressing some dimension of the Universal Divine Intelligence commonly known as God. The one people on Earth who at one time understood this better than any other were Black People. They were the first to perceive it and even though many of us are presently cut off from the ancient knowledge and science of the eternals, we can still find our way back to it. For most of us still have some sense of the Eternal Presence within us.

Some sincere European scholars, such as Gerald Massey, Godfrey Higgins, Albert Churchward and a few others, have been able intellectually, though on the surface level, to correlate the signs and symbols of the ancient Afrikan High Culture Scientists with the religious imagery of the "modern" world, but they have not been able to understand them spiritually. Apparently that is for us to do. On the other hand, Euro-centric scholars attempting to interpret the secret knowledge of the ancient Black Race in the light of Greek-centric western culture and Europeanized Judeo-Christianity or any other kind of essentially white-supremist dogma is like dwarfs nibbling at the heels of sleeping giants.

Now the giants are awakening and we must be about the business of setting the record straight in a collective as well as a personal sense. A careful and diligent study of world history reveals that by reason of our preeminence on Earth—for Afrikans were the first humans on the planet— Black People are the direct descendents

203

of Almighty God; therefore, we must act like it. Not in arrogant and braggadocio display, but rather through the proper utilization of the marvelous creation of our human brain computers which can contain anywhere from 10-20 billion brain cells, each capable of receiving, recording, storing, recalling and transmitting knowledge and by spiritually keeping ourselves in tune with the Divine Universal Intelligence and attuned to the goodness in our people.

It was not our objective here to convince anyone of the existence of a universal Creative Force or to proselytize any of our readers into devotedly believing in any of the many deity manifestations which have been perceived and expressed in throughout the ages. But rather to simply state the reality that the movement of the Primal Cosmic Energy is revealed according to an individual's perception of the hand of Divine Order moving in the midst of things in their life's experience and collectively in direct relationship to a people's historical and cultural understanding of the omnipotent cycle of natural law. This, therefore, places an individual's experience with and belief in the Creator on a very personal level and not logically subject to debate.

Our main purpose has been to focus on Astro-Mythological concepts of Cosmic Habit Force as comprehended in tangible and measurable scientific and historical evidence. Yet, there is still the very real and undeniable, though unmeasurable, spiritual dimension of the cosmos as is so vitally evident on the personal level in the secret self of one's psychic life which, though not generally understood in today's world, was clearly understood by the ancient Afrikan, and that is why they were able to develop such a highly complex science and society.

We do not mean to suggest that the awareness of the spiritual sphere is non-existent today. For there are those among us who definitely are attuned and most of us have flashes of psychic phenomena at various times in our lives, but none of this is on the level it was or can be. That is why Article One of the New Afrikan Creed, ''I believe in the spirituality, humanity and genius of Black people, and in our new pursuit of these values'', is so apropos.[439]

Afrikan people were the first to recognize and define the spiritual qualities in man and nature. This was mainly inspired by their conceptualization of Ma'at, the ''feminine wisdom'', principle which may go back as far as 100,000 years before the present. For a discussion and historical overview of this topic, see *Afrikan Woman: The Original Guardian Angel* by this author.

The priests of ancient Kemetan High Culture Science taught that the object of all evolution and learning was to achieve total oneness with the Divine Mind. On the human level, this was to be accomplished in part by divesting one's self of ultra-materialistic external influences and superficial ego-states. One of the methods they used to reconcile man's spiritual nature with his biological being and thereby achieve divine equilibrium was through the practice and personal development of the Ten Virtues.

1) Control of thought

2) Control of action

3) Steadfastness (fortitude)

4) Identity with higher ideals (temperance)

5) Evidence of a mission (goal and purpose)

6) Evidence of a call to spiritual order (deep insight)

7) Freedom from resentment (courage)

8) Confidence in the power of the Master Teacher (fidelity to one's qualified instructors)

9) Confidence in one's own learning abilities

10) Preparedness for initiation (scholarly pursuit)

For more information on the Ten Virtues, we suggest reading *Stolen Legacy*, Chapter Three. Note that at the top of the list of the Ten Virtues is control of thought. Of the several basic concepts we have learned from our examination of the Memphite Theology, among the most compelling in this author's estimation are; 1) thought is the beginning of all things, 2) conditions are the outward expression of thought, 3) change of thought patterns result in the eventual change of conditions and circumstances.

On this theme, we shall draw this work to its conclusion with some thoughts on the awesome magic of the mind.

- The process by which thoughts become things is rooted in the One Intelligence from which all things are made. Everything is conscious and has a form that is determined by the awareness entraped within.

- Human beings are truly mental creatures and those animal qualities they possess are residual only. Left over from an evolution whose great thrust in the first place was its effort to produce mind.

- When one makes up in their mind that intellect is superior to and supersedes matter, is to take the most important step of all in the living of a serene and effective life. The soul grows within even as the body decays without and one who is able in the end to merge his/her sense of being with that of the Secret Self has perpetuated himself/herself into eternity, has achieved immortality. The individual may achieve this through a proper relationship between the ego and the Universal Mind by immersing the lesser ego in his/her wider being and becoming one with The One.

- A psychological transformation is not possible without a spiritual awakening and before one can change one's kind and type of thinking, it is first necessary for one to alter their conception of self.[440]

A positive self-concept is the main determinant in one's quality of life. That is why the rediscovery and reclamation of our true historical reality is so vitally important to us because it aids us in establishing the proper "concept of self".

Dear Readers, I have truly enjoyed taking this journey with you as we have mentally and spiritually traveled to so many fabulous places and learned so many wonderful things. Until we meet again let us close with a benediction in the form of an affirmation.

Realizing that our wise ancestors perceived that the ultimate purpose of all learning was to enable us to become more god-like and be in harmony with the spheres, I apply my Divinely implanted powers to liberate the mind and expand the consciousness. From this day forward I will never be the same. Therefore, I march into the future joyfully, helping to "create a better world and a better condition than man has yet known" Amen.

NOTES AND BIBLIOGRAPHY

1. *Black Christian Nationalism: New Directions for the Black Church*, Albert B. Cheage, Jr., William Morrow & Company, Inc., New York. 1972, pp. xxv-xxvi.
2. *Man, God, and Civilization*, John G. Jackson, University Books, Inc., New Hyde Park, N.Y. 1972, p. 36.
3. *The Destruction of Black Civilization*, Chancellor Williams. Third World Press, Chicago, Illinois. 1974, p. 89.
4. *Introduction to Black Civilizations*, John G. Jackson, The Citadel Press, Seacaucus, New Jersey. 1970, pp. 3-4.
5. *Introduction to Black Studies*, Maulana Karenga, Kawaida Publications, Inglewood, Calif. 1982, pp. 50-51.
6. *The Destruction of Black Civilization*, Chancellor Williams. (See above), p. 89.
7. *The African Origin of Civilization: Myth or Reality*, Cheikh Anta Diop, Lawrence Hill & Company, New York and Westport, Paris 1955, New York, p. 25.
8. *Wonderful Ethiopians of the Ancient Cushite Empire*, Drusilla Dunjee Houston, 1926. Republished by Black Classics Press, Baltimore, Md. 1985, p. 275.
9. From an interview with Professor Abena Walker, author of *African Concepts of Education* Study Course on Ernest White's Crosstalk, WUDC, Wash. D.C. May, 1988.
10. *Africa: Mother of "Western Civilization"*, Yosef ben Jochannon. Republished by Black Classics Press, Baltimore, Md. 1989.
11. *Sex and Race*, Volume III, Joel A. Rogers, Helga M. Rogers, New York, N.Y. 1967, p. 136.
12. *Stolen Legacy*, George G.M. James, Philosophical Library, N.Y.C. 1954. Reprinted by Julian Richardson Associates, San Francisco, Calif. 1976, p. 159.
13. *Introduction to Black Studies*, Maulana Karenga (See above), p.48.
14. *Authorized Version of the Holy Bible*, Romans, Chapter 12:2 (KJV).
15. *Wonderful Ethiopians of the Ancient Cushite Empire*, Drusilla Dunjee Houston, (See above), p. 2.
16. *Authorized Version of the Holy Bible*, Jeremiah Chapter 31:33 (KJV).
17. *Funk & Wagnall's New Encyclopedia*, Volume 18. 1983, p. 231.
18. *Man, God, and Civilization*, John G. Jackson, (See above), p. 110.
19. *The Woman's Encyclopedia of Myths and Secrets*, Barbara G. Walker, Harper & Row Publisher, San Francisco, Calif. 1983.
20. *The Random House Encyclopedia*, Random House Inc., 201 East 50th Street, New York, N.Y. 10022. 1983, pp. 832, 833.

21. *Black Athena: The Afroasiatic Roots of Classical Civilization*, Volume I. Martin Bernal, Rutgers University Press, New Brunswick, NJ, 1987, p. 182.
22. *The Mystery-Religions and Christianity*, Samuel Angus University Books, New Hyde Park, N.Y. 1966, p. 73.
23. *The Origin and Evolution of Religion*, Albert Churchward, George Allen and Unwin Ltd. London, 1924. Reprinted by Health Research, P.O. Box 70, Mokelume Hill, Calif. 1986, p. 54.
24. Bernal, *op. cit.* p. 182.
25. *The Random House Encyclopedia, op. cit.* p. 834.
26. *The Origin and Evolution of Religion*, Albert Churchward (See above), p. 48.
27. *Ibid.*, p. 47.
28. *The Mysteries of Osiris' Ancient Egyptian Initiation*, R. Swinburne Clymer, The Philosophical Publishing Co., Quakertown, Penna. 1951, p. xiii; *Isis Unveiled*, Volume II, H.P. Blavatsky, Theosophical University Press, Pasadena, Calif. 1960, p. 493; Bernal *op. cit.*, p. 181.
29. Clymer, *op. cit.*, p. xiii.
30. *Black Male/Female Relationships*, Article The Neurological Misadventure of Primordial Man, by Edgar J. Ridley, Julia Hare — publisher, San Francisco, Calif. Autumn, 1982, p. 56.
31. *Ibid.*, p. 58.
32. *Ibid.*, pp. 60, 61, 62.
33. *Ibid.*, p. 58.
34. *Ibid.*, p. 58.
35. *Ibid.*, p. 62.
36. *The Origin and Evolution of Religion*, Albert Churchward (See above), p. 186.
37. *Afrikan Woman: The Original Guardian Angel*, Ishakamusa Barashango, Fourth Dynasty Publishing Company, Silver Spring, Md. 1989, Chapter 4.
38. *Ancient Egyptian Religion*, Henri Franfort, Harper & Row Publishers, N.Y.C. 1948, p. 15.
39. *Anacalypsis*, Volume I, Godfrey Higgins, London, 1836. Reprinted by Health Research, Mokelumne Hill, Calif. 1972, p. 35.
40. *Man, God, and Civilization*, (See above), p. 92.
41. Blavatsky, *op. cit.*, p. 406.
42. *The Random House Encyclopedia, op. cit.*, p. 835.
43. Drusilla Dunjee Houston, *op. cit.*, p. 18. Higgins, Volume II. p. 256.
44. *The African Origin of Civilization: Myth or Reality*, (See above), p. 194.
45. *Afrikan People and European Holidays: A Mental Genocide*, Book Two, Ishakamusa Barashango, Fourth Dynasty Publishing Company, Silver Spring, Md. 1983, p. 11.

46. Higgins, Volume II, *op. cit.*, p. 30.
47. *Ibid.*, p. 167.
48. Clymer, *op. cit.*, p. 273.
49. Bernal, *op. cit.*, p. 117.
50. *The Origin and Evolution of Religion,* Albert Churchward, (See above), p. 34.
51. Drusilla Dunjee Houston, *op. cit.*, p. 28.
52. *The History of Ancient Egypt: An Afrocentric Worldview,* A paper by A. Josef Ben Levi, King-Kennedy College, Chicago, Ill. p. 8.
53. Diop, *op. cit.*, 91.
54. *The Rebirth of African Civilization,* Chancellor Williams, Public Affairs Press, Wash., D.C. 1961, p. 2.
55. *Man, God, and Civilization,* John G. Jackson, (See above), p. 145.
56. *The Rebirth of African Civilization,* Chancellor Williams, *op. cit.*, p. 15.
57. Diop, *op. cit.*, p. 140.
58. *World's Great Men of Color,* Volume I, J.A. Rogers, Helga M. Rogers, New York, N.Y. 1947, p. xvi.
59. *Ancient Egyptian Religion,* Henri Franfort, (See above), p. 25.
60. *The Origin and Evolution of Religion,* Albert Churchward, (See above), p. 185.
61. Blavatsky, Volume I. *op. cit.*, p. 533.
62. *Man, God, and Civilization,* John G. Jackson, (See above), pp. 142-143.
63. *Ibid.*, p. 110.
64. Blavatsky, Volume I. *op. cit.*, p. 544.
65. *Stolen Legacy,* George G.M. James, Philosophical Library, N.Y.C. 1954. Reprinted by Julian Richardson Associates, San Francisco, Calif. 1976, p. 28.
66. *Ancient Egytian Religion,* Henri Franfort, (See above), p. 25.
67. *The Origin and Evolution of Religion,* Albert Churchward, (See above), pp. 18, 32.
68. *Ibid.*, pp. 33-34.
69. Drusilla Dunjee Houston, *op. cit.*, pp. 81-82.
70. *The Origin and Evolution of Religion,* Albert Churchward, (See above), p. 33.
71. Blavatsky, Volume I. op. cit., pp. 23-24.
72. Angus, *op. cit.*, p. 71; Frankfort, *op. cit.*, p. 25.
73. The November, 1982 edition of *The Journal of African Civilization,* Transaction Books, Rutgers-The State University, New Brunswick, NJ 08903, p. 64. A paper by Charles S. Finch.
74. George G.M. James, *op. cit.*, p. 27.
75. Barbara G. Walker, *op. cit.*, p. 725.
76. *The Random House Encyclopedia, op. cit.*, p. 1829; Drusilla Dunjee Houston, *op. cit.*, p. 83.

77. *Man's Religions*, John B. Noss, Macmillan Publishing Co., Inc., New York, N.Y., Collier Macmillan Publishers, London, England: Fifth Edition 1974, p. 36.
78. Frankfort, *op. cit.*, p. 110.
79. Diop, *op. cit.*, p. 109.
80. George G.M. James, *op. cit.*, pp. 154-155.
81. Frankfort, *op. cit.*, p. 51.
82. *The Introduction to African Civilizations*, Jackson *op. cit.*, p. 10.
83. Barbara B. Walker, *op. cit.*, p. 731.
84. *Egyptian Mythology*, Veronica Ions, The Hamlyn Publishing Group Ltd. London, New York, Sydney, Toronto. 1968, p. 50.
85. *The Egyptian Book of the Dead*, E.A. Wallis Budget, Dover Publications, Inc., New York. 1967, p. cxvi.
86. Drusilla D. Houston, *op. cit.*, p. 160.
87. The November, 1982 edition of *The Journal of African Civilization*, Transaction Books, Rutgers-The State University, New Brunswick, NJ 08903, pp. 137, 139, 140.
88. *Blacks in Science: Ancient and Modern*, Ivan Van Sertima, Transaction Books, New Brunswick (U.S.A.) and London (U.K.), 1983. pp. 20, 58, 65-66.
89. *Man, God, and Civilization*, John G. Jackson, (See above), pp. 243-244.
90. Drusilla D. Houston, *op. cit.*, p. 160.
91. *The World and Africa*, W.E. Burghardt DuBois, International Publishers, New York, 1946, 1965, p. 98.
92. *African Presence In Early Asia*, Ivan Van Sertima/Runoko Rashidi; Transaction Books, New Brunswick (U.S.A.) nd Oxford (U.K.) 1985, p. 163.
93. Drusilla D. Houston, *op. cit.*, pp. 161-162.
94. *Great African Thinkers*, Volume I. Ivan Van Sertima/Cheikh Anta Diop, Transaction Books, New Brunswick (U.S.A.) and Oxford (U.K.). 1987, p. 235.
95. *Man, God, and Civilization*, John G. Jackson, (See above), pp. 245, 246.
96. *The Destruction of Black Civilization*, Chancellor Williams, Third World Press, Chicago, Ill. p. 15.
97. *When God Was A Woman*, Merlin Stone, Harcourt Brace Jovanovich Publishing, San Diego, New York, London. 1976, p. 200.
98. *Ibid.*, p. 210.
99. *The Great Mother*, Eric Neumann, Princeton University Press, 1963, p. 159.
100. Martin Stone, *op. cit.*, p. 3.
101. *Man, God, and Civilization*, John G. Jackson (See above), p. 242.
102. *Mysteries*, Colin Wilson, G.P. Putnam's Son's, New York, 1978, pp. 141-142.

103. *Man, God, and Civilization*, John G. Jackson, (See above), p. 242.
104. Merlin Stone, *op. cit.*, p. 219.
105. John B. Noss, *op. cit.*, p. 47.
106. Merlin Stone, *op. cit.*, p. 97.
107. *Funk & Wagnall's Standard Reference Encyclopedia*, Volume 22 Standard Reference Works Publishing Company, Inc., New York, 1967, p. 8311.
108. Merlin Stone, *op. cit.*, p. 58.
109. *Cradle of Civilization*, Samuel Noah Kramer, Time-Life Books, New York, 1967, p. 119.
110. Drusilla D. Houston, *op. cit.*, p. 151.
111. *Ibid.*, p. 132.
112. *Ibid.*, p. 130.
113. *Ibid.*, p. 130.
114. *Ibid.*, pp. 4-5.
115. *Ibid.*, pp. 111-112.
116. *Ibid.*, p. 113.
117. *Ibid.*, p. 113.
118. *The Origin and Evolution of Religion*, Albert Churchward, (See above), p. 361; Drusilla D. Houston, *op. cit.*, p. 112; John B. Noss, op. cit., p. 508; Drusilla D. Houston, *op. cit.*, pp. 114, 123.
119. *The Origin and Evolution of Religion*, Albert Churchward, (See above), p. 360.
120. Drusilla D. Houston, *op. cit.*, p. 121.
121. *Ibid.*, p. 130.
122. *Ibid.*, p. 114.
123. *Ibid.*, p. 131.
124. *Ibid.*, pp. 130, 131.
125. *Ibid.*, p. 123.
126. *Ibid.*, p. 114.
127. *Ibid.*, p. 123.
128. *Ibid.*, p. 116.
129. *Washington Post* Newspaper, Sunday, January 20, 1991. Article entitled "Mauritanias Persecution of Blacks" by Jack Anderson and Dale Van Atta.
130. *African Genesis*, Leo Frobenius/Douglas C. Fox, Turtle Island Foundation, Berkeley, Calif. 1983, p. 20.
131. *The Iceman Inheritance: Prehistoric Source of Western Man's Racism, Sexism and Aggression*, Michael Bradley, Warner Books, Inc., New York, N.Y. 10019, July, 1981, pp. 8-9, 18.
132. *Ibid.*, p. 20.
133. *Blacks in Science: Ancient and Modern*, Ivan Van Sertima (See above), pp. 8-9.
134. John B. Noss, *op. cit.*, p. 509.

211

135. *African Origins of the Major "Western Religions"*, Yosef ben Jochannan, Alkebulan Books, N.Y.C., 1970, p. 212.
136. Eric Neumann, *op. cit.*, p. 260.
137. Merlin Stone, *op. cit.*, p. 206; John B. Noss, *op. cit.*, p. 509.
138. *African Origins of the Major "Western Religions"*, Yosef ben Jochannan, (See above), p. 212.
139. Barbara G. Walker, *op. cit.*, p. 51.
140. *African Origins of the Major "Western Religions"*, Yosef ben Jochnnan, (See above), p. 67.
141. Drusilla D. Houston, *op. cit.*, pp. 137, 149.
142. *Ibid.*, pp. 145, 151.
143. *Ibid.*, pp. 115, 116.
144. Joel A. Rogers, Volume I. *op. cit.*, pp. 95-96.
145. *World's Great Men of Color*, Volume I, Joel A. Rogers, Helga M. Rogers, 1270 Fifth Avenue, New York, N.Y. 10029, p. 74.
146. As quoted in *God, The Bible and The Man's Destiny*—I. Barashango, Fourth Dynasty Publishing Company, Silver Spring, Md. 20910, p. 148.
147. *The Muslim Dictionary*, Sura 1:37; Sura xli:8; Sura xvi:3; Sura xxxv:12.
148. *The Encyclopedia Britannica*, Volume 6, 4th Edition, 1939, p. 708.
149. Drusilla D. Houston, *op. cit.*, p. 272.
150. *The Random House Encyclopedia, op. cit.*, p. 985.
151. *Drusilla D. Houston, op. cit.*, p. 267.
152. *Ibid.*, p. 171.
153. Diop, *op. cit.*, pp. 106-107; *Black Manhood: The Building of Civilization by the Black Man of the Nile*, Kieta Tarharka Sundiata, University Press of America, Inc., Wash., D.C. 1979, p. 230.
154. Drusilla D. Houston, *op. cit.*, pp. 255-256.
155. Diop, *op. cit.*, p. 265; Drusilla D. Houston, *op. cit.*, p. 255; Rogers, Volume I, *op. cit.*, pp. 59-60.
156. Drusilla D. Houston, *op. cit.*, p. 264.
157. *Ibid.*, p. 265.
158. *Afrikan People and European Holidays: A Mental Genocide*, Book Two, Ishakamusa Barashango, (See above), pp. 28-30.
159. Drusilla D. Houston, *op. cit.*, pp. 265-266.
160. *African Presence In Early Asia*, Ivan Van Sertima/Runoko Rashidi, *op. cit.*, p. 171.
161. Drusilla D. Houston, *op. cit.*, p. 255.
162. *Ibid.*, p. 272.
163. Diop, *op. cit.*, p. 222.
164. *Ibid.*, p. 10.
165. Sundiata, *op. cit.*, p. 135.
166. *Herodotus The Histories*, Penguin Books Inc., 7110 Ambassador Road, Baltimore, Md. 21207, 1971, pp. 182-183.

167. *Ibid.*, pp. 184-185.
168. Sundiata, *op. cit.*, p. 136.
169. Diop, *op. cit.*, pp. 112, 113.
170. Barbara G. Walker, *op. cit.*, pp. 14-15.
171. *Man, God, and Civilization,* John G. Jackson, (See above), p. 97.
172. Drusilla D. Houston, *op. cit.*, p. 267.
173. Barbara G. Walker, *op. cit.*, p. 664.
174. *Ibid.*, p. 664.
175. *Man, God, and Civilization,* Johrf G. Jackson, (See above), p. 100.
176. Merlin Stone, *op. cit.*, p. 74.
177. Barbara G. Walker, *op. cit.*, p. 663.
178. *Ibid.*, p. 663.
179. *Drusilla D. Houston, op. cit.*, p. 216.
180. *African Presence In Early Asia,* Ivan Van Sertima/Wayne B. Chandler, *op. cit.*, p. 89.
181. *Drusilla D. Houston, op. cit.*, p. 216.
182. *Ibid.*, p. 211.
183. *African Presence In Early Asia,* Ivan Van Sertima/Runoko Rashidi, *op. cit.*, p. 171; *Ibid.*, Wayne B. Chandler, *op. cit.*, p. 80.
184. *Ibid.*, Rashidi, p. 171; *Ibid.*, Chandler, p. 80.
185. *Our Oriental Heritage,* W. Durant, Simon and Schuster, 650 Fifth Avenue, New York, N.Y. 10020, 1963, p. 396.
186. J.A. Rogers, Volume I, *op. cit.*, p. 268.
187. *Man, God, and Civilization,* John G. Jackson, (See above), p. 247; DuBois, *op cit*, p. 177; W. Durant, *op. cit.*, p. 396.
188. Barbara G. Walker, *op. cit.*, pp. 580, 626, 627.
189. Higgins, Volume I, *op. cit.*, p. 335.
190. Barbara G.Walker, *op. cit.*, p. 840.
191. *Ibid.*, p. 670.
192. *Ibid.*, pp. 627-628.
193. *Ibid.*, p. 572.
194. M. Stone, *op. cit.*, p. 72.
195. B.G. Walker, *op. cit.*, p. 493.
196. *Ibid.*, p. 488.
197. *Ibid.*, p. 490.
198. *Ibid.*, p. 491.
199. *Authorized Version of the Holy Bible,* John, Chapter 1:1; (KJV); B.G. Walker, *op. cit.*, p. 489.
200. *Ibid.*, p. 491.
201. *Ibid.*, p. 572.
202. *Ibid.*, p. 492.
203. *Ibid.*, p. 490.
204. *Ibid.*, p. 489.

205. *Afrikan People and European Holidays: A Mental Genocide*, Book I, Ishakamusa Barashango, (See above), p. 30; D.D. Houston, *op. cit.*, p. 134.
206. B.G. Walker,*op. cit.*, p. 491.
207. *Afrikan People and European Holidays: A Mental Genocide*, Book Two, Ishakamusa Barashango, (See above), p. 11.
208. *A Book of The Beginnings*, Gerald Massey, Volume I. Reprinted by Health Research, Mokelumne Hill, Calif. 1987, pp. 453, 455, 441, 439, 446.
209. B.G. Walker, *op. cit.*, p. 491.
210. *Ibid.*, pp. 894, 571.
211. *Ibid.*, pp. 336-337.
212. *Ibid.*, p. 224.
213. *Ibid.*, p. 225; D.D. Houston, *op. cit.*, p. 267.
214. *100 Amazing Facts About The Negro*, J.A. Rogers, Helga M. Rogers, New York, N.Y. 10029, 1970, pp. 4, 21.
215. B.G. Walker, *op. cit.*, p. 899.
216. *Ibid.*, pp. 894, 899.
217. *Ibid.*, pp. 1098, 1096.
218. *Ibid.*, pp. 401-402.
219. *Ibid.*, p. 543.
220. *Ibid.*, p. 543.
221. *Ibid.*, p. 929.
222. *Ibid.*, p. 930.
223. *Ibid.*, p. 929.
224. *Ibid.*, p. 627.
225. D.D. Houston, *op. cit.*, pp. 258, 267,.
226. *The Encyclopedia Britannica*, Volume 7, 4th Edition, 1939, p. 21.
227. B.G. Walker, *op. cit.*, p. 1052.
228. *Ibid.*, p. 526; *African Presence In Early Asia*, Ivan Van Sertima/Wayne B. Chandler, *op. cit.*, p. 235.
229. B.G. Walker, *op. cit.*, p. 580.
230. *Ibid.*, p. 58.
231. D.D. Houston, *op. cit.*, p. 250.
232. *Ibid.*, p. 229.
233. *African Presence In Early Asia*, Ivan Van Sertima/Runoko Rashidi, *op. cit.*, pp. 36-37.
234. *Ibid.*, V.T. Rajshekar, p. 237.
235. B.G. Walker, *op. cit.*, p. 35.
236. *Ibid.*, p. 544.
237. *Ibid.*, p. 936.
238. *Ibid.*, p. 1097.
239. *Ibid.*, p. 936.
240. *Ibid.*, p. 935.

241. *Ibid.*, p. 936.
242. *Loves Picture Book*, Volume III. Ove Brusendorf and Poul Henningsen, Lyle Stuart, Inc., New York, 1960, p. 73.
243. D.D. Houston, *op. cit.*, pp. 234, 235, 247, 251, 258-259.
244. *African Presence In Early Asia*, Ivan Van Sertima, *op. cit.*, pp. 13, 235; Brusendorf/Henningsen, *op. cit.*, p. 73.
245. *Nile Valley Civilizations*, Ivan Sertima/Runoko Rashidi, The Journal of African Civilization Ltd., Inc., *op. cit.*, 1989, p. 217.
246. *African Presence In Early Asia*, Ivan Van Sertima/Wayne B. Chandler, *op. cit.*, p. 235.
247. B.G. Walker, *op. cit.*, p. 936.
248. *Ibid.*, pp. 869-870.
249. *Ibid.*, p. 116.
250. *Ibid.*, p. 115.
251. *Ibid.*, p. 115.
252. D.D. Houston, *op. cit.*, p. 247.
253. Wayne B. Chandler, *op. cit.*, p. 235.
254. *African Presence In Early Asia*, Ivan Van Sertima/John G. Jackson, *op. cit.*, p. 108.
255. D.D. Houston, *op. cit.*, . 235.
256. *Man, God, and Civilization*, John G. Jackson, (See above), p. 132.
257. J.A. Rogers, Volume I. *op. cit.*, p. 265.
258. B.G. Walker, *op. cit.*, p. 515.
259. *Ibid.*, p. 516; D.D. Houston, *op. cit.*, p. 250.
260. *Chariots of The Gods Unsolved Mysteries of the Past*, Erich Von Daniken, Bantam Books Inc., New York, 1969, pp. 56-59.
261. B.G. Walker, *op. cit.*, p. 123.
262. D.D. Houston, *op. cit.*, p. 252.
263. B.G. Walker, *op. cit.*, p. 124.
264. J.A. Rogers, Volume I. *op. cit.*, p. 266; Higgins, Volume I, *op. cit.*, p. 364.
265. As quoted in *God, The Bible and The Black Man's Destiny*—I. Barashango, (See above), p. 3.
266. As quoted in DuBois, *op. cit.*, pp. 177-178.
267. D.D. Houston, *op. cit.*, p. 241.
268. J.A. Rogers, Volume I, *op. cit.*, p. 265.
269. V.T. Rajshekar, *op. cit.*, p. 224.
270. M. Stone, *op. cit.*, p. 72.
271. *World Book Encyclopedia*, Volume 19, 1965 Edition, p. 232.
272. *African Presence In Early Asia*, Ivan Van Sertima/Runoko Rashidi, *op. cit.*, p. 34; *The Encyclopedia Britannica*, Volume 23, 4th Edition, 1939.
273. D.D. Houston, *op. cit.*, pp. 246, 251, 247.
274. *Ibid.*, p. 250.

275. W.B. Chandler, *op. cit.*, p. 93; *Afrique Histoire*, Volume 4 number 1, Yoga is One of the Links Between Indu and African Culture. An article by Genevieve Khane, pp. 20-25.
276. W.B. Chandler, *op. cit.*, pp. 95, 97.
277. *Ibid.*, pp. 82, 90.
278. *Man, God, and Civilization*, John G. Jackson, (See above), p. 247.
279. W.B. Chandler, *op. cit.*, p. 87.
280. As quoted by Gersham Williams in *African Presence In Early Asia*, Ivan Van Sertima, *op. cit.*, pp. 117-118.
281. W.B. Chandler, *op. cit.*, p. 2335.
282. D.D. Houston, *op. cit.*, p. 216.
283. *African Presence In Early Asia*, Ivan Van Sertima/Runoko Rashidi, *op. cit.*, p. 244; D.D. Houston, *op. cit.*, p. 235.
284. W.B. Chandler, *op. cit.*, p. 83; V. T. Rajshekar, *op. cit.*, p. 236.
285. D.D. Houston, *op. cit.*, p. 251.
286. *Ibid.*, p. 249.
287. *Afrikan People and European Holidays: A Mental Genocide*, Book Two, Ishakamusa Barashango, (See above), pp. 10-11, 15.
289. DuBois, *op. cit.*, p. 179.
290. As quoted in *Sex and Race*, Volume I, J.A. Rogers, (See above), p. 266.
291. *Man, God, and Civilization*, John G. Jackson, (See above), pp. 244-245.
292. *The Signs and Symbols of Primordial Man*, Albert Churchward, *op. cit.*, p. 209.
293. M. Stone, *op. cit.*, p. 42.
294. *Documents From Old Testament Times*, D. Winton Thomas, Harper & Row Publishers, New York, 1958, p. 14.
295. M. Stone, *op. cit.*, pp. 42-43.
296. *The Origin and Evolution of Religion*, Albert Churchward, (See above), p. 184.
297. D.D. Houston, *op. cit.*, p. 197.
298. M. Stone, *op. cit.*, p. 42.
299. D.D. Houston, *op. cit.*, p. 197.
300. *The Origin and Evolution of Religion*, Albert Churchward, (See above), p. 185.
301. *Ibid.*, p. 59.
302. D. Winton Thomas, *op. cit.*, p. 5.
303. *Ibid.*, pp. 3-13; John B. Noss, *op. cit.*, p. 48.
304. W. Dorant, *op. cit.*, pp. 236-237.
305. D. Winton Thomas, *op. cit.*, p. 16.
306. Blavatsky, Volume I, *op. cit.*, p. 533.
307. Yosef ben Jochannon, *A Chronology of The Bible*.
308. *Blacks in Science: Ancient and Modern*, Ivan Van Sertima, *op. cit.*, p. 13.
309. G. Massey, *op. cit.*, p. 454.

310. B.G. Walker, *op. cit.*, p. 999.
311. *Ibid.*, p. 998.
312. *Ibid.*, p. 999.
313. D. Winton Thomas, *op. cit.*, p. 4.
314. E. Neumann, *op. cit.*, p. 213.
315. D. Winton Thomas, *op. cit.*, p. 14.
316. E. Neumann, *op. cit.*, p. 213.
319. *Funk & Wagnall's Standard Desk Dictionary*, Volume 2, 1979, p. 625.
320. *The Origin and Evolution of Religion*, Albert Churchward, (See above), p. 132.
321. *The Religions of the Ancient World*, George Rawlinson, Hurst and Company, New York. Reprinted 1974 by Health Research, Mokelumne Hill, Calif. p. 57.
322. *The Encylopedia Britannica*, Volume 14, 4th Edition, 1939, p. 873.
323. *Funk & Wagnall's New Encyclopedia*, Volume 3, 1983, p. 176.
324. Rawlinson, *op. cit.*, p. 55.
325. E. Neumann, *op. cit.*, p. 214.
326. *Ibid.*, p. 214; Rawlinson, *op. cit.*, p. 56.
327. E. Neumann, *op. cit.*, p. 215.
328. B.G. Walker, *op. cit.*, pp. 999, 491.
329. *Ibid.*, p. 998.
330. *Ibid.*, pp. 998-999.
331. E. Neumann, *op. cit.*, p. 226.
332. M. Stone, *op. cit.*, p. 200.
333. B.G. Walker, *op. cit.*, p. 537.
334. *Authorized Version of the Holy Bible*, Isaiah Chapter 27:1 (KJV).
335. *Harper's Bible Dictionary*, M.S. and J.L. Miler, Harper & Row Publishers, N.Y.C. 1961, p. 390.
336. *Seventh-Day Adventist Bible Dictionary*, Siegfried H. Horn, Review and Herald Publishing Association, Washington, D.C. 1960, p. 649.
337. B.G. Walker, *op. cit.*, p. 999.
338. E. Neumann, *op. cit.*, p. 214.
339. M. Stone, *op. cit.*, p. 200.
340. *Ibid.*, p. 198; *Authorized Version of the Holy Bible*, Psalms Chapter 74:13-14 (KJV); Ibid., Job Chapter 41:1-10.
341. Rawlinson, *op. cit.*, p. 48.
342. *Funk & Wagnall's Encyclopedia*, Volume 3, 1983, p. 176.
343. B.G. Walker, *op. cit.*, p. 581.
344. *The Encyclopedia Britannica*, Volume 14, 4th Edition, 1939, p. 873.
345. Rawlinson, *op. cit.*, p. 43.
346. *The Random Encyclopedia*, *op. cit.*, p. 2403.
347. *Cradle of Civilization*, Samuel Noah Kramer, *op. cit.*, p. 119.

348. *The Encyclopedia Britannica,* Volume 10, 4th Editiion, 1939, p. 108.
349. Charles S. Finch, November 1982 edition of *The Journal of African Civilization, op. cit.,* p. 57.
350. Trawick, *op. cit.,* p. 42.
351. *The Origin and Evolution of Religion,* Albert Churchward, (See above), p. 185.
352. B.G. Walker, *op. cit.,* p. 99.
353. M. Stone, *op. cit.,* pp. 7-8.
354. *God, The Bible and The Black Man's Destiny*—I. Barashango, (See above), pp. 8, 9, 69-71.
355. Trawick, *op. cit.,* p. 16.
356. B.G. Walker, *op. cit.,* p. 98.
357. *Philosophy and Opinions of Marcus Garvey,* A.J. Garvey, Julian Richardson Associates, San Francisco, Calif. 1967.
358. Higgins, Volume I, *op. cit.,* p. 807.
359. *African Origins of the Major "Western Religions",* Yosef ben Jochannon, (See above), pp. 73-137; *God, The Bible and The Black Man's Destiny*—I. Barashango, (See above), pp. 142-146.
360. Higgins, Volume I, *op. cit.,* pp. 97-98.
361. B.G. Walker, *op. cit.,* p. 99.
362. Higgins, Volume II, *op. cit.,* p. 390.
363. Trawick, *op. cit.,* p. 13.
364. B.G. Walker, *op. cit.,* p. 184.
365. D.D. Houston, *op. cit.,* p. 192.
366. *The Origin and Evolution of Religion,* Albert Churchward, (See above), p. 306.
367. *Ibid.,* p. 242.
368. B.G. Walker, *op. cit.,* p. 185.
369. Trawick, *op. cit.,* p. 46.
370. *Ibid.,* p. 45.
371. *Ibid.,* p. 46.
372. *The Origin and Evolution of Religion,* Albert Churchward, (See above), p. 319.
373. *The Signs and Symbols of Primordial Man,* Albert Churchward, (See bove), p. 27.
374. *The Origin and Evolution of Religion,* Albert Churchward, (See above), pp. 245, 262.
375. *Ibid.,* p. 262.
376. B.G. Walker, *op. cit.,* p. 184.
377. Higgins, Volume I, *op. cit.,* p. 35.
378. *Afrikan Woman: The Original Guardian Angel,* I. Barashango, *op. cit.,* pp. 48, 56, 43-44.
379. Trawick, *op. cit.,* p. 43.

380. *The Encyclopedia Britannica*, Volume 6, 4th Edition, 1939, p. 147.
381. B.G. Walker, *op. cit.*, p. 288; J.A. Rogers, Volume I, *op. cit.*, p. 28.
382. *God, The Bible and The Black Man's Destiny*—I. Barashango, (See above), p. 23.
383. M. Stone, *op. cit.*, p. 197.
384. *The Encyclopedia Britannica*, Volume 1, 4th Edition, 1939, p. 148.
385. *Holy Bible (KJV)* Genesis 2:18-20.
386. M. Stone, *op. cit.*, p. 197.
387. *Encyclopedia Britannica*, Volume 6, 1939, p. 148.
388. M. Stone, *op. cit.*, p. 59.
389. *The Jerusalem Bible*, Doubleday & Company, Inc., Garden City, New York, 1966, Jeremiah 44:15-19.
390. G.G.M. James, *op. cit.*, pp. 140, 182.
391. *100 Amazing Facts About the Negro*, J.A. Rogers, (See above), p.9 #51.
392. Charles S. Finch, November, 1982 Edition of *The Journal of African Civilization*, *op. cit.*, p. 64.
393. *Foundations of the Black Nation*, I.A. Obadele I, New Afrikan Creed No. 9, p. 152.
394. G.G.M. James, *op. cit.*, p. 118.
395. *Ibid.*, p. 102.
396. *The Origin and Evolution of Religion*, Albert Churchward, (See above),, p. 184.
397. E.A. Budge, *op. cit.*, pp. xci-xciii.
398. *Man, God, and Civilization*, John G. Jackson, (See above), p. 5.
399. Diop, *op. cit.*, pp. 108-109.
400. *The Origin and Evolution of Religion*, Albert Churchward (See above), pp. 185-186.
401. *Holy Bible (KJV)* Genesis 1:9-10.
402. *Ibid.*, Matthew 5:14-16.
403. *Ibid.*, Luke 12:32; *Ibid.*, Deuteronomy 28:13.
404. G.G.M. James, *op. cit.*, p. 40.
405. *The Jersusalem Bible*, Doubleday & Company, Inc., Garden City, New York, 1966. The Book of Wisdom 7:22-30; 8:1, pp. 1014-1015. Wisdom "She is a breath of the power God" Wisdom 7:22.
406. *The Teachings of Ptahhotep: The Oldest Book in the World*, Asa Hilliard III, Larry Williams and Nia Damili, Blackwood Press and Company, Inc., Atlanta, Georgia, Box 115311, 1987, p. 19; The Teachings of Kegemni as recorded in Franfort, *op. cit.*, pp. 60-85.
407. B.G. Walker, *op. cit.*, p. 562.
408. *The Living Bible*, Tyndale House Publishers, Wheaton, Illinois. Coverdale House Publishers Ltd. London, England. Distributed by Doubleday and Company, Inc. Proverbs 8:1-3, 6-8, 10-12, 14-16, 20-26, 32, 35.

409. *Holy Bible (KJV)* Ecclesiastes 1:4.
410. *Ibid.,* Psalms 27:13.
411. Colin Wilson, *op. cit.,* p. 102.
412. G.G.M. James, *op. cit.,* p. 102.
413. *The Culture of Ancient Egypt,* John A. Wilson, The University of Chicago Press, Chicago, Ill. 1965, p. 60.
414. G.G.M. James, *op. cit.,* p. 147.
415. *Ibid.,* p. 143.
416. *Ibid.,* p. 144.
417. *Ibid.,* p. 149.
418. *New Standard Encyclopedia,* Volume —Standard Education Society, Inc., Chicago, Ill. 1961, p. -464.
419. G.G.M. James, *op. cit.,* p. 150.
420. *World Book Encyclopedia,* Volume A, *op. cit.,* p. 844.
421. John A. Wilson, *op. cit.,* p. 60.
422. G.G.M. James, *op. cit.,* p. 103.
423. *The Living Bible,* (See above), Psalms 148:1-5.
424. *Holy Bible (KJV)* Psalms 19:1-3.
425. *Ibid.,* Colossians 1:15-17, 26.
426. John G. Jackson, November, 1982 Edition of *The Journal of African Civilization, op. cit.,* p. 72.
427. G.G.M. James, *op. cit.,* pp. 154-155, 183.
428. *John G. Jackson, November, 1982 Edition of The Journal of African Civilization, op. cit.,* p. 79.
429. *Rameses II and the African Origin of Civilization,* Video Tape, The Third Eye, P.O. Box 226064, Dallas, Texas 75222.
430. G.G.M. James,*op. cit.,* p. 118.
431. *Holy Bible (KJV)* Genesis 1:6-7.
432. *Ibid.,* Genesis 1:1-5.

433. G.G.M. James, *op. cit.,* p. 146.
434. *Ibid.,* pp. 119, 147.
435. *Ibid.,* p. 183.
436. *Ibid.,* p. 150.
437. *Holy Bible (KJV)* Phillipians 4:7-8.
438. G.G.M. James, *op. cit.,* pp. 150-151.
439. *Foundations of the Black Nation,* I.A. Obadele I, New Afrikan Creed No. 1, p. 152.
440. Paraphrased by I. Barashango based on excerpts from *The Magic In Your Mind,* U.S. Anderson, Wilshire Book Company, Hollywood, Calif. 1966, pp. 140-141, 146, 150.

ANNOUNCING

Four Powerful and Enlightening Publications

Afrikan People
and
European Holidays:
A Mental Genocide

Rev. Ishakamusa Barashango
BOOK I

Afrikan People
and
European Holidays:
A Mental Genocide

Rev. Ishakamusa Barashango
BOOK TWO

These Books represent a serious study into the historical background and cultural significance of European holidays and the devastating impact and damaging effects they have on the Black experience.

Afrikan People & European Holidays: A Mental Genocide Book I

Takes an indepth look at Thanksgiving and Christmas providing some answers to such questions as what are the true aims and purposes of Thanksgiving Day and Xmas? Who were the people called Pilgrims and where did they come from? Why isn't there as many "Indians" living in America today as there were when the Pilgrims landed? Who was the Catholic bishop who recommended that Afrikans be captured and brought to the Americas as slaves, to replace the Red men who were being killed by the hundreds of thousands? Where did the celebration of Xmas originate and what European pagan festival did it replace? What is the origin of the first Xmas tree and who trimmed it? Who was Santa Claus and what is his criminal background? Who really benefits from the money spent during the holiday season? And many others. After analyzing each of these European Holidays Book I introduces and elucidates the significance of the meaningful and lovely celebrations of *Umoja Karamu* (Unity Feast) and *Kwanzaa* (Festival of The First Fruits), demonstrates the historical roots and meaning of these Black Holy Days, what they stand for and how they should be celebrated. Now available to you
—$12.95

Afrikan People & European Holidays:
A Mental Genocide Book II

Exposes the misleading idealisms we were taught about European History and the founding fathers of the U.S.A. Putting in proper perspective the romanticism and sentimental imagery programmed into our psyche by the public school and media systems of this society. The well documented pages of Book II tells the historical truth about what really took place. This work answers such questions as what were the real reasons for the American Revolutionary War and what was the status of Black People in the thirteen colonies at the time? Why did George Washington and other American patriotic leaders have so little success at getting the average white colonists to fight in their Revolutionary War? What promises were made by the British on one hand and the colonist on the other to get the black man to fight on either side? How many of America's founding fathers were slave holders and/or involved in slave smuggling and the Afrikan slave trade? After the thirteen colonies won independence what became of the over whelming number of Black People who played a major role in this saga and what kind of impact did this have on the United States slave economy? These and many other pertinent facts leading up to and surrounding the events of "America's Independence Day: The Fourth-of-you-lie" are comprehensively presented in Book II as it takes you on an exciting panoramic journey through a narrative outline of the history of the British Empire. In order to provide you with a full grasp of the real meaning of the subject matter it became necessary for the author to pursue a degree of detail and during the course of this investigation some amazing facts were brought to light. For example did you know that Afrikan People dominated the Earth for untold thousands of years and took their high culture learning systems and advanced civilizations to the European continent? Even if you were previously aware of this phenomena we are certain that you will find the chapter titled "Ancient Afrikan Scientist Bring Civilization To The British Isles" to be very revealing and mentally stimulating to the true seeker of knowledge and understanding. This and all the other fact filled chapters in this work provide excellent material for introduction to the study of European history from a Black perspective. Book II is highly recommended for classroom study and personal self-improvement and knowledge gathering projects. Now available to you —$14.95

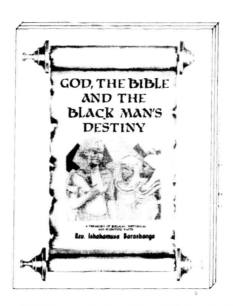

God, The Bible and the Black Man's Destiny

Confirms the fact that it was the Afrikan who first conceptualized and fashioned the greatest moral society ever known to man and established the basic principles and body of knowledge that the positive aspects of all other religious and social philosophies were later built upon, This solid foundation laid down by the Black man and woman in Ancient times was and is the source from which came all the worlds learning, art, science and culture in general. This book mentally and spiritually takes you on an illuminating journey which answers many questions of the following nature: Who were the first people on Earth and what great civilizations did they establish? What were the earliest revelations of the Creator to this planet and how were they manifested to the original inhabitants? Who really wrote the Bible and which ancient writings and teachings is it based upon? What was the real historical mission of Jesus Christ and what was the name of the original liberation movement founded by him? What are the Afrikan Roots of the origins of Buddhism, Judaism, Christiantiy and Islam? And so much more. This profusely documented and dynamic book is compiled and arranged with the format of a question and answer study guide into 23 chapters which puts the factual information on these subjects right at your fingertips. *God, the Bible and the Black Man's Destiny* now brings this once hidden knowledge to you in the langauge of everyday people. No matter what your religious affiliation and/or beliefs through the reading of this study guide you will probably acquire a greater knowledge and understanding of the bible and its place in Black History than perhaps you have ever known before. Handsomely bound and well illustrated —$19.95

A NEW BOOK BY
Rev. Dr. Ishakamusa Barashango

Afrikan Woman
the
Original Guardian Angel

A collection of writings on the Black Woman's creation of and on-going contribution to world civilization. This work sets forth documented proof that the original Afrikan Woman is the mother of all living. She was also the first to develop agricultural science, to create an alphabet and mathematics, to devise scripts for writing and to establish educational and social systems. In essence, she was the spiritual impetus for all scientific investigation in the ancient world.

The Black Woman was also the first builder of houses, constructor of cities, establisher of laws and governance and the creator of the market place. In fact, all the elements of civilization that humans hold dear initially emnated from her, that is why she was revered as an angel in antiquity. Now available to you. —$14.95

Barashango And Associates
❈ Lecture Series ❈

AFRIKAN ORIGIN OF HUMAN HISTORY AND CIVILIZATION

1. *Afrikan Origin Of The Human Species*
2. *In The Beginning Was The Black Race*
3. *Portrait Of The Eternal people*
4. *Black Woman: Queen Mother Of Universe*

BLACK HISTORICAL FACTS ABOUT THE BIBLE

5. *How To Find Black History In The Bible*
6. *Amazing Black Facts Of The Bible: An Historical Outline*
7. *The Bible: Word Of God Or Work Of Man?*
8. *Afrikan Warriors In The Bible*
9. *Great Black Women In The Bible Pt. 1*
10. *Great Black Women In The Bible Pt. 2*

BLACK HISTORICAL FACTS ABOUT JESUS

11. *The Real Jesus Was A Black Man*
12. *The Marital Life Of Jesus And His Son Barrabas*
13. *A Black Revolutionary Called Jesus*
14. *Black Historical Facts On The Life Of Jesus Volume I*
15. *Black Historical Facts On The Life Of Jesus Volume II*

AN AFRIKAN CENTERED HISTORICAL PERSPECTIVE ON RELIGION

16. *Afrikan Origin Of The Christian Church*
17. *Overcoming The Holocaust Of A Slave Religion*
18. *How The White Man Uses Religion As A Brainwashing Tool*
19. *How To Recognize Satan's Preachers In The Pulpit*

THE AFRIKAN LIBERATION MOVEMENT

20. *The Gospel According To Ol' Nat The Prophet*
21. *And The Word Of The Lord Came By Marcus Garvey*
22. *Dr. King And The Gospel Of Black Liberation*
23. *Resurrecting The Hidden Cosmic Powers Of The Afrikan Mind*

AFRIKAN PEOPLE AND EUROPEAN HOLIDAYS

24. *Afrikan People And European Holidays: A Mental Genocide (Misgiving Day)*
25. *Afrikan People And European Holidays: A Mental Genocide (Xmas)*
26. *It's Madness! Black People And White Folks Holidays (Hip Hop Rendition)*
27. *Christopher Columbus DID NOT Discover America*
28. *Should Black People Be Celebrating "Thanksgiving" Day?*
29. *A Cold Turkey Withdrawal From The Christmas Addiction*
30. *Come On Black People Let's Deal With This Easter Thang!*

ALL THE AUDIO TITLES IN THE ℬ&𝒜
Lecture SERIES ARE FULL 90 MINUTE
TAPES $10.00 Each

The Temple of The Black Messiah
Message Series Presenting
Dr. Ishakamusa Barashango
*AFRIKAN CENTERED PERSPECTIVES
ON THE BIBLE, GOD, JESUS,
CHRISTIANITY AND DOCTRINES*

AFRIKAN CENTERED MENTAL AND SPIRITUAL DEVELOPMENT

#10. Afrikan Centered Prayer And It's Power To Change Things

#11. Using The Power Of Afrikan Centered Meditation To Take Control In Your Life

#16. The Power Of A Cosmic State Of Mind

#17. Tapping The Awesome Powers Of The Afrikan Mind

#18. The Power Of Ancient Afrikan Spiritual Principles

#12. Perfect The Spiritual Martial Arts, Protect Yourself From The Enemy

#15. Use Your Spiritual Powers And Take Possession Of Your Life

#19. Using Our Divine Power To Do Amazing Things

HELPING AFRIKAN PEOPLE FREE THEMSELVES FROM A " PLANTATION THEOLOGY"

#2. ...And If The *Truth* Be Told Black Folks Need To Free their Minds

#9. ...See Black Folks Acting Strange Remember "An Enemy Has Done This"

#20. "We Have The Task Of Unbrainwashing An Entire Race Of People"

ALL THE AUDIO TITLES IN THE *Temple Of The Black Mesiah* SERIES ARE FULL 60 or 90 MINUTE TAPES $7.00 Each

Selected Titles Published
By
AFRIKAN WORLD BOOKS

Pale Fox (M. Griaule...$29.95

Kupigana Ngumi (Shaha Mfundishi Maasi)........................$19.95

Yurugu (Marimba Ani)..$29.95

Let The Circle Be Unbroken (Marimba Ani).......................$9.95

Melanin: a key to freedom (Richard King).........................$16.95

Spiritual Warriors are Healers (Mfundishi Salim)..............$29.95

The Isis Papers the keys to the colors
(Dr. Frances Cress Welsing)...$16.95

Blacked Out Through Whitewash (Suzar)...........................$49.00

Opening To Spirit (Caroline Shola Arewa).........................$29.95

Afrikan People and European Holidays vol # 1
(Ishakamusa Barashango)...$12.95

The Philosophy Of Maat Kemetic-Soulism (Maaxeru Tep)...........$25.00

The Exhuming Of A Nation (Noble Drew AIi)....................$49.95

In The Beginning That Never Began
(A1mighy God Dawud Allah)..$10.00

Man Heal Thyself (Queen Afua)...$20.00

The City Of Wellness (Queen Afua)...................................$28.00

ENF: State of Nation Address to S.A. Rastafari
(E.S.P. McPherson)..$29.95

Over 50,000 Popular & Hard To Find Books

AFRIKAN WORLD BOOKS
P.O. Box 16447
Baltimore, MD 21217
Tel# (410) 383 2006
www.afrikanworldbooks.com

AFRIKAN WORLD BOOKS
2217 Pennsylvania Ave.
Baltimore, MD. 21217
Phone (410) 383-2006
Fax (410) 383-0511

The Official Distributor of Books and Tapes by Dr. Ishakamusa Barashango

Afrikan World Books also distributes Over 50,000 titles of other informational and educational books and materials relevant to Afrikan consciouness and liberation.